Introduction to Human–Computer Interaction

Introduction to Human–Computer Interaction

Mark McFadden

Larsen & Keller
www.larsen-keller.com

Introduction to Human–Computer Interaction
Mark McFadden
ISBN: 978-1-64172-636-8 (Hardback)

 **Larsen & Keller**

Published by Larsen and Keller Education,
5 Penn Plaza,
19th Floor,
New York, NY 10001, USA

Cataloging-in-Publication Data

Introduction to human–computer interaction / Mark McFadden.
    p. cm.
Includes bibliographical references and index.
ISBN 978-1-64172-636-8
1. Human-computer interaction. 2. Human engineering.
3. Human computation. I. McFadden, Mark.
QA76.9.H85 I58 2022
004.019--dc23

For more information regarding Larsen and Keller Education and its products, please visit the publisher's website www.larsen-keller.com

Table of Contents

Preface

The design and use of computer technology pertaining to the interfaces between human users and computers are explored within the domain of human-computer interaction. The designing of technologies which allows humans to interact with computers in new ways is explored in this field. It also observes the ways in which humans interact with computers. Human-computer interaction is an amalgamation of a variety of fields such as behavioral sciences, design, media studies and computer science. Research within this field is further divided into various subfields. Some of these are augmented reality, user customization, social computing, embedded computation and brain-computer interfaces. The various sub-fields of human-computer interaction along with technological progress that have future implications are glanced at in this book. It will also provide interesting topics for research which interested readers can take up. This textbook is appropriate for students seeking detailed information in this area as well as for experts.

A short introduction to every chapter is written below to provide an overview of the content of the book:

Chapter 1 - Human-computer interaction is concerned with the researches in the design as well as the utilization of computer technology, primarily focusing on the interfaces between users and computers. This is an introductory chapter which will introduce briefly all the significant aspects of human-computer interaction; **Chapter 2** - There are different models, theories and guidelines in human-computer interaction. These includes human-computer interaction guidelines, basic model for human-computer interaction, user modeling in HCI, cognitive models, security and human-computer interaction, dialog designs, etc. The topics elaborated in this chapter will help in gaining a better perspective about human-computer interaction; **Chapter 3** - The platform where interaction between human and computer occurs is called a user interface. Some of the aspects that fall under its domain are user interface layer, user interface plug-in modules, user interface toolkit, visual design in HCI, user interface usability testing and evaluation methods, ethics of user experience design, etc. This chapter closely examines these aspects of user interface layer and development toolkit to provide an extensive understanding of the subject; **Chapter 4** - Computer systems characterized by notable amount of interactivity between humans and computer are referred to as interactive systems. This chapter delves into components of development framework such as model, view and controller, wimp interface, post-WIMP interface, multimodel interface and gestures and image recognitions to provide an extensive understanding of this subject; **Chapter 5** - Human-computer interaction can be applied to various areas such as virtual reality, locomotives, game design, vehicle information system, hospitality, business management, finance, etc. The topics elaborated in this chapter will help in gaining a better perspective about these applications of human-computer interaction.

Finally, I would like to thank my fellow scholars who gave constructive feedback and my family members who supported me at every step.

Mark McFadden

Human-Computer Interaction:
An Introduction

Human-computer interaction is concerned with the researches in the design as well as the utilization of computer technology, primarily focusing on the interfaces between users and computers. This is an introductory chapter which will introduce briefly all the significant aspects of human-computer interaction.

Computer is a device for processing, storing, and displaying information. Computer once meant a person who did computations, but now the term almost universally refers to automated electronic machinery.

The first computers were used primarily for numerical calculations. However, as any information can be numerically encoded, people soon realized that computers are capable of general-purpose information processing. Their capacity to handle large amounts of data has extended the range and accuracy of weather forecasting. Their speed has allowed them to make decisions about routing telephone connections through a network and to control mechanical systems such as automobiles, nuclear reactors, and robotic surgical tools. They are also cheap enough to be embedded in everyday appliances and to make clothes dryers and rice cookers "smart." Computers have allowed us to pose and answer questions that could not be pursued before. These questions might be about DNA sequences in genes, patterns of activity in a consumer market, or all the uses of a word in texts that have been stored in a database. Increasingly, computers can also learn and adapt as they operate.

Computers also have limitations, some of which are theoretical. For example, there are undecidable propositions whose truth cannot be determined within a given set of rules, such as the logical structure of a computer. Because no universal algorithmic method can exist to identify such propositions, a computer asked to obtain the truth of such a proposition will (unless forcibly interrupted) continues indefinitely—a condition known as the "halting problem. "Other limitations reflect current technology. Human minds are skilled at recognizing spatial patterns—easily distinguishing among human faces, for instance—but this is a difficult task for computers, which must process information sequentially, rather than grasping details overall at a glance. Another problematic area for computers involves natural language interactions. Because so much common knowledge and contextual information is assumed in ordinary human communication, researchers have yet to solve the problem of providing relevant information to general-purpose natural language programs.

Importance of Human-Computer Interaction

In every day we interact with many thing like cell phone, TV remote, Ac remote, Keyboard, Mouse and other devices like ATM, web or mobile application which is part of our life. Sometimes we take time to understand the design and sometimes we don't take time it understands it about poor and good design. Interaction is the connection between the user and the device or application. Interaction design is concerned with designing interactive products to support people in their everyday and working lives. Interaction design is now big business every company wants it now a day.

User interface is one of the most important elements of software, which attract the user toward the application. Interaction refers to an abstract model by which humans interact with the computing device and interface is a choice of software. HCI refers to both interaction and interface. HCI give the idea of user experience UX in which we can improve the computing devices and application for the user. HCI is a design that should produce a good relation between the user, the device and the services which is performed by the device in order to achieve a certain task, both in quality and optimality of the services. In aircraft HCI is needed because we need good human interaction and clearly describe the functionality of aircraft software and hardware toward the pilot. HCI is an important factor when designing any of these systems or interfaces ATM machines, train ticket, hot drinks, banking software ,management software ,aircraft and cars. Good use of HCI principles and techniques is not only important for the user which uses your software, but it is very high priority for software development companies. Develop or improve Safety, Utility, Effectiveness, Efficiency, Usability and Appeal of systems that include computers. If a software product is unusable, frustration, bad functionality or interface, no person will use the program by choice, and at the end of result sales will be negative. If the user cannot understand any functionality, company miss the important functionality or not user friendly interface that cause may be very high because computers are used by non-technical people. Toward this end, technologies such as the graphical user interface, virtual environments, speech recognition, gesture and handwriting recognition, multimedia presentation, and cognitive models of human learning and understanding are developed and applied as part of HCI research lab.

Jobs in Global and Local Market Human-Computer Interaction

The job HCI is designed interactive design for the user in which user can easily understand all the functionality of the device or software like which button is mostly use, Design UI/UX jobs of HCI. User Experience Researcher: identifies user wants or needs through a number of different qualitative and quantitative methods. Product Designer, Product Manager, Visual Designer, and User Interface qualitative and quantitative methods, goes from user needs to a product idea that addresses those needs and also where the most important button place, what the function must be involve in device or software Engineer. In HCI we identify user wants or needs through a number of different according the state rule and laws.

Global

- Human Factors Engineer/Researcher.
- Human Factors Design Engineer.
- User Experience Researcher.
- Human-Computer Interaction and Visualization Scientist.
- User Experience Researcher.
- UX Researcher, News.

Local

- Tenure-Track Faculty Positions Human-Computer Interaction and Design.
- Assistant Professor: Human-Computer Interaction, Deep Learning, or Artificial Intelligence User Experience Designer.

- User Experience Researcher.

- UX Researcher for android.

The Human-Computer Interaction

Human-Computer interaction (HCI) is a multidisciplinary field of study focusing on the design of computer technology and, in particular, the interaction between humans (the users) and computers. While initially concerned with computers, HCI has since expanded to cover almost all forms of information technology design.

Meteoric Rise of HCI

HCI surfaced in the 1980s with the advent of personal computing, just as machines such as the Apple Macintosh, IBM PC 5150 and Commodore 64 started turning up in homes and offices in society-changing numbers. For the first time, sophisticated electronic systems were available to general consumers for uses such as word processors, games units and accounting aids. Consequently, as computers were no longer room-sized, expensive tools exclusively built for experts in specialized environments, the need to create human-computer interaction that was also easy and efficient for less experienced users became increasingly vital. From its origins, HCI would expand to incorporate multiple disciplines, such as computer science, cognitive science and human-factors engineering.

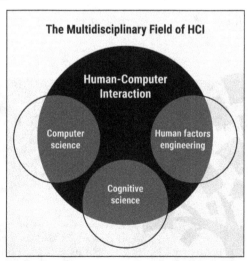

HCI soon became the subject of intense academic investigation. Those who studied and worked in HCI saw it as a crucial instrument to popularize the idea that the interaction between a computer and the user should resemble a human-to-human, open-ended dialogue. Initially, HCI researchers focused on improving the usability of desktop computers (i.e., practitioners concentrated on how easy computers are to learn and use). However, with the rise of technologies such as the Internet and the smartphone, computer use would increasingly move away from the desktop to embrace the mobile world. Also, HCI has steadily encompassed more fields:

> "It no longer makes sense to regard HCI as a specialty of computer science; HCI has grown to be broader, larger and much more diverse than computer science itself. HCI expanded from its initial focus on individual and generic user behavior to include social and organizational computing, accessibility for the elderly, the cognitively and physically impaired, and for all people, and for the widest possible spectrum of human experiences and activities. It expanded from desktop office applications to include games, learning and education, commerce, health and medical applications, emergency planning and response, and systems to support collaboration and community. It expanded from early graphical user interfaces to include myriad interaction techniques and devices, multi-modal interactions, tool support for model-based user interface specification, and a host of emerging ubiquitous, handheld and context-aware interactions."

UX Value of HCI and its Related Realms

HCI is a broad field which overlaps with areas such as user-centered design (UCD), user interface (UI) design and user experience (UX) design. In many ways, HCI was the forerunner to UX design.

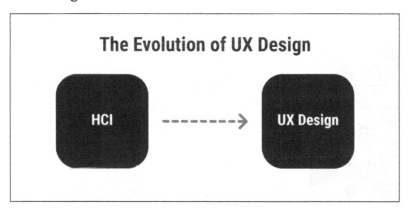

Despite that, some differences remain between HCI and UX design. Practitioners of HCI tend to be more academically focused. They're involved in scientific research and developing empirical understandings of users. Conversely, UX designers are almost invariably industry-focused and involved in building products or services—e.g., smartphone apps and websites. Regardless of this divide, the practical considerations for products that we as UX professionals concern ourselves with have direct links to the findings of HCI specialists about users' mindsets. With the broader span of topics that HCI covers, UX designers have a wealth of resources to draw from, although much research remains suited to academic audiences. Those of us who are designers also lack the luxury of time which HCI specialists typically enjoy. So, we must stretch beyond our industry-dictated constraints to access these more academic findings. When you do that well, you can leverage key insights into achieving the best designs for your users. By "collaborating" in this way with the HCI world, designers can drive impactful changes in the market and society.

Usability in Human-Computer Interaction

Usability is the measure of a product's potential to accomplish the goals of the user. In information technology, the term is often used in relation to software applications and Web sites, but it can be used in relation to any product that is employed to accomplish a task (for example, a toaster, a car dashboard, or an alarm clock). Some factors used in determining product usability are ease-of-use, visual consistency, and a clear, defined process for evolution.

Usability testing is a method by which users of a product are asked to perform certain tasks in an effort to measure the product's ease-of-use, task time, and the user's perception of the experience. Usability testing can be done formally, in a usability lab with video cameras, or informally, with paper mock-ups of an application or Web site. Changes are made to the application or site based on the findings of the usability tests. Whether the test is formal or informal, usability test participants are encouraged to think aloud and voice their every opinion. Usability testing is best used in conjunction with user-centered design, a method by which a product is designed according to the needs and specifications of users.

The last several years, the usability of Web sites has become a hot topic for Web developers. Many major Web sites employ usability engineers to ensure that they have an easy-to-use, friendly site that provides a positive customer experience.

Principles of Usable Design

A well designed user interface is comprehensible and controllable, helping users to complete their work successfully and efficiently, and to feel competent and satisfied. Effective user interfaces are designed based on principles of human interface design. The principles listed below are consolidated from a wide range of published sources.

Usefulness

- Value: The system should provide necessary utilities and address the real needs of users.

- Relevance: The information and functions provided to the user should be relevant to the user's task and context.

Consistency

- Consistency and standards: Follow appropriate standards/conventions for the platform and the suite of products. Within an application (or a suite of applications), make sure that actions, terminology, and commands are used consistently.

- Real-world conventions: Use commonly understood concepts, terms and metaphors, follow real-world conventions (when appropriate), and present information in a natural and logical order.

Simplicity

- Simplicity: Reduce clutter and eliminate any unnecessary or irrelevant elements.

- Visibility: Keep the most commonly used options for a task visible (and the other options easily accessible).

- Self-evidency: Design a system to be usable without instruction by the appropriate target user of the system: if appropriate, by a member of the general public or by a user who has the appropriate subject-matter knowledge but no prior experience with the system. Display data in a manner that is clear and obvious to the appropriate user.

Communication

- Feedback: Provide appropriate, clear, and timely feedback to the user so that he sees the results of his actions and knows what is going on with the system.

- Structure: Use organization to reinforce meaning. Put related things together, and keep unrelated things separate.

- Sequencing: Organize groups of actions with a beginning, middle, and end, so that users know where they are, when they are done, and have the satisfaction of accomplishment.

- Help and documentation: Ensure that any instructions are concise and focused on supporting the user's task.

Error Prevention and Handling

- Forgiveness: Allow reasonable variations in input. Prevent the user from making serious errors whenever possible, and ask for user confirmation before allowing a potentially destructive action.

- Error recovery: Provide clear, plain-language messages to describe the problem and suggest a solution to help users recover from any errors.

- Undo and redo: Provide "emergency exits" to allow users to abandon an unwanted action. The ability to reverse actions relieves anxiety and encourages user exploration of unfamiliar options.

Efficiency

- Efficacy: (For frequent use) Accommodate a user's continuous advancement in knowledge and skill. Do not impede efficient use by a skilled, experienced user.

- Shortcuts: (For frequent use) Allow experienced users to work more quickly by providing abbreviations, function keys, macros, or other accelerators, and allowing customization or tailoring of frequent actions.

- User control: (For experienced users) Make users the initiators of actions rather than the responders to increase the users' sense that they are in charge of the system.

Workload Reduction

- Supportive automation: Make the user's work easier, simpler, faster, or more fun. Automate unwanted workload.

- Reduce memory load: Keep displays brief and simple, consolidate and summarize data, and present new information with meaningful aids to interpretation. Do not require the user to remember information. Allow recognition rather than recall.

- Free cognitive resources for high-level tasks: Eliminate mental calculations, estimations, comparisons, and unnecessary thinking. Reduce uncertainty.

Usability Judgment

- It depends: There will often be tradeoffs involved in design, and the situation, sound judgment, experience should guide how those tradeoffs are weighed.

- A foolish consistency: There are times when it makes sense to bend or violate some of the principles or guidelines, but make sure that the violation is intentional and appropriate.

References

- Computer: britannica.com, Retrieved 08 July, 2019

- Importance-of-Human-Computer-Interaction-HCI-320409133: researchgate.net, Retrieved 25 June, 2019

- Human-computer-interaction: interaction-design.org, Retrieved 15 March, 2019

- Usability: whatis.techtarget.com, Retrieved 23 April, 2019

- Principles-for-usable-design: usabilitybok.org, Retrieved 08 January, 2019

2

Human-Computer Interaction: Theories and Evaluation

There are different models, theories and guidelines in human-computer interaction. These includes human-computer interaction guidelines, basic model for human-computer interaction, user modeling in HCI, cognitive models, security and human-computer interaction, dialog designs, etc. The topics elaborated in this chapter will help in gaining a better perspective about human-computer interaction.

Human-Computer Interaction Guidelines

Shneiderman's Eight Golden Rules

Ben Shneiderman, an American computer scientist combined few implied facts about designing and came up with below eight common guidelines:

- Strive for Consistency.
- Cater to Universal Usability.
- Offer Informative feedback.
- Design Dialogs to yield closure.
- Prevent Errors.
- Permit easy reversal of actions.
- Support internal locus of control.
- Reduce short term memory load.

These guidelines are useful for normal designers and also for interface designers. These eight guidelines can be used to distinguish a good interface design from a bad one. These are useful in experimental assessment to identify improved Graphical User Interfaces.

Norman's Seven Principles

For accessing the interaction between human and computers, Donald Norman in 1988 has proposed seven principles to be used for transforming complex tasks. Below are the seven principles of Norman:

- Make use of both knowledge in world & knowledge in the head.
- Shorten the task structures.
- Create things visibly.
- Get the mapping right.
- Change constrains into advantages.
- Design for Error.
- When everything else fails – Standardize.

Heuristic Evaluation

Heuristics evaluation is a systematic procedure for checking user interface for usability problems. When a usability problem is detected in design, they will be addressed as an integral part of constant design processes. Heuristic evaluation method consists of some usability principles such as Nielsen's ten Usability principles.

Nielsen's Ten Heuristic Principles for Human-Computer Interaction

- Visibility of system status.
- Match between system and real world.
- User control and freedom.
- Consistency and standards.
- Error prevention.
- Recognition rather than Recall.
- Flexibility and efficiency of use.
- Aesthetic and minimalist design.
- Help diagnosis and recovery from errors.
- Documentation and Help.

General Interaction

Guidelines for general interaction are complete advices which mainly focus on general instructions like:

- Being consistent.

- Offering significant feedback.

- Asking for authentication of any non-trivial critical action.

- Authorizing easy reversal of most actions.

- Reducing the amount of information to be remembered in between actions.

- Seeking competence in dialogue, motion and thought.

- Excusing mistakes.

- Classifying activities by function and establishing screen geography accordingly.

- Delivering context sensitive help services.

- Using simple action verbs or short verb phrases to name commands.

Information Display

Information offered by the HCI must not be unfinished or uncertain or else the application will not meet the user requirements. For providing better display, below guidelines are prepared:

- Display information which is only applicable to the present context.

- Don't load the user with heavy data; rather use a presentation layout to allow rapid integration of information.

- Make use of standard labels, standard abbreviations and probable colors.

- Allow the user in maintaining visual context.

- Create meaningful error messages.

- Make use of upper and lower case, indentation and text grouping to aid in understanding.

- Make use of windows (if available) to classify different types of information.

- Make use of analog displays for characterizing the information which is more easily integrated with this form of representation.

- Consider the available geography of the display screen and use it proficiently.

Data Entry

Below guidelines focus on data entry which is another important aspect of HCI:

- Lessen the number of input actions that are needed by the user.

- Maintain steadiness between information display and data input.

- Allow the user to customize the input.

- Interaction must be flexible but also tuned to the user's favored mode of input.

- Disable unsuitable commands in the context of current actions.

- Let the user to control the interactive flow.

- Provide help to assist with all input actions.

- Remove "mickey mouse" input.

Human-Computer Interaction Standards

Types of Standard for HCI and Usability

Standards related to usability can be categorised as primarily concerned with:

- The use of the product (effectiveness, efficiency and satisfaction in a particular context of use),

- The user interface and interaction,

- The process used to develop the product,

- The capability of an organisation to apply user centred design.

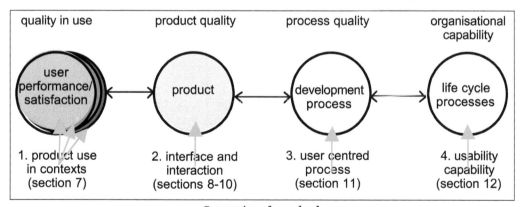

Categories of standard.

Figure above illustrates the logical relationships: the objective is for the product to be effective, efficient and satisfying when used in the intended contexts. A prerequisite for this is an appropriate interface and interaction. This requires a user centred design process, which to be achieved consistently requires an organisational capability to support user centred design.

Development of ISO Standards

Standards for HCI and usability are developed under the auspices of the International Organisation for Standardisation (ISO) and the International Electrotechnical Commission (IEC). ISO and IEC comprise national standards bodies from member states. The technical work takes place in Working Groups of experts, nominated by national standards committees but expected to act as independent experts.

The standards are developed over a period of several years, and in the early stages the published documents may change significantly from version to version until consensus is reached. As the standard becomes more mature, from the Committee Draft Stage onwards, formal voting takes place by participating national member bodies and the draft documents provide a good indication of what the final standard is likely to look like.

Basic Model for Human-Computer Interaction

In order to depict a taxonomy of multimodal human-computer interaction we will have to clarify a number of concepts and issues. The first assumption is that there are minimally two separate *agents* involved, one human and one machine. They are physically separated, but are able to exchange information through a number of information channels. As schematically shown in figure, we will make the following definitions.

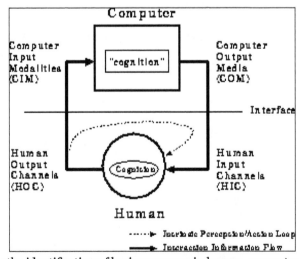

A model for the identification of basic processes in human-computer interaction.

There are two basic processes involved on the side of the human user: Perception and Control. Note that we take the perspective of the human process throughout this document. With respect to the Perceptive process, we can make a distinction between:

- Human Input Channels (HIC).

- Computer Output Media (COM).

Within the *Control process*, we can make a distinction between:

- Human Output Channels (HOC) and
- Computer Input Modalities (CIM).

Then, within both of the agents, a cognitive or computational component can be identified, which processes the incoming input information and prepares the output. Also, at this intermediate cognitive level, intentional parameters will influence the processing, either implicitly, such as by design, in the case of non-intelligent agents, or explicitly, as in humans or in more sophisticated agents containing an explicit representation of goals and "beliefs". With respect to the machine, it should be noted that here the design is known, whereas for the human cognitive apparatus, the architecture must be inferred and cannot be observed directly.

Instead of the word modality at the human input side, and the word media at the human output side, we have chosen for the word *channel*, which also allows for a more clear distinction between the abbreviations (HOC → CIM → COM → HIC → HOC ...) which can also be pronounced as:

- HOC: Human output to computer.
- CIM: Computer input from man.
- COM: Computer output to man.
- HIC: Human input from computer.

User Modeling in HCI

User models are defined as models that systems have of users that reside inside a computational environment. They should be differentiated from mental models that users have of systems and tasks that reside in the heads of users, in interactions with others and with artifacts.

An Early Success Example of User Modeling

The WEST system represents an early pioneering effort to explore issues associated with user modeling. WEST was a coaching system for a game called "How the West was Won" that was modeled on "Chutes and Ladders." The players rotate three spinners and have to form an arithmetic expression from the three numbers that turn up on the spinners using +,-,*, / and appropriate parentheses (and they have to specify what the value of the expression is). So, for example, a player who gets a 2, 3, and 4 on the spinners, might form the expression (2+3)*4 = 20 and move forward 20 spaces. If players land on a town (towns occur every 10 spaces), they move forward to the next town. If they land on a chute, they slide to the end of the chute. If they land on an opponent, that opponent is sent back two towns. The optimal strategy is to figure out all the possible moves and take the one that puts you farthest ahead of your opponents. But empirical analyses showed that students did not use this strategy; they were much more likely to rely on a strategy such as adding the two smallest numbers and multiplying by the largest.

The WEST coach analyzed students' moves in terms of the optimal strategy and could rate the moves with respect to that strategy. It watched to see if the students consistently followed a lessthan-optimal strategy, such as not taking opportunities to land on a town or chute or opponent. If the WEST coach detected such a pattern, it would intervene at an opportune time, when the student's move was far from optimal, and it would point out how the student could have done much better. It then would give the student a chance to take the move over.

In the context of WEST, the following problems of user modeling were explored:

- Shared context: Computer coaches are restricted to inferring the students' shortcomings from whatever they do in the context of playing the game or solving the problem;

- Initiative and intrusiveness: The user model was used (1) to make a judgment of when to give valuable advice and make relevant comments to students without being so intrusive as to destroy the fun of the game; and (2) to avoid the danger that students will never develop the necessary skills for examining their own behavior and looking for the causes of their own mistakes because the coach immediately points out the students' errors;

- Relevance: WEST developed the paradigm "coaching by issues and examples." By assessing the situational context and acting accordingly, students were coached in a way in which they could see the usefulness of the issue at a time when they were most receptive to the idea being presented. Based on the information contained in the user model, the system used explicit intervention and tutoring strategies to enable the system to say the "right" thing at the "right" time.

Although the WEST system explored some of the basic concepts of user modeling, it did so in the context of a very simple domain in which outcomes were limited to the combinatorics of a few variables. The approach worked well because the computer expert (as one component of the overall system) operating in a "closed-world" can play an optimal game, and it can determine the complete range of alternative behaviors. Low level, individual events were easy to interpret. The user model was incrementally constructed by exploiting many events occurring in the same domain.

High-functionality Applications

High-functionality applications (such as UNIX, MS-Office, Photoshop, Eudora, etc.) are used to model parts of existing worlds and to create new worlds. They are complex systems because they serve the needs of large and diverse user populations. If you asked 100 different people what features they would like to have in a particular application, you would end up with a very large number of features. The design of HFAs must address three problems: (1) the unused functionality must not get in the way; (2) unknown existing functionality must be accessible or delivered at times when it is needed; and (3) commonly used functionality should be not too difficult to be learned, used, and remembered.

We have conducted a variety of empirical studies to determine the usage patterns of HFAs, their structure, and their associated help and learning mechanisms. All of these studies have led us to the identification of the qualitative relationships between usage patterns of HFAs as illustrated in figure.

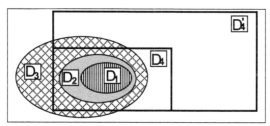

Levels of Users' Knowledge about a High-functionality Application.

The ovals in figure represent users' knowledge about the system's concepts set. D_1 represents concepts that are well known, easily employed, and used regularly by a user. D_2 contains concepts known vaguely and used only occasionally, often requiring passive help systems. D_3 represents concepts users believe to exist in the system. The rectangle D_4 represents the functionality provided by the system. The "D_3 and not D_4" domain represents concepts in the user's mental model that they expect to exist, although they do not exist in the actual system. End-user modification and programming support is needed to empower users to add this functionality.

As the functionality of HFAs increases to D_4, little is gained for users unless there are mechanisms to help them relate the additional functionality to their needs. Most users do not want to become technical experts — they just want to get their tasks done. The area of D_4 that is not part of D_3 is of specific interest to research in user modeling. This is system functionality, whose existence is unknown to users. For the "D_4 and not D_3" domain, information access (the user-initiated location of information when they perceive a need for an operation) is not sufficient, but information delivery (the system volunteering information that it inferred to be relevant to the users' task at hand) is required. Active help systems and critics are required to point out to users functionality that may be useful for their tasks and to help users avoid getting stuck on suboptimal plateaus.

Figure shows usage patterns of HFAs without taking specific tasks of users into account. There is no reason for users to worry about additional existing functionality in D_4 if this functionality is not relevant to their tasks. However, if the system does provide functionality in D_4 related to users' tasks, it is desirable to avoid having users unable to perform the task or do so in a suboptimal or error-prone way because they do not know about this functionality. In figure the gray rectangle T represents the information that is relevant to the users' task at hand, and the dots represent different pieces of functionality. Passive support systems supporting information access can help users to explore pieces of functionality that are contained in D and T, whereas active intelligent systems supporting information delivery are needed for the functionality contained in T and not in D_3. The functionality of all dots, including the ones in D_4 outside of T is often offered by specific push systems such as "Did You Know" (DYK) systems or Microsoft's "Tip of the Day". This approach suffers from the problem that concepts get thrown at users in a decontextualized way.

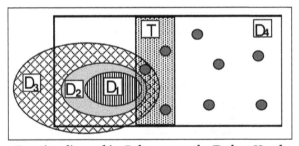

Functionality and its Relevance to the Task at Hand.

Expertise in HFA. "Experts" (users who know everything about a system) no longer exist in HFAs. In HFAs, being an "expert" is at best an attribute of a specific context, rather than a personal attribute. The different spaces of expertise (determined by individual interest) are illustrated in figure. In this multi-kernel model, $\{D_1, U_i\}$ means the area of functionality that is well known to a particular user U_i; for example: U_1 knows about the equation editor, U_2 knows about mail-merge functionality, U_3 uses a bibliography system for references, and U_4 is familiar with collaborative writing tools. This view provides a rationale why HFAs exist in this world: because designers need to write software for millions of users (at design time) for a large space of different tasks to be known only at use time.

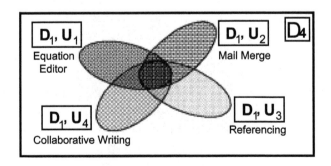

Distributed Expertise in HFAs.

HFAs create challenging learning problems that are representative for numerous complex systems. As illustrated with the above figures, nobody learns these systems completely, but users acquire some base functionality and learn additional functionality on demand. User-modeling techniques can effectively support learning on demand by helping users to identify opportunities to learn additional functionality relevant to their task at hand and to avoid people becoming stuck on suboptimal plateaus. User modeling techniques based on logged user data can support the organization-wide learning of HFAs. Typical knowledge workers have become so deluged with information that they find it increasingly difficult to access the information they need — the sheer volume of irrelevant information makes it difficult to find information that is relevant. This challenge is particularly important in the context of organizational memory systems, because most of these systems will contain too much information for browsing to be effective. The Invision project was an early user modeling approach to use explicitly represented models of the knowledge and information needs of members of the organization to improve organizational communication and organizational learning.

Future Challenges of User Modeling in HCI

User modeling in HCI faces a number of interesting challenges, including the following ones:

1. Increase the payoff of user modeling: There is little to be gained if expensive mechanisms are used to achieve minimal improvements in usability and usefulness (e.g., our empirical investigations have shown that few users, even trained computer scientists, take advantage of the MS-Word macro adaptation mechanisms). The payoff or utility of cognitive artifacts can be characterized by the quotient of "value / effort." To increase the payoff, we have two options: (1) increase the value by showing that future systems relying on user models are more usable and more useful, or (2) decrease the effort associated with creating a user model (for example, by exploiting usage data).

2. Differentiate between user modeling and task modeling: In many cases, we are not interested in user modeling in any general sense, but only in user performance and background knowledge with respect to tasks in a certain domain. In this case, an adequate user model can be restricted to a small set of user attributes related to a specific task.

3. Support different modeling techniques: Many user modeling approaches failed because they relied too much on one specific technique. There is evidence that substantial leverage can be gained by integrating modeling (e.g., with specification components, with questionnaires) with implicit modeling (e.g., analysing user performance on tasks, inferring the knowledge background and interests based on previous interactions).

This enriched synthesis can be further complemented by asking users (in otherwise open environments, such as HFAs and design environments) to solve specific problems in which the selection of the problem is driven by specific needs of the user modeling component.

4. Dealing with user models containing wrong, outdated, and inadequate information: User models represent a world that is outside the computational environment. The mapping of external information (particularly if we rely on inferred rather than observed behavior) to the internal model may be wrong to start with, but even under the assumption that it is an adequate representation at some point of time, it may become outdated by external changes of which the model is unaware. How, when, and by whom can a wrong user model be identified? Who will have the authority and the knowledge to change the model, and which modification mechanisms will be available to do so?

5. Develop criteria to judge the adequacy of user modeling in different domains: Assuming that user modeling is useful in some domains but not in others, which criteria do we have to distinguish these domains?

6. Capturing the Larger Context: Suchman argues convincingly that "interaction between people and computers requires essentially the same interpretive work that characterizes interaction between people, but with fundamentally different resources available to the participants. People make use of linguistic, nonverbal, and inferential resources in finding the intelligibility of actions and events, which are in most cases not available and not understandable by computers." This raises the interesting challenges: (1) How can we capture the larger (often unarticulated) context of what users are doing (especially beyond the direct interaction with the computer system)? (2) How can we increase the "richness of resources" available for computer programs attempting user modeling to understand (what they are told about their users) and to infer from what they are observing their users doing (inside the computational environment and outside).

7. Ubiquitous computing, embedded communication, and usage data make an attempt to reduce the unnecessary separation of computational artifacts from the physical objects they represent and from the discussions surrounding them (this separation created computational environments that are "deaf, blind, and quadriplegic agents" History and interaction patterns document how artifacts were developed and which actions and contributions individual users have made. Circumstantial indexing, for example, is a powerful retrieval technique used by human collaborators that allows users to remember events in terms of things they did, not necessarily in terms of things that happened to objects.

8. User Modeling and Control: A consequence of any smart behavior of systems is that agents (humans or computers) can guess wrong and perform hidden changes that users do not like. Current systems often lack the possibility or at least the transparency for users to turn off these "smart" features, which can get more in the way than help.

Systems, even smart ones, are aware of only a fraction of the total problem-solving process their human partners undergo, and they cannot share an understanding of the situation or state of problem-solving of a human. Whereas these drawbacks of smart systems may be only annoying in HFAs such as word processors, they are unacceptable in other collaborative human-computer systems, such as airline cockpit computers serving as intelligent agents. Billings argues convincingly that in computerized cockpit design each intelligent agent in a human-computer system must have knowledge of the intent and the rationale of the actions of the other agents. To avoid these drawbacks, intelligent systems should provide malleable tools that empower rather than diminish users, giving them control over tasks necessary for everyday life. There are situations in which we desire automation and intelligence (for example, few people will have the desire to compile their programs themselves) — but the decision as to what should be automated and what not should be under the control of the people affected by the system.

Privacy and User Models. We live in a world where more and more events take place and are tracked in some computational environment and recorded in a user model, just to name a few examples: telephone calling cards, shopping cards at supermarkets, book ordering at electronic book stores, websites visited, active badges worn by humans. Numerous organizations compile user models of our behavior and actions — and there is the great danger that this information can be misused. It will be a major challenge to find ways to avoid misuses, either by not allowing companies to collect this information at all or by finding ways that the individual users have control over these user models.

Cognitive Models

Cognitive modeling is an area of computer science that deals with simulating human problem-solving and mental processing in a computerized model. Such a model can be used to simulate or predict human behavior or performance on tasks similar to the ones modeled and improve human-computer interaction.

Cognitive modeling is used in numerous artificial intelligence (AI) applications, such as expert systems, natural language processing, neural networks, and in robotics and virtual reality applications. Cognitive models are also used to improve products in manufacturing segments, such as human factors, engineering, and computer game and user interface design.

Types of Cognitive Models

Some highly sophisticated programs model specific intellectual processes. Techniques such as discrepancy detection are used to improve these complex models.

Discrepancy detection systems signal when there is a difference between an individual's actual state or behavior and the expected state or behavior as per the cognitive model. That information is then used to increase the complexity of the model.

The cognitive machines they've created have the capacity to infer user intent -- which is not always consistent with behavior - store information from experiences similarly to human memory, and call upon expert systems for advice when they need it.

Another type of cognitive model is the neural network. This model was first hypothesized in the 1940s, but it has only recently become practical thanks to advancements in data processing and the accumulation of large amounts of data to train algorithms.

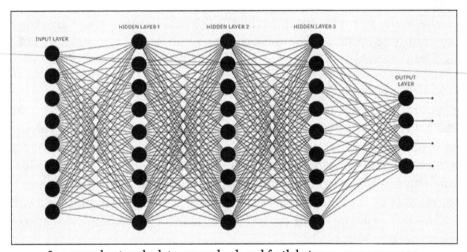

In a neural network, data passes back and forth between many neurons.

Neural networks work similarly to the human brain by running training data through a large number of computational nodes, called artificial neurons, which pass information back and forth between each other. By accumulating information in this distributed way, applications can make predictions about future inputs.

Reinforcement learning is an increasingly prominent area of cognitive modeling. This approach has algorithms run through many iterations of a task that takes multiple steps, incentivizing actions that eventually produce positive outcomes, while penalizing actions that lead to negative ones. This is a primary part of the AI algorithm which bested the top human Go players in 2016.

These models, which can also be used in natural language processing and smart assistant applications, have improved human-computer interaction, making it possible for machines to have rudimentary conversations with humans.

Potential Limitations of Cognitive Modeling

Despite advancements in applying cognitive models to artificial intelligence, it still falls short of its true goal of simulating human thinking. In neural networks, for example, algorithms must see thousands - or even millions - of examples of training data before they can make predictions about similar data in the future. Even then, they can only make inferences about the narrow topic area on which they trained.

This is very different from how human brains work. The human brain uses a combination of context and more limited experience to make generalizations about new experiences, something even the most advanced cognitive models can't do today.

The most advanced biological research into the human brain still lacks a complete picture of how it works. Even if that baseline information is established, transposing human thought processes onto computer programs is another leap entirely.

Modelling Rich Interaction

We operate within an ecology of people, physical artifacts and electronic systems, and this rich ecology has recently become more complex as electronic devices invade the workplace and our day-to-day lives. We need methods to deal with these rich interactions.

- Status-event analysis is a semi-formal, easy to apply technique that:

    - Classifies phenomena as event or status.

    - Embodies naïve psychology.

    - Highlights feedback problems in interfaces.

- Aspects of rich environments can be incorporated into methods such as task analysis:

    - Other people.

    - Information requirements.

    - Triggers for tasks.

    - Modeling artifacts.

    - Placeholders in task sequences.

- New sensor-based systems do not require explicit interaction, this means:

    - New cognitive and interaction models.

    - New design methods.

    - New system architectures.

Security and Human-Computer Interaction

Privacy is developing as an important element for interactive systems. Many applications exists which offers some security tasks. This is necessary in all those applications that are working over internet and involves security threats. An application must be secure enough to provide protection from these security threats. But for the user must have all the knowledge about the system/application. The HCI design-user interface need to be address in different ways like application should be smart enough that people may understand how to secure their information. Some users are not experienced enough and are not able to change setting according to their need so they are forced to use default setting. They are not aware of how to change security settings as the designer has not kept in mind all the HCI principles.

In order to inspect and evaluate the principle of HCI only computer related information is not enough. Many other skills are required. A developer must design a suitable user interface where learnability and efficiency will be high. The extreme objective of HCI is to advance the communication between human and computer. It may be attained by designing applications that all the features must be used by users. The usability of system decreases when security measures have to be taken serious like, Password must be used to access valid access. The password is more complex and longer, can be alphanumeric, and then system is safer. So, if guides are produced that improve the HCI-Sec aspects of an application, it may be easier to use security options. The stability of HCI-Sec is to make the system stronger, more reliable and more reliable.

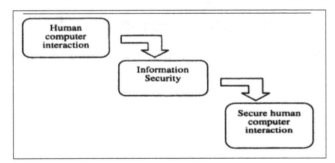

Human-Computer Interaction Influence.

Secure Human-Computer interaction is most needed feature for e-commerce environments. Users want to assure that the interface by which they enter their credit card information for transaction will be protected against unauthorized modification

Information Security

IS is discussed in five services that are integrity, non-repudiation, authorization, confidentiality, identification & authentication. These services are necessary to guarantee that data is ensured and secured. Identification & authentication is the initial move towards implementing security. Authorization is the next stage is to decide whether the confirmed matter has the privilege to get to the computer facilities being referred to. All material must be severely available to authorized users only. Confidentiality is that only authorized parties will be able to access information. Confidentiality is necessary but integrity should be guaranteed too. So only the authorized user will be able to change the content. Non-repudiation is that no act of changing content can damage information security. These services must be accessible, visible, and functional from the perspective of Human-Computer interaction to obtain information security.

HCI for Information Security Technology

People are responsible for security issues which results in computer systems failure. It is possible to advance or enhance the execution of information security by means of consideration to some aspects. First of all understand the problem which occurs while providing secure interaction. Next complexity reduces security. Information security is only provided when all the features are visible to user and he knows how to use it.

HCI-S Guidelines

Here are some HCI rules that presentation should follow to have correct HCI features. Ten important guidelines were formed and applications were estimated against for each one of them.

Perceptible organization state and safety purposes: All the security related function must be visible to the user he should not have to search them in order to apply changes. The system should always keep clients educated about what is happening, through suitable feedback within sensible time. Much of the time, the display of the present security state can be utilized to give clients reflexive feedback of data security. Visibility of the system security state contributes to the working of trust and is therefore one standard for effective human-machine connection in security applications. Security must be visible without being nosy, as clients would prefer documents, dynamic symbols when security capacities are being executed on a system.

- Security should be easily used: Interface should be designed in a way that it requires less effort to use of security features. The interface ought to be carefully compose and require negligible exertion so as to make utilization of security highlights. Moreover the security settings ought not to be set in a few distinct areas inside the application, since it will be hard for the client to find every last one of them.

- Suitable for advanced as well as first time users: Applications are developed for use of both new and experienced users. So show enough information for an experienced user and detailed information for new user. There must be both shortcuts as well as defined methods for any function in application so that new user uses well defined methods to perform the work and experienced user may use shortcuts. Application may be simple and shortcut must be available for advanced users.

- Avoid heavy use of technical vocabulary or advanced terms: Many people who uses applications may not have good vocabulary or language skills. If the designer uses feature containing difficult vocabulary user will definitely get confused in selecting the appropriate function according to his need, so use easy words and vocabulary in order to avoid misunderstandings.

- Handle errors appropriately: Good error messages are suspicious interaction design which avoids a problem from happening in the first place. Therefore, system should not contain error-prone elements and should forestall possible user errors. Errors produced by the use of security feature could be prohibited and minimized.

- Allow customization without risk to be trapped: New as well as old users are sometime not aware of proper functionality of some features. Exit path must be available if any function are chosen by mistake because in case if user experience wrong selection and no immediate exit he will never use any security feature until he is not properly aware of it. Need of exit path is necessary.

Example: In many applications there is back button or if we press esc button on keyboard we are out of that particular area.

- Easy to setup security settings: Security setting are basic need of user. To implement security as needed by clients all the settings available must be easy to understand, visible and vocabulary should be easily understandable. It should be easy so that anyone can change settings according to their needs.

- Suitable Help and documentation for the available security: Help and documentation must be provided for new users. Provide clients quick access to help resources. Organize help around their tasks and goals. Make complete and accurate help. Write all appropriate thing in the documents.

- Make the user feel protected: Guarantee the users that his work is ensured by the application. Recovery from sudden blunders must be considered and the application ought to guarantee that clients won't lose their information. Applications ought to give the client the most recent security includes with a specific end goal to feel ensured. Besides some type of notice would be helpful on the off chance that a security update is available.

- Security should not reduce performance: It is said that if we increase security, usability decreases and if usability increases security decreases. So, enhance security features but also keep performance in mind by using efficient algorithms.

Assessment of Existing Applications

On the basis of HCI-S guidelines applications are accessed. Applications are evaluated and compared. The applications are Norton Antivirus, McAfee Virus Scan, Agnitum's Outpost Firewall, Opera, Mozilla Firefox web-browser, and Microsoft Word. Each application was verified against 10 guidelines. The grading technique applied for all the applications were from 0 to 5, as recorded in table.

Table: Grading Technique.

Grade	Reason
0	Application diverges completely from guideline.
1	Application significantly diverges from guideline.
2	Application has paid attention to guideline but still have major problems.
3	Application has paid attention to guideline but still have minor problems.
4	Application follows guideline in some sections.
5	Application completely follows guideline in all possible sections.

A summary of score for each application achieved from each of the 10 guidelines is shown below in table.

	Firefox	Outpost	Mc Afee	Norton	Ms word	Open
Visible system state and security functions	2	3	4	2	3	3
Security should be easily used	4	3	3	4	3	3
Suitable for advanced as well as first time users	5	2	2	4	4	2
Avoid technical vocabulary or advanced terms,	2	0	4	2	1	3
Handle errors appropriately	3	2	3	2	4	4

Allow customization without risk to be trapped	2	2	0	2	1	2
Easy to setup security settings	2	5	5	2	3	5
Suitable security help and documentation	0	1	1	5	4	5
Make the user feel protected	3	4	4	3	4	3
Security should not reduce performance	3	4	1	3	4	4
TOTAL (50)	26	26	27	29	31	34

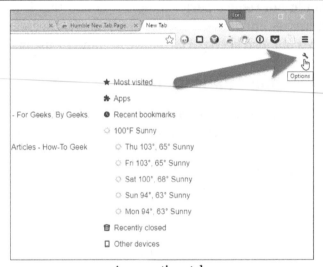

A new options tab.

Cognitive Task Analysis

Cognitive task analysis (CTA) techniques seek to model the mental activity of a task operator. With the rise of computing artifacts, the focus of CTA has changed from supporting the tutoring of operators, to modeling knowledge application, to modeling cognitive processes. Descendants of knowledge-based approaches include GOMS, and produce quantitative temporal behavioural predictions for well-defined interfaces. The increasing pace of design and the dominance of small design teams have led to a demand for more flexible techniques. A CTA in ICS requires a prior task analysis to have been conducted, but the analyst then identifies the configuration of cognitive processes necessary to transform information about the task, through the phases of goal formation, action specification, and action execution; for novices, occasional (normal), and expert operators. The availability of procedural knowledge, experiential, and abstracted memories influence the ease of processing, and the scope a design offers for their development informs ease of learning and skill acquisition. The location of a particular form of buffered processing predicts subjective awareness of different aspects of the task, and of task complexity. Two notations supporting analysis are described. The close coupling of the analytic approach and the underlying theory enables a CTA in ICS to provide supportive evaluation, allowing iterative redesign. It is also allowing further research linking ICS to formal models of systems analysis (Syndetics) and to other methods of TA, namely TKS, to extend both techniques to collaborative and multiple task performance.

Rationale for Cognitive Task Analysis

The pace of technological change and the ubiquity of computer-based devices has brought about a significant change in the focus of task analysis over the past 20 years. Cognitive task analysis (CTA) began by recognizing that the key to skilled task performance lay in the possession and appropriate use by the operator of task-relevant knowledge and sought to develop models of the required knowledge to improve the tutoring of operators and speed the progression of an individual from task novice to task expert. Psychological theories of learning and knowledge structuring, such as Newell's SOAR architecture, gave rise to the realization that the task could itself be designed to facilitate knowledge acquisition, and so CTA began to be seen as a stage in task design, modifying the task device or structure, rather than as something to be done to modify the operators' knowledge.

The descendants of knowledge-based approaches to CTA are represented by the GOMS methods). Initially, such methods were aimed at optimizing tasks for expert performance, as they were implicitly following a large-scale industrial model of both design and use. This required a structured methodology for CTA suitable for use in the design process and for dealing with end products that would be used repeatedly by highly skilled operators (products in which a fraction of a second of execution time saved could result in billions of dollars of costs saved).

Toward the end of the 1980s, dissatisfaction with the cost and effort of employing such methods, together with a recognition that not all task design fitted this mold, led to a search for analytical methods that could be used on a smaller scale. This was partly driven by the rise of small information technology (IT) firms and the in-house development of IT, where the design and implementation of computer applications was often carried out by one or two individuals. The pace of change in IT was another factor, since many IT applications were used now not by experts but only occasionally by people who were at best infrequent users of each of a large number of computer-supported tasks. This and the need for tasks to be user friendly and allow people to "walk up and use them" changed the focus away from designing for expert use toward designing tasks to be comprehensible by novices, supporting the recall of task steps during infrequent use.

In such a rapidly changing technological world, the rationale for CTA has become clear. Technology, devices, tasks, and even the knowledge of the human operator will vary widely, but one thing remains unchangeable: the human cognitive architecture. Even if the content of our memories and skills changes with time, the way that we process information, form and recall memories, and automate our skills does not change. Analysts ought to be able to make use of supportive methods based on cognitive psychology to fit the design of tasks to this single unchanging factor.

For a method to be applicable in the fast-paced world of small-scale IT development, it needs to be usable alongside a wide range of other approaches and at almost any stage of design, from initial task conception through to postdesign firefighting and usability evaluation. It has to be very tolerant in the amount of detailed design and domain information that it requires. It should also be able to guide designers explicitly toward improvements and changes in their initial ideas rather than just giving evaluative output. In other words, it must provide supportive evaluation for iterative redesign.

One such approach has been evolving steadily since the mid-1980s, largely with the sup- port of the European Union, through the international basic research projects Amodeus and Amodeus 2. These projects brought together cognitive psychologists, computer scientists, IT designers, and design re- searchers to explore their interrelationships and involvement in Human-Computer interaction (HCI).

ICS is not designed as a theory to support task analysis or design but is a general purpose representation of cognitive operations. It is a theory of cognitive function derived from empirical research in psychology and is open to empirical testing. In addition to the HCI applications of Amodeus, it has been used within clinical psychology and as a basic cognitive model within experimental psychology. For HCI designers, a handbook has been published for use in master's degree HCI courses and tutorials at HCI conferences given to teach the approach to entrants to the IT industries in Europe. A CTA in ICS attempts to identify the cognitive resources that an individual operator would need to employ in performing a task. Having identified these resources, the analysts can note conflicts where a single resource is required to do different things or is required by competing simultaneous tasks. The availability of prior knowledge to support processing can be estimated systematically, and the scope that processing allows for the progressive development of knowledge can be assessed. The behavioral consequences of the analysis are qualitative rather than the quantitative, time-based products of GOMS, since they highlight points in the task where processing demands are high and so where errors may occur. Support for redesign is implicit but guided by the analysts' under- standing of the theoretical concepts that they have used in building the CTA. A close coupling between the underlying theory and the analytical process is seen by the proponents of ICS as a key strength.

Because ICS addresses only the cognitive operations of a single user, it has not yet been applied to tasks in which several people collaborate, and because it takes as its starting point a description of the task to be designed, it does not include a conventional task analysis phase. Collaborative tasks can in principle be understood by modeling the processing of each individual, but owing to its form ICS allows a more ambitious scaling up of the approach. The ICS architecture has been influenced by ideas about information processing drawn from computer science, and the generic nature of the components of the overall system has allowed parallels to be drawn with formal models of systems analysis known as interactors. This has been used to develop a quasi-formal analytical method called syndetics in which a computing system and the human cognitive architecture are modeled conjointly as interactors, no distinction being made within the model as to the human or technological origin of particular interactors.

In principle, a syndetic analysis could be applied to collaborative working, with individuals being classed as interactors within the work group. TKS is a knowledge-based method of task decomposition, and there are some interesting parallels with the way that knowledge is formed and abstracted in ICS. TKS has also conventionally addressed the individual task operator, and current research is exploring a combination of ICS and TKS to support their joint extension to collaborative and multiple task performance.

Interacting Cognitive Subsystems

Models within cognitive psychology have usually been developed to describe the mental functions necessary for a particular phenomenon, such as face perception, reading, semantic memory, working memory, and so on. Typically, these models consist of box and arrow diagrams and in a sense are similar to a hierarchical task analysis conducted on aspects of human thought: The boxes represent things that logically have to be done, and each box can potentially be broken down into smaller units. Arrows drawn between boxes can represent either process relationships such as "this function enables that function" or "this function requires that function." The cognitive architecture represented by ICS is different and sometimes difficult for those experienced in cognitive psychology to grasp (perhaps for the same reason, it seems easier for computer scientists to follow the ideas). It starts from the assumption that mental operations can be thought of independently of the functional roles they support and that a limited number of general purpose operations can be used to perform all cognitive tasks. Phenomena such as short-term memory, semantic memory, attention, perception, and executive control arise from the activity of these operations, but the operations themselves are not specific to these phenomena. The boxes in ICS are not functions that need to be carried out but information-processing operations that carry out functions, and the arrows indicate a flow of information between operations.

The general purpose operation that ICS carries out is the transformation of a mental representation from one form, in which it describes a particular class of information about the world, into another form, in which it describes a different class of information. In performing this operation, ICS will store the incoming representation in a local form of long-term memory called the image record and will access proceduralized knowledge acquired from previous experiences with the incoming information to try to produce the appropriate output representation. In general within cognitive psychology, proceduralized knowledge is knowledge about how to do something that has become so well learnt that the action can be carried out without conscious effort. In ICS, proceduralized knowledge is embedded within the transformation processes, and it allows them to produce an output for a particular input without accessing the image record. If it is poorly developed, ICS may try to access previous experiences that are similar to the incoming representation from the image record, to elaborate and refine it. Finally, if the output representation that is produced is used successfully in task performance, the procedural knowledge relating the incoming and output representations is updated or strengthened, as appropriate. A key aspect of CTA in ICS is identifying the demands on proceduralized knowledge, the scope for its development (that is, skill acquisition), the support provided by the image record contents, and the scope for its development (that is, schematic abstraction in memory).

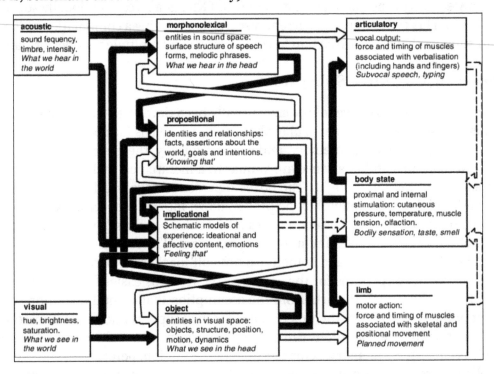

These three basic operations—storage, transformation, and revival of information by memory—are grouped together within a "subsystem" dedicated to the processing of one par- ticular class of information. (Stored information is said to be "revived by memory" rather than "retrieved from memory" because memory is seen as an active entity rather than a passive store.) The overall system is built up of nine such subsystems, each one taking as its incoming representation either information from the sensory organs (the eyes and ears, which sense distal information sources, and bodily sensations, which sense proximal information sources such as taste, smell, temperature, and body states) or crucially, cognitive information that has been output by another subsystem. Together these nine subsystems operate in parallel to continually process a flow of information. Figure details the subsystems and shows how they are linked together.

Two important features of the organization of the system should be noted: (a) Each subsystem produces more than one class of information but not all possible types (in fact, no more than three types), and (b) most subsystems have more than one source of incoming information.

The nine subsystems of ICS and the classes of information processed at each subsystem. The arrows indicate the potential flows of information, showing how the output of one subsystem can be used as the incoming representation of another subsystem. Black arrows represent "abstractive" flow, white arrows "elaborative" flow. Dashed arrows are indirect, because they represent information exchange mediated by changes in the body.

Looking in more detail at the nine classes of information encompassed within the scope of ICS, First, there are three sensory subsystems, two on the left of figure operating on Acoustic and Visual sensations and one on the right operating on Body State sensations. Second, there are four central subsystems operating on different levels of interpreted meaning derived from the sensory information. These are the Morphonolexical and Object subsystems, which primarily process information from their respective sensory subsystems, and the Propositional and Implicational subsystems, which deal with increasingly abstract levels of meaning. Third, there are two effector subsystems, Articulatory and Limb, whose output is used to execute physical actions in the world.

No subsystem does much on its own. Just seeing something, for example, is a flow of information from the eyes through the Visual subsystem (which extracts both quantitative featural and qualitative affective information from the sensation and discards a lot of the sensory detail), the Object subsystem (which identifies objects and their spatial and activity relationships), the Propositional subsystem (which infers the meaning of the objects being seen and the actions they are performing and their relevance to the self and one's goals), and the Implicational subsystem (which detects conformance or violation of goals, revises current goals, and produces affective responses in the body, subsequently detected by the Body State subsystem). This is the simplest flow, leaving out any mental naming (Morphonolexical), vocalization (Articulatory), or motor activity (Limb) and thus any interaction with the seen object. Any cognitive task will inevitably require the involvement of processes within several subsystems, and so the CTA must consider the procedural knowledge available for each process and the image record contents of each subsystem.

At first sight, figure looks like a rather redundant way of building a stimulus-response architecture, with several stages intervening between sensation and action. As the arrows indicate, however, flow is not limited to this single direction. In particular, the four central subsystems can all take some of each others' outputs as additional inputs, allowing loops of processing as well as top-down internal initiation of thought and action. Taking the nature of the information processed by the different subsystems into account, we can distinguish two types of transformation: abstractive and elaborative.

Abstractive transformations build "higher level" classes of information from more detailed classes, and the transformations from the Visual subsystem through to the Implicational subsystem described in the example of seeing were all of this type. They all involve combining the basic units of description of the incoming class to produce some higher level of description. This higher level becomes the basic unit of description in the output representation, with the constituent detail of the incoming information being discarded. Thus, an Object level of representation contains organizational details such as shape, orientation, and overall color that have been inferred from the more detailed Visual level of representation, but it does not contain the minute textural details or variation in color caused by lighting. Abstractive flows between subsystems are indicated by black arrows in figure.

Elaborative transformations work in the opposite direction. That is, the basic units of description are broken down into their constituent elements, and any higher level organization is lost. An elaborative transformation works to add in detail that was not present at the higher level of description. The elaborative flows are shown by the white arrows in figure. Some of them correspond to what might be seen as the response side of a stimulus-response flow of processing, such as those from Morphonolexical to Articulatory and from Object to Limb, but others operate purely within the architecture, with information flowing from the Implicational to the Propositional subsystem and thence to the Morphonolexical and Object subsystems. The hierarchical, structured nature of information is a central concept in ICS.

Coupling these iterative and combinative flow patterns with each subsystem's independent access to memory means that ICS is able to encompass the rich variety of human cognitive experience. It also means that there is seldom just one way to do anything, which threatens to make CTA using the full model a frustratingly noncommittal exercise. Luckily, the simplest way of processing information through the architecture is associated with greater speed of execution, less ambiguity of behavioral output, and less subjective effort. Therefore, the more complex the alternate processing route required, the worse the results in terms of the conventional metrics of usability or task design.

A CTA in ICS is a more qualitative exercise than the quantitative assessments typically resulting from models such as those in the GOMS tradition. Every CTA results in a family of different cognitive task models, and each model is a snapshot of the cognitive activity of a particular user who is at a specific phase in the task, has a given level of expertise at the task, and is working within a specific task context. The three levels of user expertise shown in figure are simply nominal, representing people who have no previous experience of the task in question (the "novice" level), a great deal of experience (the "expert" level), or some experience (the "normal" level, which would be the level of a typical person). Although the very short term dynamics of cognitive activity are represented within a single model (which gives access to conventional interface design information such as "Will users notice this button?"), consideration of the relationships between models for different phases of activity within a task can address the short-term dynamics of task performance (e.g., "Will users do the elements of this task in an appropriate order?"). Finally, the relationships between models for different levels of user expertise can inform the analyst about the longer term dynamics, such as likely patterns of learning, development of preferred patterns of use, and persistent errors.

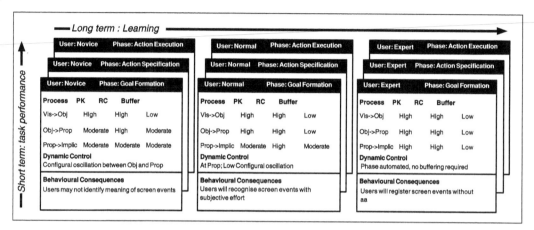

Figure: A family of cognitive task models for novice, normal, and expert users at three phases of task performance. Each model details the configuration of processes, the status of their procedural knowledge, record contents, and requirements for memory access, together with the implications for dynamic control of cognition and likely behavioral consequences. A single model represents the very short-term dynamics of cognition; a stack of three phases represents the short-term dynamics of task performance; and changes across the three stacks represent long-term dynamics, or task learning.

The Process of Actainics

The family of cognitive task models illustrated in figure indicate that conducting a CTA in ICS requires the analysts to identify the level of expertise of the individual they are concerned with as well as the phase of task performance. Within a phase, the analysts have to identify the configuration of subsystems that will be involved in the flow and hence the transformation processes operating within each subsystem (indicated in figure by the "Process" column in each model). For each process, the analysts must consider the degree of existing proceduralized knowledge that is available (the "PK" column) and the availability of experiential image record contents that may be recruited to assist in strengthening the incoming representation (the "RC" column). In situations where there is little proceduralized knowledge and weak record contents to support the transformation, the process will attempt to operate in a buffered mode. In this mode, the process, instead of working directly on the incoming information supported by record contents, works solely on record contents.

The fourth column in the models describes the likelihood that each process will attempt to work in buffered mode. This is an important indication of the subjective effort that will be felt in task performance, because it operates like a bottleneck in the flow of information and gives rise to focal awareness of the information being processed. Subjectively, the individual feels that he or she is having to concentrate on whatever aspect of the task is being buffered. Tasks that have little proceduralized knowledge may require the buffer to move back and forth between two or even more subsystems (oscillation), making the individual feel that he or she is having to switch attention between several different aspects of the task. In contrast, a task for which proceduralized knowledge is available for the complete flow may not require buffering and may be able to be performed automatically, or at least without the individual needing to concentrate on it. Identifying the need for buffering allows this degree of dynamic control of cognition to be assessed.

Once these three classes of information have been established for each phase, the interrelationships of the phases of activity can be considered. The three phases of goal formation (realizing that something needs to be done), action specification (working out how to accomplish a goal), and action execution (carrying out actions to meet a goal) can, in the simplest tasks, be sequential, but neither real life nor ICS require a strict serial ordering.

In practice, an individual is usually doing several things at once, and there may be multiple cues in the world or in the individual's active cognitive content that indicate a new goal. While actions are specified to meet these goals, the task context may change, leading to a modification of the goal (i.e., a further round of goal formation). While actions are executed to meet the goal, the task context needs to be evaluated to refine the actions, modify plans (i.e., further action specification), and perhaps form subsidiary goals (i.e., yet more goal formation). Within any one task, it is more likely that these three phases will be richly interleaved than serial, and it is also conceivable that the phases of different tasks may be interleaved as the individual divides his or her effort between them. Interleaving of tasks and interleaving of phases of activity may be straightforward if the configurations of the processes that they require differ, and the tasks and phases may even be able to continue in parallel if they do not compete for the same resource (i.e., the same transformation processes or image records). However, as soon as competition occurs, then the architecture needs to be able to shift between different flows of information, adding the costs of disengagement and reengagement.

CTA in ICS consists of identifying four aspects of cognitive resources:

- The configuration of transformation processes in the flow of information between subsystems.

- The proceduralized knowledge available for each process (and potential change).

- The image record contents available within each subsystem (and potential change).

- The dynamic control in terms of locus of buffer and interleaving of phases or tasks.

Constructing a CTA

Constructing configurations of ICS transformation processes is the first step in a CTA. Once each process has been noted, the next step is to consider the degree of proceduralized knowledge available to support the processes' actions and what record contents might be available to supplement it. Because knowledge acquisition is the development of record contents and then proceduralized knowledge, it generally results in one process learning to produce an output directly from its input without needing to engage in loops with other subsystems or accessing its own image record contents. The configurations for normal task operators and then experts will usually be compressions of the novice configuration. By starting with the novice pattern, as in the examples in the, the configurations for the more practiced classes of operator can be inferred relatively easily.

Learning and Errors

The characteristic patterns of learning and skill acquisition also emerge directly from this process of modeling. Development of record contents and proceduralized knowledge will be greatest in the subsystems that have the most buffering, and reliance on memory access in these subsystems means that the task is effectively "controlled" by the class of information that they operate on. Errors and confusions between similar entities within the task will be most likely to occur at this level. Changes in the task that alter the information being used to control the task, perhaps by modifying the nature or grouping of the task entities, will have differing degrees of impact depending on the relationship between the changes and the level at which task control resides. If the changes are at the same level of information as the task control, then they will be most disruptive, since all that has been gained by buffered processing and the construction of new record contents will have to be relearnt. If the changes occur at a different level, then they may be easily accommodated, since all that will have to be relearnt will be mappings in what were presumably well-proceduralized processes.

For example, suppose that someone has learnt to associate several task steps by learning an Implicational relationship between them: They might all share some common functional attribute such as "deletion" or "coloring." This relationship would be represented in ICS by the development of proceduralized knowledge in the Implicational-to-Propositional process, so that forming the implicational representation of deletion or coloring would allow the Implicational-to-Propositional process to derive abstract propositional task steps. The Propositional subsystem would receive this information stream, subsequently using its Propositional to - Morphonolexical process to output verbal names for the task steps. Redesigning the task to change the verbal forms required for task execution will have little detrimental effect, provided that the task attributes required for goal formation are not altered, because all that the individual will have to learn will be new Propositional-to-Morphonolexical mappings (which might already exist). Adding a new task step that fits the same implicational form as the existing steps will also not be problematic, although it might be occasionally omitted while learning is taking place. Changing the sequence in which the task steps have to be executed or interspersing new steps that do not fit the same implicational mold as the learnt steps will be very detrimental, since the controlling implicational representations will have to be relearnt. The operator will need to regress to the novice level for this task yet will also have existing but now incorrect record contents that must be overcome in learning rather than having nothing interfere, as a true novice would.

Controlling Attention

Tasks that require the operator to notice some event in the world and to carry out a single response are nice to model but rare in practice. It is more often the case that the operator must search the world for task-relevant information to form task goals; specify the actions with reference to other, perhaps dynamic attributes of task entities; and execute their actions in a changing world while monitoring the behavior of other task entities to ensure that their planned actions and inferred goals are accurate. We can do all this because we can direct our attention around the world, actively seeking information from different sensory streams and from different entities within those streams. Attention is task motivated and is task directed. The ICS architecture allows us to model this without requiring an attention module or having to postulate a central executive that controls and schedules actions. The location of buffered processing accounts for the level of information that provides the sense of focal awareness, but the explanation for how we can control attention within this level relates to the abstraction and elaboration of information as it is transformed by the processes in the different subsystems.

The generic information-processing architecture of ICS subsystems allows us to use a generic representational notation for the structure of information regardless of its class or content. Whatever the class, information consists of basic units of meaning. At the Object level, for example, the basic units are entities in visual space; at the Propositional level, they will be the abstract identities of entities and their interrelationships. In a conventional computer interface window, the Object basic units might be graphical icons, checkboxes, text labels, or parts of the window frame itself (e.g., Word Icon–PDF Icon–Word Icon). At a Propositional level, they might be the identities recognized from these Objects and their interrelationships. These basic units will each have a detailed constituent structure. Objects consist of parts that can include other smaller objects and ultimately parts such as edges, corners, surfaces (e.g., one form of Word icon consists of a blue italic W on a document icon that holds some small lines of text); Propositions can be subdivided into attributes and relationships (e.g., task steps can be broken down into subtasks and their sequencing down to and even beyond the keystroke level). Basic units also group together into higher order units, or assemblies (to give an A-B-C hierarchy of structure, as shown in figure. Objects group together to form regions of a scene (the icons are part of an array, which is part of a window, which is part of the display); Propositions assemble together to form sequences of related knowledge (the task steps are part of an overall goal).

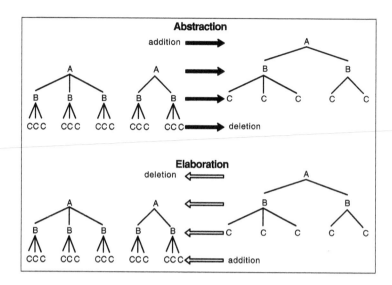

In the figure above, Information at all levels in ICS is composed of basic units of meaning (B) that have constituent substructures (C) and can be clustered into higher order assemblies (A). Abstraction between subsystems uses the assemblies to derive the basic units of the output representation; elaboration uses the constituent substructures. Abstraction adds new higher order assemblies in the output representation while losing the detail of the input's constituent structures; elaboration adds new detailed constituent structures in the output while losing the higher order assemblies from the input.

Each transformation process changes the qualitative nature of the information being output, but the chunks of information that correspond to the basic units of the output representation relate to the input representation in a straightforward way. A process that is abstracting information (the black arrows in is using the assemblies from its input representation to form the basic units of its output representation, whereas a process that is elaborating information (the white arrows) is using the constituent structures of its input to form the basic units of its output representation. Each process discards information. In particular, the output of an abstractive process does not include the constituent structure of its input representation, and the output representation of an elaborative process does not include the assembly units of its input. Each process also needs to add in new information that was not present in its input. An abstractive process needs to construct new, higher order assemblies to group together the basic units, and an elaborative process needs to construct new, more detailed constituent structures for each basic unit it is outputting. This "new" information is to some extent inherent in the input information, but it is effectively the contribution of memory, either through use of record contents or proceduralized knowledge. Cognitive processing is the repeated application of memory to refine information.

When a subsystem is receiving two inputs simultaneously, one might be from an elaborative process, the other from an abstractive process. One will be rich in the detailed constituent structure of the information (because it is derived from the basic units of information used in the prior process) but have weak assembly information (because it has been inferred from memory); the other will have detailed assembly information but be weak in the constituent structures. Together they may blend to complement each other. They can only do this, though, if their basic units are coherent; where they are, the detailed hierarchical information may overwrite the weaker information. Basic units that are in one stream but not the other may not be included in the blended representation or may be included but with either a weak degree of detail or a weak linking in to the organization of the other basic units.

This idea of hierarchical structure, abstraction, and elaboration allows the model to include an analysis of when streams of information are coherent and can blend and when they are incoherent and must be alternately processed or processed separately by different processes within a subsystem. It also gives the model a way of representing thematic changes in processing such as those that reflect a change in attentional focus within a subsystem. Focal awareness (and hence attention) is determined by the location of the buffer, and the content of awareness is the information that is being buffered. Attention shifts between different classes of information reflect changes of the buffer between subsystems, but when attention shifts within a subsystem, the unit of information that is being buffered changes instead. Since the subsystem itself cannot alter its inputs it must follow from a change in the information arriving on the input array. There are consequently two types of attentional shift: an exogenous shift that is caused by a change in the content of an abstracted stream, driven ultimately by a change in the external world, and an endogenous shift that is caused by a change in the content of an elaborated stream, driven by internal processing.

Both exogenous and endogenous shifts in attention can also be modeled using the ideas of hierarchical structure. Although there can be several basic units at a level of representation, one will be the current topic of processing and hence the psychological subject of awareness in the subsystem (and if buffered, of the whole architecture). The other basic units are in awareness (but less focally), as predicate elements of the topic. These terms are taken from the systemic grammar of Halliday but can be interpreted generally to cover all classes of information, not just linguistic representations. Also in awareness are the topic's assembly structure and constituent structure. Changes in attention can be made to any of the other basic units (i.e., within the predicate structure), to the assembly of the topic (i.e., "up" the hierarchy in an abstraction), or to the constituent structure of the topic (i.e., "down" the hierarchy in an elaboration).

Graphical Notation to Represent Attentional Shifts

Shifts in attention can only occur when there is a change in the stream of information being processed. Endogenous streams can change when the output from a process that is feeding into the subsystem retopicalizes on a different element because of a change in the activity of the process (i.e., a different rule within the process gains control of the output). Endogenous shifts in attention are therefore are a consequence of activity in at least two subsystems. Figure illustrates the nature of attentional shifts in the object level of representation when a computer user attends to various elements of a graphical user interface. Each row of the figure shows the elements of the representation that are currently in awareness: at the left, the assembly of the current topic; on its right, the topic and its predicate basic units; and at the right, the constituent structure of the current topic. Time is represented on the vertical axis, with each successive row representing a new state of attention in the subsystem.

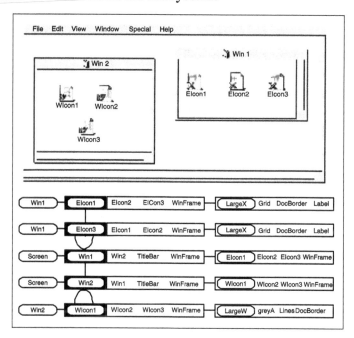

A transition path diagram (TPD) representing successive shifts in attention around a simple window interface. Each row in the TPD represents a moment in time, with the assembly, basic units, and constituent structure that are in awareness at a particular level of representation (here the object level). Time is represented vertically, so reading the diagram from top to bottom reveals successive shifts in attention, first to an element in the predicate of the initial topic, then to their shared assembly unit. There is then a transition to a predicate of this higher order unit, followed by a transition down into its substructure.

The nature of the shift in attention between each row is indicated by the symbol joining the successive topics. A vertical bar represents a shift to an element of the predicate structure (that is, within a level). Note that the assembly unit remains the same because all basic units within the attentional focus are part of the same higher order unit, but also note that the constituent structure in awareness alters to reflect the detail of the new topic. An abstraction up the hierarchy to make the previous assembly unit the new topic is marked by a U-link. The previous basic units become the constituent structure, and new predicate elements enter awareness, together with a new assembly unit that groups them together with the topic. An abstraction down the hierarchy into the constituent structure of the topic results in the previous topic becoming the new assembly unit. One of the elements of the constituent structure becomes the new topic, with the others forming its predicate, and the new constituent structure depends on the topic.

Figure represents shifts in visual attention around a scene. The figure represents the transitions that are made over time and so is called a Transition Path Diagram (TPD).

Although the basic units of the representation move up and down, the quality of the information represented does not change: It remains at the Object level. The process mapping this into a Propositional output, though, will be changing the quality of the information as well as its level—as will the process mapping it to the Limb subsystem. TPDs can be drawn for any of the nine levels of information processed in ICS, although the nature of the units represented will vary. In a Morphonolexical TPD, the units are phonemes or sound entities. In a Propositional TPD, the units are entities, their properties, and their relationships. In an Implicational TPD, the units are schematic patterns of affect and feeling.

TPDs are of most use in CTA in supporting reasoning about the need for oscillation between different configurations within task performance and in determining how well the structure of the information presented by the world conforms to the expectations of the operator, as represented by the task goals. Parallel TPDs drawn for Object and Propositional levels can allow the analyst to check that changes in the visual information available to the operator (or the operator's attentional shifts around an unchanging scene) match changes in the task goals (at the Propositional level), check that appropriate information is available just when the operator needs it, and determine whether this information might in fact force an exogenous shift in attention and so aid in goal formation. Parallel TPDs drawn for the Morphonolexical and Object subsystems can show how well sound and vision will support each other (that is, do sound events occur at appropriate times, given the influence of the POP loop on the Object structure?). Further details about the use of TPDs can be found in Barnard and May.

Applying CTA in ICS

Drawing TPDs is helpful for an analyst who is becoming familiar with the ideas of CTA in ICS. With practice, though, the ideas about structure become second nature, and the notation plays a secondary role (namely, it helps the analyst explain the reasoning behind the analysis to others on the design team or to those who have commissioned the design). Similarly, the abbreviated lexical notation for representing configurations of processing can help an analyst spot duplicated resource requirements and possible points of blending or incoherence in the flow, but for a more experienced analyst, it will be used more for communicating and recording the CTA rather than executing it. The analytical steps of identifying the configuration of processing resources, and then their memory requirements, for the different phases of task performance and different classes of users, remains the core of the technique.

With any analytical technique, there will always be a degree of skill involved in its application. For instance, an experienced analyst will be able to draw on a history of similar analyses and jump to a conclusion without apparently engaging in any real analysis. The question of what role the theory or the analytic method play, compared with the skill of an experienced analyst, can be answered by the proof-of-concept expert system that was developed in the Amodeus projects. This was a collection of production rules that embodied a limited amount of knowledge about the domain of HCI and ICS and was thus able to produce CTAs for several scenarios of common HCI problems. Three classes of rules were written: The first class asked questions about the scenario to aid in building an abstract task description; the second embodied ICS principles and used this task description to produce a family of cognitive task models (CTMs); the third deduced some behavioral consequences from the CTMs. No learning was possible (the rules were not modified automatically), and there was no skill in using the system (apart from learning how to describe the task when applying the first class of rules), and despite the limited nature of the third class of rules, it was found that the system could make interpretable and sensible predictions about novel scenarios other than those that its rules had been written to encompass.

Future Developments

The descriptions used the terms operator and task device rather than user and computer or interface to reinforce the generality of the approach. The human cognitive architecture existed long before computers and graphical user interfaces, and a method that describes task performance in cognitive terms should be applicable just as much to the design of real artifacts and tools and to communicative tasks where several people exchange information without using any artifacts at all. Communicative tasks are often mediated by IT, though, and methods originally scoped to deal with individual HCI tasks are being examined to see how they can change their focus to be applied to collaborative situations in which group goals must be shared and other individuals' knowledge and goals must be recognized if task performance is to be successful.

Syndetics represents agents in an interaction as discrete, independent interactors that exchange information and attempt to coordinate their activity, whether they be humans, machines, or software components. It has been used to model conjoint human-machine software systems such as intelligent whiteboards with gesture recognition, and it has been argued that it is potentially extensible to command-and-control situations as varied as a missile defence room on a naval warship and the routing of the Roman armies by the Carthaginian army at Cannae.

One of problems in the wider field of task analysis is relating cognitive task analysis to higher levels of analysis. For example, how do constraints that work in the individual mind and the technologies it has to support its work affect the behavior of a group or team? Going a step further, how do constraints at the level of the group or team affect the wider organization? The problem is one of communication between different levels of analysis. Traditional forms of task analysis embed task analysis for an individual within a team task analysis, which is in turn embedded in an analysis of the wider workflow within the overall organization. Attempts to build models that work across multiple levels of analysis have often foundered on the difficulty of relating the analytical approaches that apply at these different levels. Syndetic modeling and the framework of systems analysis that supports it attempt to resolve this problem by couching the input and output of each level of analysis within the same notational form and by identifying two kinds of theory.

All systems, in abstract terms, consist of a number of entities that interact to constrain the overall behavior of the system, and the task of a type 1 theory is to explain the way that these interactors behave. In task analysis, there will be different type 1 theories for explaining an individual's cognitive behavior (such as ICS), the behavior of a group or team (perhaps a task analysis model), and the workflow in an organization (perhaps a social psychology model). No system operates in isolation, however, for systems must themselves interact with other systems. A human interacts with other humans, with computers, with tools, and with organizations, among other entities. As well as consisting of interactors, then, each system is itself an interactor. To understand the workings of any system of interactors, it is necessary to know the external, observable behavior of other systems with which it interacts, but it is not necessary for a single type 1 theory to be able to model the internal behavior of those systems. That is the job of other type 1 theories scoped specifically for those interactors. A theory of the second kind (a type 2 theory) specifically relates these levels of analysis to one another. In task analysis, then, there needs to be a type 2 theory to explain how inferences about an individual task analysis can be taken up by the theory that addresses team tasks and another type 2 theory to explain how the results of team task analyses can be taken up by organization-level theories.

Recognizing the need for both types of theories is a crucial step, because it allows a theory that is restricted to a particular level of analysis to obtain information and insights from beyond its own analytic scope (by using type 2 theory to communicate with a type 1 theory of a different level of analysis). Equally, the inferences and conclusions of a type 1 theory at one level can be communicated to and have an effect on other levels of analysis. The current situation is that type 1 theories are far more common than type 2 theories. Indeed, there seems to be a reluctance by the theorists who have developed type 1 theories even to recognize that building type 2 theories to relate their work to that of other theorists is advantageous and strengthens their own approach.

The potential benefit that the syndetic approach offers is in understanding the way that these different levels relate together via type 2 theoretical interfaces. Using the same principles of abstraction and elaboration that ICS applies to the exchange of information within and between its cognitive subsystems, it is possible to argue that each level of theoretical analysis has a basic unit of analysis (whether this be a software entity, cognitive process, person, team, or organization) and a constituent structure and that these units can be assembled into higher order units. Successful communication between levels of analysis requires the recognition of mappings between the basic units of one level and another level's constituent structures (for an abstractive mapping) or assembly structures (for an elaborative mapping).

Just as a cognitive model such as ICS works with a configuration of mental processes, so a group or team can be regarded as configured to support particular interactions within the team and between that team and another. Figure shows a purely hypothetical analysis of a manufacturing company, with its inputs and outputs and internal departmental structure. When the structure of one of the departments, which deals with incoming raw materials, is considered in more detail, the functions that it carries out are noted. Each of these functions is carried out by a human employee, whose cognitive processes can be modeled by ICS subsystems. The number and arrangement of the components of the manufacturing company and the raw materials department both mirror that of ICS. Realistic systems would not, of course, have this form. For figurative purposes only, the arrangement serves to make clear the analogy of the mappings between different levels and also the potential for applying, by extension, the same basic notations (e.g., configural definitions and TPDs) to the analysis of interactions within each level.

We can think of the parallels at the level of the more abstract concept of "interactors." At one level of analysis, the interactors are mental processes within the cognitive system; at the next level, they are people in a team; and at the highest level depicted, they are whole departments. The hierarchical decompositions, configural definitions used for ICS and the TPDs, could all potentially be applied at each level. In figure each level contains what amounts to a control loop, where the behavior of the basic unit is partly determined by interactions among its constituents and partly constrained by the assembly of external interactors that the system engages with.

In this syndetic analysis, the manufacturing company is an interactor that exchanges information (and physical objects) with other interactors at the same level of granularity. These are basic units at an economic level of analysis. The constituent structure of the company consists of the major functions that need to be carried out, and these functions become the basic units of a lower level of organizational analysis. At this level, the company is the assembly, the departments are the basic units, and the roles carried out within each department are the constituents. Organizational theory provides the appropriate type 1 body of theory. At the next level of analysis down, the roles map onto humans, who are the basic units, and each unit interacts with other entities such as other people, computers, tools, and so on. Within each human, the constituent structure of cognitive subsystems can be seen, and so on. If desired, computational models of the activity within a process could be postulated, even neural models of their implementation within the brain. The key is that different theories and methods of analysis can operate at each level, but communication between them is only comprehensible once the mappings between units of analysis are made explicit. If mappings cannot sensibly be made, then it is likely that at least one level of analysis is missing, in which case the mappings are attempting to bridge too great an abstractive or elaborative gulf.

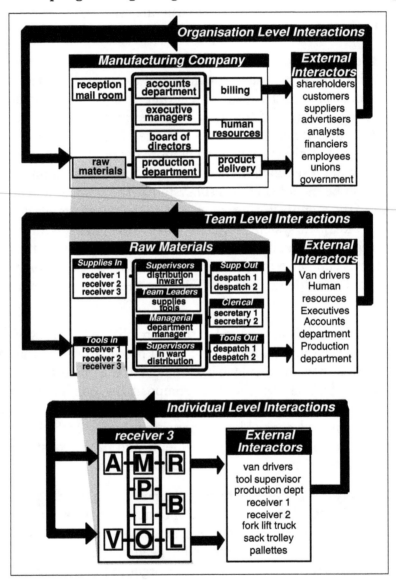

In a syndetic model, a manufacturing company interacts with its world (consisting of other interactors at the same level of granularity), and it consists of a number of departments. Each department fulfills a number of roles, and each role is carried out by a human. The humans interact with their world (consisting of other interactors), and their cognitive behavior is modeled by postulating a number of subsystems.

This division of analysis into levels, each with its own body of type 1 theory and way of dividing the world up into analyzable entities, helps us to resolve the otherwise problematic absence of a task analysis phase in the CTA in ICS approach.

Because ICS is a cognitive model of an individual, it does not make any theoretical sense to try to extend its scope to include task analysis, especially since there are already many well-explored methods and theories in this area. No one theory is grand enough to explain everything in a manner that is economical enough to be applicable. What is required is a coherent interface between levels. To link a cognitive task analysis with wider methods of task analysis, the interface can be an approach in which the basic unit of analysis is a human, the constituent structure is cognitive in nature, and mappings can be built between this cognitive structure and the information levels of ICS. The task analytic method can then be strengthened by abstraction from the outputs of ICS (being given a rationale for the cognitive behavior of its human), and ICS can be strengthened by elaboration from the outputs of the task analytic method (being given a rationale for the structure of the tasks being modeled).

TKS is a task analytic method that provides exactly the sort of type 2 theoretical interface between system levels that we need. It produces a task description in terms of the structures of knowledge of task operations and task entities that an individual needs to possess to work with a well-defined subset of external interactors. TKS effectively specifies what is required to make the lowest level of control loop shown in figure function, whereas ICS specifies only the internal interactors of the mental architecture. TKS includes notions of abstraction of task knowledge that is grounded in the external interactors, be the other members of the team or technological artifacts available for use or under design. These can then be related to the abstraction and elaboration of information within ICS and its re-representation at multiple levels of processing. In TKS, the controlling knowledge about an entity or a task step is contingent upon the task context. This itself originates in the properties of teams and artifacts. In ICS, the finer levels of "cognitive control" are similarly constrained by the location of the buffered process or the level of information that is in focal awareness. It is hoped that bringing these two approaches together will offer benefits to both, by offering ICS a link to a well-tested form of task analysis and providing TKS with analytical tools for reasoning about the abstraction and elaboration of task knowledge. These benefits are thought to be important in allowing the two approaches to be extended to situations where a person is performing multiple tasks at the same time or where several people are collaborating on a single task. In these situations, the analysis needs to take into account the conflicting demands of two task sequences and knowledge structures or the demands of the communication of task knowledge and of the assessment by one individual of the states of knowledge and intentions of others engaged in the task. This requires that both the prior task analysis feeding into ICS and the cognitive basis of task knowledge be given firmer foundations.

Developments along these lines show that, although CTA in ICS is a helpful problem-solving technique that can provide support to those who need to understand human cognitive processing in task performance, it is also an extensible technique that can deal with the changing demands of design. Its supportive nature and its extensibility are both consequences of the close relationship between the application representation and the underlying science base (the cognitive theory of ICS). These form a reciprocal pair, analogous to processing loops in ICS, with advances in one driving developments in the other. Research and application of task analytic techniques are not only of practical importance but have a crucial role to play in feeding back information to cognitive psychology and theories of systems analysis.

Dialog Designs

A dialog is the construction of interaction between two or more beings or systems.

In HCI, a dialog is studied at three levels:

- Lexical – Shape of icons, actual keys pressed, etc., are dealt at this level.

- Syntactic – The order of inputs and outputs in an interaction are described at this level.

- Semantic – At this level, the effect of dialog on the internal application/data is taken care of.

Dialog Representation

To represent dialogs, we need formal techniques that serve two purposes:

- It helps in understanding the proposed design in a better way.

- It helps in analysing dialogs to identify usability issues. E.g., Questions such as "does the design actually support undo?" can be answered.

Formalism

There are many formalism techniques that we can use to signify dialogs. we will discuss on three of these formalism techniques, which are:

- The state transition networks (STN).

- The state charts.

- The classical Petri nets.

State Transition Network

STNs are the most spontaneous, which knows that a dialog fundamentally denotes to a progression from one state of the system to the next.

The syntax of an STN consists of the following two entities:

- Circles – A circle refers to a state of the system, which is branded by giving a name to the state.

- Arcs – The circles are connected with arcs that refers to the action/event resulting in the transition from the state where the arc initiates, to the state where it ends.

STN Diagram

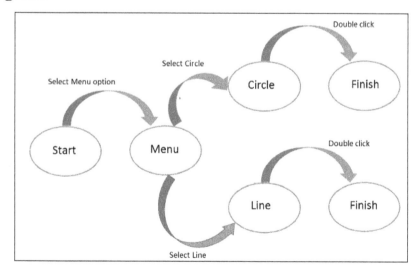

State Charts

State Charts represent complex reactive systems that extend Finite State Machines (FSM), handle concurrency, and add memory to FSM. It also simplifies complex system representations. State Charts has the following states:

- Active state – The present state of the underlying FSM.

- Basic states – These are individual states and are not composed of other states.

- Super states – These states are composed of other states.

Let us see the State Chart Construction of a machine that dispense bottles on inserting coins.

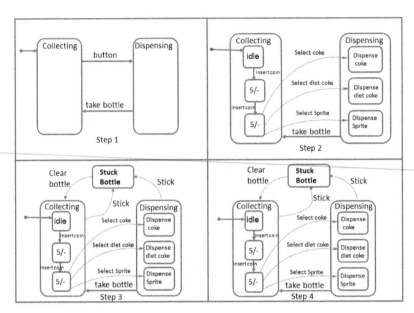

The above diagram explains the entire procedure of a bottle dispensing machine. On pressing the button after inserting coin, the machine will toggle between bottle filling and dispensing modes. When a required request bottle is available, it dispense the bottle. In the background, another procedure runs where any stuck bottle will be cleared.

Petri Nets

Petri Net is a simple model of active behavior, which has four behavior elements such as – places, transitions, arcs and tokens. Petri Nets provide a graphical explanation for easy understanding.

- Place – This element is used to symbolize passive elements of the reactive system. A place is represented by a circle.

- Transition – This element is used to symbolize active elements of the reactive system. Transitions are represented by squares/rectangles.

- Arc – This element is used to represent causal relations. Arc is represented by arrows.

- Token – This element is subject to change. Tokens are represented by small filled circles.

Visual Thinking

Visual materials has assisted in the communication process since ages in form of paintings, sketches, maps, diagrams, photographs, etc. In today's world, with the invention of technology and its further growth, new potentials are offered for visual information such as thinking and reasoning. As per studies, the command of visual thinking in human-computer interaction (HCI) design is still not discovered completely. So, let us learn the theories that support visual thinking in sense-making activities in HCI design.

An initial terminology for talking about visual thinking was discovered that included concepts such as visual immediacy, visual impetus, visual impedance, and visual metaphors, analogies and associations, in the context of information design for the web.

As such, this design process became well suited as a logical and collaborative method during the design process. Let us discuss in brief the concepts individually.

Visual Immediacy

It is a reasoning process that helps in understanding of information in the visual representation. The term is chosen to highlight its time related quality, which also serves as an indicator of how well the reasoning has been facilitated by the design.

Visual Impetus

Visual impetus is defined as a stimulus that aims at the increase in engagement in the contextual aspects of the representation.

Visual Impedance

It is perceived as the opposite of visual immediacy as it is a hindrance in the design of the representation. In relation to reasoning, impedance can be expressed as a slower cognition.

Visual Metaphors, Association, Analogy, Abduction and Blending

- When a visual demonstration is used to understand an idea in terms of another familiar idea it is called a visual metaphor.

- Visual analogy and conceptual blending are similar to metaphors. Analogy can be defined as an implication from one particular to another. Conceptual blending can be defined as combination of elements and vital relations from varied situations.

The HCI design can be highly benefited with the use of concepts. The concepts are pragmatic in supporting the use of visual procedures in HCI, as well as in the design processes.

Direct Manipulation Programming

Direct manipulation has been acclaimed as a good form of interface design, and are well received by users. Such processes use many source to get the input and finally convert them into an output as desired by the user using inbuilt tools and programs.

"Directness" has been considered as a phenomena that contributes majorly to the manipulation programming. It has the following two aspects.

- Distance.
- Direct Engagement.

Distance

Distance is an interface that decides the gulfs between a user's goal and the level of explanation delivered by the systems, with which the user deals. These are referred to as the *Gulf of Execution* and the *Gulf of Evaluation*.

The Gulf of Execution

The Gulf of Execution defines the gap/gulf between a user's goal and the device to implement that goal. One of the principal objectives of Usability is to diminish this gap by removing barriers and follow steps to minimize the user's distraction from the intended task that would prevent the flow of the work.

The Gulf of Evaluation

The Gulf of Evaluation is the representation of expectations that the user has interpreted from the system in a design. As per Donald Norman, *The gulf is small when the system provides information about its state in a form that is easy to get, is easy to interpret, and matches the way the person thinks of the system.*

Direct Engagement

It is described as a programming where the design directly takes care of the controls of the objects presented by the user and makes a system less difficult to use.

The scrutiny of the execution and evaluation process illuminates the efforts in using a system. It also gives the ways to minimize the mental effort required to use a system.

Problems with Direct Manipulation

- Even though the immediacy of response and the conversion of objectives to actions has made some tasks easy, all tasks should not be done easily. For example, a repetitive operation is probably best done via a script and not through immediacy.

- Direct manipulation interfaces finds it hard to manage variables, or illustration of discrete elements from a class of elements.

- Direct manipulation interfaces may not be accurate as the dependency is on the user rather than on the system.

- An important problem with direct manipulation interfaces is that it directly supports the techniques, the user thinks.

Item Presentation Sequence

In HCI, the presentation sequence can be planned according to the task or application requirements. The natural sequence of items in the menu should be taken care of. Main factors in presentation sequence are:

- Time.
- Numeric ordering.
- Physical properties.

A designer must select one of the following prospects when there are no task-related arrangements:

- Alphabetic sequence of terms.
- Grouping of related items.
- Most frequently used items first.
- Most important items first.

Menu Layout

- Menus should be organized using task semantics.
- Broad-shallow should be preferred to narrow-deep.
- Positions should be shown by graphics, numbers or titles.
- Subtrees should use items as titles.
- Items should be grouped meaningfully.
- Items should be sequenced meaningfully.
- Brief items should be used.
- Consistent grammar, layout and technology should be used.
- Type ahead, jump ahead, or other shortcuts should be allowed.
- Jumps to previous and main menu should be allowed.
- Online help should be considered.

Guidelines for consistency should be defined for the following components:

- Titles.
- Item placement.
- Instructions.
- Error messages.
- Status reports.

Form Fill-in Dialog Boxes

Appropriate for multiple entry of data fields:

- Complete information should be visible to the user.
- The display should resemble familiar paper forms.
- Some instructions should be given for different types of entries.

Users must be familiar with:

- Keyboards.
- Use of TAB key or mouse to move the cursor.
- Error correction methods.
- Field-label meanings.
- Permissible field contents.
- Use of the ENTER and RETURN key.

Form Fill-in Design Guidelines:

- Title should be meaningful.
- Instructions should be comprehensible.
- Fields should be logically grouped and sequenced.
- The form should be visually appealing.
- Familiar field labels should be provided.
- Consistent terminology and abbreviations should be used.
- Convenient cursor movement should be available.
- Error correction for individual characters and entire field's facility should be present.
- Error prevention.

- Error messages for unacceptable values should be populated.

- Optional fields should be clearly marked.

- Explanatory messages for fields should be available.

- Completion signal should populate.

References

- Guidelines-in-hci, human-computer-interface-tutorial- 25507: wisdomjobs.com, Retrieved 26 January, 2019

- Human-Computer-Interaction-and-Security-HCI-Sec- 325291084: researchgate.net, Retrieved 19 June, 2019

- Dialog-design, human-computer-interface: tutorialspoint.com, Retrieved 09 July, 2019

- Horvitz, E., Jacobs, A., & Hovel, D. (1999) "Attention-Sensitive Alerting." In Proceedings of UAI '99, Conference on Uncertainty and Artificial Intelligence (Stockholm, Sweden), Morgan Kaufmann, San Francisco, pp. 305-313

3

User Interface and Development Toolkit

The platform where interaction between human and computer occurs is called a user interface. Some of the aspects that fall under its domain are user interface layer, user interface plug-in modules, user interface toolkit, visual design in HCI, user interface usability testing and evaluation methods, ethics of user experience design, etc. This chapter closely examines these aspects of user interface layer and development toolkit to provide an extensive understanding of the subject.

User Interface

A user interface is that portion of an interactive computer system that communicates with the user. Design of the user interface includes any aspect of the system that is visible to the user. Once, all computer user were specialists in computing, and interfaces consisted of jumper wires in patch boards, punched cards prepared offline, and batch printouts. Today a wide range of nonspecialists use computers, and keyboards, mice, and graphical displays are the most common interface hardware. The user interface is becoming a larger and larger portion of the software in a computer system—and a more important portion, as broader groups of people use computers. As computers become more powerful, the critical bottleneck in applying computer-based systems to solve problems is now more often in the user interface, rather than the computer hardware or software.

Because the design of the user interface includes anything that is visible to the user, interface design extends deep into the design of the interactive system as a whole. A good user interface cannot be applied to a system after it is built but must be part of the design process from the beginning. Proper design of a user interface can make a substantial difference in training time, performance speed, error rates, user satisfaction, and the user's retention of knowledge of operations over time. The poor designs of the past are giving way to elegant systems. Descriptive taxonomies of users and tasks, predictive models of performance, and explanatory theories are being developed to guide designers and evaluators. Haphazard and intuitive development strategies with claims of "user friendliness" are yielding to a more scientific approach. Measurement of learning time, performance, errors, and subjective satisfaction is now a part of the design process.

Design of a User Interface

Design of a user interface begins with task analysis—an understanding of the user's underlying tasks and the problem domain. The user interface should be designed in terms of the user's terminology and conception of his or her job, rather than the programmer's. A good understanding of the cognitive and behavioral characteristics of people in general as well as the particular user population is thus important. Good user interface design works from the user's capabilities and limitations, not the machine's; this applies to generic interfaces for large groups of people as well as to designing special interfaces for users with physical or other disabilities. Knowledge of the nature of the user's work and environment is also critical. The task to be performed can then be divided and portions assigned to the user or machine, based on knowledge of the capabilities and limitations of each.

Levels of Design

It is useful to consider the user interface at several distinct levels of abstraction and to develop a design and implementation for each. This simplifies the developer's task by allowing it to be divided into several smaller problems. The design of a user interface is often divided into the conceptual, semantic, syntactic, and lexical levels. The conceptual level describes the basic entities underlying the user's view of the system and the actions possible upon them. The semantic level describes the functions performed by the system. This corresponds to a description of the functional requirements of the system, but it does not address how the user will invoke the functions. The syntactic level describes the sequences of inputs and outputs necessary to invoke the functions described. The lexical level determines how the inputs and outputs are actually formed from primitive hardware operations.

The syntactic-semantic object-action model is a related approach; it, too, separates the task and computer concepts from the syntax for carrying out the task. For example, the task of writing a scientific journal article can be decomposed into the sub-tasks for writing the title page, the body, and the references. Similarly, the title page might be decomposed into a unique title, one or more authors, an abstract, and several keywords. To write a scientific article, the user must understand these task semantics. To use a word processor, the user must learn about computer semantics, such as directories, filenames, files, and the structure of a file. Finally, the user must learn the syntax of the commands for opening a file, inserting text, editing, and saving or printing the file. Novices often struggle to learn how to carry out their tasks on the computer and to remember the syntactic details. Once learned, the task and computer semantics are relatively stable in human memory, but the syntactic details must be frequently rehearsed. A knowledgeable user of one word processor who wishes to learn a second one only needs to learn the new syntactic details.

User Interface Management Systems

A user interface management system (UIMS) is a software component that is separate from the application program that performs the underlying task. The UIMS conducts the interaction with the user, implementing the syntactic and lexical levels, while the rest of the system implements the semantic level. Like an operating system or graphics library, a UIMS separates functions used by many applications and moves them to a shared subsystem. It centralizes implementation of the user interface and permits some of the effort of designing tools for user interfaces to be amortized over many applications and shared by them. It also encourages consistent "look and feel" in user interfaces to different systems, since they share the user interface component. A UIMS also supports the concept of dialogue independence, where changes can be made to the interface design (the user-computer dialogue) without affecting the application code. This supports the development of alternative user interfaces for the same application (semantics), which facilitates both iterative refinement of the interface through prototyping and testing and, in the future, alternative interfaces for users of different physical or other disabilities. A UIMS requires a language or method for specifying user interfaces precisely; this also allows the interface designer to describe and study a variety of possible user interfaces before building any. UIMSs are emerging as powerful tools that not only reduce development effort, but also encourage exploratory prototyping.

Syntactic Level Design: Interaction Styles

The principal classes of user interfaces currently in use are command languages, menus, forms, natural language, direct manipulation, virtual reality, and combinations of these. Each interaction style has its merits for particular user communities or sets of tasks. Choosing a style or a combination of styles is a key step, but within each there are numerous minute decisions that determine the efficacy of the resulting system.

Command Language

Command language user interfaces use artificial languages, much like programming languages. They are concise and unambiguous, but they are often difficult for a novice to learn and remember. However, since they usually permit a user to combine constructs in new and complex ways, they can be more powerful for advanced users. For them, command languages provide a strong feeling that they are in charge and that they are taking the initiative rather than responding to the computer. Command language users must learn the syntax, but they can often express complex possibilities rapidly, without having to read distracting prompts. However, error rates are typically high, training is necessary, and retention may be poor. Error messages and on-line assistance are difficult to provide because of the diversity of possibilities and the complexity of relating tasks to computer concepts and syntax. Command languages and lengthier query or programming languages are the domain of the expert frequent users (power users), who often derive satisfaction from mastering a complex set of concepts and syntax.

Command language interfaces are also the style most amenable to programming, that is, writing programs or scripts of user input commands.

Menu

Menu-based user interfaces explicitly present the options available to a user at each point in a dialogue. Users read a list of items, select the one most appropriate to their task, type or point to indicate their selection, verify that the selection is correct, initiate the action, and observe the effect. If the terminology and meaning of the items are understandable and distinct, users can accomplish their tasks with little learning or memorization and few keystrokes. The menu requires only that the user be able to recognize the desired entry from a list rather than recall it, placing a smaller load on long-term memory. The greatest benefit may be that there is a clear structure to decision making, since only a few choices are presented at a time. This interaction style is appropriate for novice and intermittent users. It can also be appealing to frequent users if the display and selection mechanisms are very rapid. A principal disadvantage is that they can be annoying for experienced users who already know the choices they want to make and do not need to see them listed. Well-designed menu systems, however, can provide bypasses for expert users. Menus are also difficult to apply to "shallow" languages, which have large numbers of choices at a few points, because the option display becomes too big. For designers, menu selection systems require careful task analysis to ensure that all functions are supported conveniently and that terminology is chosen carefully and used consistently. Software tools to support menu selection help in ensuring consistent screen design, validating completeness, and supporting maintenance.

Form Fill-in

Menu selection usually becomes cumbersome when data entry is required; form fill-in (also called fill-in-the-blanks) is useful here. Users see a display of related fields, move a cursor among the fields, and enter data where desired, much as they would with a paper form for an invoice, personnel data sheet, or order form. Seeing the full set of related fields on the screen at one time in a familiar format is often very helpful. Form fill-in interaction does require that users understand the field labels, know the permissible values, be familiar with typing and editing fields, and be capable of responding to error messages. These demands imply that users must have some training or experience.

Natural Language

The principal benefit of natural language user interfaces is, of course, that the user already knows the language. The hope that computers will respond properly to arbitrary natural language sentences or phrases has engaged many researchers and system developers, but with limited success thus far. Natural language interaction usually provides little context for issuing the next command, frequently requires "clarification dialog," and may be slower and more cumbersome than the alternatives. Therefore, given the state of the art, such an interface must be restricted to some subset of natural language, and the subset must be chosen carefully—both in vocabulary and range of syntactic constructs. Such systems often behave poorly when the user veers even slightly away from the subset. Since they begin by presenting the illusion that the computer really can "speak English," the systems can trap or frustrate novice users. For this reason, the techniques of human factors engineering can help. A human factors study of the task and the terms and constructs people normally use to describe it can be used to restrict the subset of natural language in an appropriate way, based on empirical observation. Human factors study can also identify tasks for which natural language input is good or bad. Although future research in natural language offers the hope of human-computer communication that is so natural it is "just like talking to a person," such conversation may not always be the most effective way of commanding a machine. It is often more verbose and less precise than computer languages. In settings such as surgery, air traffic control, and emergency vehicle dispatching, people have evolved terse, highly formatted languages, similar to computer languages, for communicating with other people. For a frequent user, the effort of learning such an artificial language is outweighed by its conciseness and precision, and it is often preferable to natural language.

Direct Manipulation

In a graphical or direct manipulation style of user interface (GUI), a set of objects is presented on a screen, and the user has a repertoire of manipulations that can be performed on any of them. This means that the user has no command language to remember beyond the standard set of manipulations, few cognitive changes of mode, and a reminder of the available objects and their states shown continuously on the display. Examples of this approach include painting programs, spreadsheets, manufacturing or process control systems that show a schematic diagram of the plant, air traffic control systems, some educational and flight simulations, video games, and the Xerox Star desktop and its descendants (Macintosh, Windows, and various X Window file managers). By pointing at objects and actions, users can rapidly carry out tasks, immediately observe the results, and, if necessary, reverse the action. Keyboard entry of commands or menu choices is replaced by cursor motion devices, such as a lightpen, joystick, touchscreen, trackball, or mouse, to select from a visible set of objects and actions. Direct manipulation is appealing to novices, is easy to remember for intermittent users, encourages exploration, and, with careful design, can be rapid for power users. The key difficulty in designing such interfaces is to find suitable manipulable graphical representations or visual metaphors for the objects of the problem domain, such as the desktop and filing cabinet. A principal drawback of direct manipulation is that it is often difficult to create scripts or parameterized programs in such an inherently dynamic and ephemeral language.

In a well-designed direct manipulation interface, the user's input actions should be as close as possible to the user's thoughts that motivated those actions; the gap between the user's intentions and the actions necessary to input them into the computer should be reduced. The goal is to build on the equipment and skills humans have acquired through evolution and experience and exploit these for communicating with the computer. Direct manipulation interfaces have enjoyed great success, particularly with new users, largely because they draw on analogies to existing human skills (pointing, grabbing, moving objects in space), rather than trained behaviors.

Virtual Reality

Virtual reality environments carry the user's illusion of manipulating real objects and the benefit of natural interaction still further. By coupling the motion of the user's head to changes in the images presented on a head-mounted display, the illusion of being surrounded by a world of computer-generated images, or a virtual environment, is created. Hand-mounted sensors allow the user to interact with these images as if they were real objects located in space surrounding him or her. Augmented reality interfaces blend the virtual world with a view of the real world through a half-silvered mirror or a TV camera, allowing virtual images to be superimposed on real objects and annotations or other computer data to be attached to real objects. The state of the art in virtual reality requires expensive and cumbersome equipment and provides very low resoution display, so such interfaces are currently used mainly where a feeling of "presence" in the virtual world is of paramount importance, such as training of fire fighters or treatment of phobias. As the technology improves they will likely find wider use.

Virtual reality interfaces, like direct manipulation interfaces, gain their strength by exploiting the user's pre-existing abilities and expectations. Navigating through a conventional computer system requires a set of learned, unnatural commands, such as keywords to be typed in, or function keys to be pressed. Navigating through a virtual reality system exploits the user's existing, natural "navigational commands," such as positioning his or her head and eyes, turning his or her body, or walking toward something of interest. The result is a more natural user interface, because interacting with it is more like interacting with the rest of the world.

Other Issues

Blending several styles may be appropriate when the required tasks and users are diverse. Commands may lead the user to a form fill-in where data entry is required or pop-up (or pulldown) menus may be used to control a direct manipulation environment when a suitable visualization of operations cannot be found. The area of computer-supported cooperative work extends the notion of a single user-computer interface to an interface that supports the collaboration of a group of users.

Although interfaces using modern techniques such as direct manipulation are often easier to learn and use than conventional ones, they are considerably more difficult to build, since they are currently typically programmed in a low-level, ad-hoc manner.

Appropriate higherlevel software engineering concepts and abstractions for dealing with these new interaction techniques are still needed. Direct manipulation techniques for the actual design and building of direct manipulation interfaces are one solution. Specifying the graphical appearance of the user interface (the "look" via direct manipulation is relatively straightforward and provided by many current tools, such as Visual Basic, but describing the behavior of the dialogue (the "feel") is more difficult and not yet well supported; predefined or "canned" controls and widgets represent the current state of the art.

Lexical Level Design: Interaction Tasks, Devices and Techniques

Lexical design begins with the interaction tasks necessary for a particular application. These are low-level primitive inputs required from the user, such as entering a text string or choosing a command. For each interaction task, the designer chooses an appropriate interaction device and interaction technique (a way of using a physical device to perform an interaction task). There may be several different ways of using the same device to perform the same task. For example, one could use a mouse to select a command by using a pop-up menu, a fixed menu (palette or toolbox), multiple clicking, circling the desired command, or even writing the name of the command with the mouse.

Input Devices

Input operations range from open-ended word processing or painting programs to simple repeated ENTER key presses for page turning in an electronic document. While keyboards and mice have been the standard computer input device, there are increasingly attractive alternatives for many tasks. High-precision touchscreens have made this durable device more attractive for public access, home control, process control, and other applications. Joysticks, trackballs, and data tablets with styluses with numerous variations are also useful for various pointing and manipulation tasks. Speech input for voice mail and speech recognition for commands are effective, especially over the telephone and for the physically disabled. Other techniques for input include keys that can be dynamically labeled, speech, 3D pointing, hand gesture, whole body motion, and visual line of gaze.

Output Devices

Output mechanisms must be successful in conveying to the user the current state of the system and what actions are currently available. The CRT display has become the standard approach, but flat panel (LED, LCD, plasma, electroluminescent, and others) and hardcopy devices are alternatives. Current high-resolution screens provide approximately 1000 × 1000 pixels; but their resolution (in dots per inch) is still far cruder than a typical paper printout or photograph, and their size, far smaller than a typical user's desk, bulletin board, or other work surface. High-resolution displays can improve the readability of textual displays so that performance can match that of typewritten documents. Synthesized or digitized voice output is effective and eco-nomical, especially in telephone applications and for the physically disabled. Voice mail systems that store and forward digitized voice messages continue to grow in popularity. Other output media include animated graphics, windows, icons, active value displays, manipulable objects, hypertext and hypermedia, head-coupled dis-plays, and non-speech audio.

Types of User Interface

Natural-language Interfaces

Natural-language interfaces are perhaps the dream and ideal of inexperienced users, because they permit them to interact with the computer in their everyday, or natural, language. No special skills are required of the user, who interfaces with the computer using natural language.

The display depicted in the figure below lists three natural-language questions from three different applications. Notice that interaction with each seems very easy. For in-stance, the first sentence seems straightforward: "List all of the salespeople who met their quotas this month."

> List all of the salespeople who met their quotas this month.

    Tom Otto
    Roz Berry
    Spin Etch

> Compare the percentage of produce spoiled in each of our three stores.

    Fair Oaks   4%
    Tyson's   5%
    Metro Center   3%

> Graph the sale of DVD drives on a monthly basis for the last three years.

    Press any key to continue.

Natural-language interfaces.

The subtleties and irregularities residing in the ambiguities of English produce an ex-tremely exacting and complex programming problem. Attempts at natural-language interfacing for particular applications in which any other type of interface is infeasible (say, in the case of a user who is disabled) are meeting with some success; however, these interfaces are typically expensive. Implementation problems and extraordinary demand on computing resources have so far kept natural-language interfaces to a min-imum. The demand exists, though, and many programmers and researchers are work-ing diligently on such interfaces. It is a growth area, and it therefore merits continued monitoring.

Question-and-answer Interfaces

In a question-and-answer interface, the computer displays a question to the user on the display. To interact, the user enters an answer (via a keyboard stroke or a mouse click), and the computer then acts on that input information in a preprogrammed manner, typically by moving to the next question.

A type of question-and-answer interface called a dialog box. A dialog box acts as a question-and-answer interface within another application, in this case a PERT chart for a systems analysis project for the Bakerloo Brothers. Notice that the rounded rectangle for "Yes" is highlighted, indicating that it is the most likely answer for this situation. The main interface for this application need not necessarily be question and answer. Rather, by incorporating a dialog box, the programmer has included an easy-to-use interface within a more complicated one.

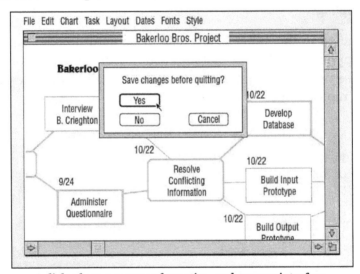

A dialog box: one type of question-and-answer interface.

Wizards used to install software are a common example of a question-and-answer interface. The user responds to questions about the installation process, such as where to install the software or features. The wizard can also ask questions and respond to the user's answers with more questions designed to narrow the scope of the problem. This is a typical way of setting up a technical support interface in order to winnow down problems and do more accurate troubleshooting.

Menus

A menu interface appropriately borrows its name from the list of dishes that can be selected in a restaurant. Similarly, a menu interface provides the user with an onscreen list of available selections. In responding to the menu, a user is limited to the options displayed. The user need not know the system but does need to know what task should be accomplished. For example, with a typical word processing menu, users can choose from the Edit, Copy, or Print options. To utilize the menu best, however, users must know which task they desire to perform.

Menus are not hardware dependent. Variations abound. Menus can be set up to use keyboard entry, light pen, touch screen, or mouse. Selections can be identified with a number, letter, or keyword, or users can click on a selection with a mouse. Consistency is important in designing a menu interface.

Menus can also be put aside until the user needs them. Figure illustration below shows how a pull-down menu is used while constructing a PERT diagram for a systems analysis project being completed for the Bakerloo Brothers. The user puts the pointer on Dates and pulls it down. Then the user puts the pointer on Calendar, selecting the option to display the project on a conventional monthly calendar.

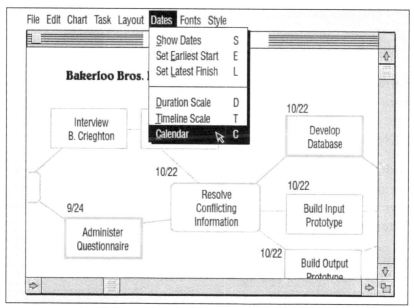

A pull-down menu is there when the user needs it.

Menus can be nested within one another to lead a user through options in a program. Nested menus allow the screen to appear less cluttered, which is consistent with good design. They also allow users to avoid seeing menu options in which they have no interest. Nested menus can also move users quickly through the program.

GUI menus are used to control PC software and have the following guidelines:

1. The main menu bar is always displayed.

2. The main menu uses single words for menu items. Main menu options always display secondary drop-down menus.

3. The main menu should have secondary options grouped into similar sets of features.

4. The drop-down menus that display when a main menu item is clicked often consist of more than one word.

5. Secondary options perform actions or display additional menu items.

6. Menu items in gray are unavailable for the current activity.

An object menu, also called a pop-up menu, is displayed when the user clicks on a GUI object with the right mouse button. These menus contain items specific for the current activity, and most are duplicate functions of main menu items.

Experienced users may be irritated by nested menus. They may prefer to use a single-line command entry to speed things up. Other users might use the shortcut abbreviations or key combinations such as Alt-. I -.P- C, which inserts a picture that is clip art in a Microsoft Office document.

Form-fill Interfaces

Form-fill interfaces consist of onscreen forms or Web-based forms displaying fields containing data items or parameters that need to be communicated to the user. The form often is a facsimile of a paper form already familiar to the user. This interface technique is also known as a form-based method and input/output forms.

Figure below shows a form-fill interface. A pull-down menu for Part No. automatically enters a Description and Unit Price for the item. When the user tabs to the Quantity field and enters the number of items being purchased, the software automatically calculates the Extended Price by multiplying Quantity by Unit Price.

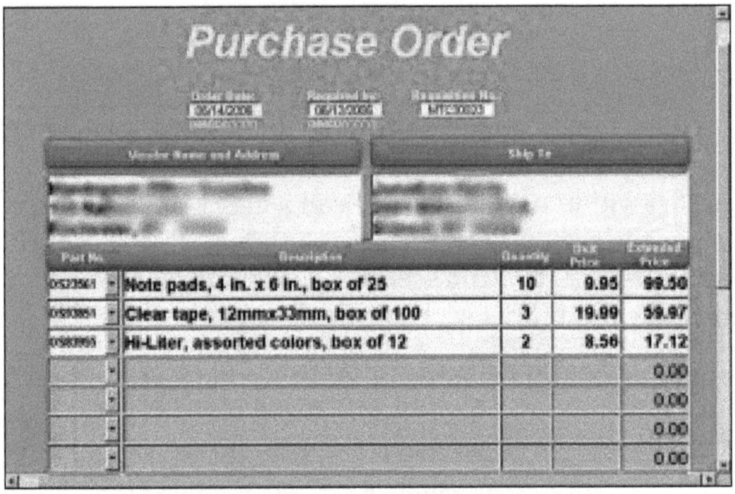

An example of the form-fill interface.

Forms for display screens are set up to show what information should be input and where. Blank fields requiring information can be highlighted with inverse or flashing characters. The cursor is moved by the user from field to field by a single stroke of an arrow key. This arrangement allows movement one field backward or one field forward by clicking the appropriate arrow key. It provides the user good control over data entry. Web-based forms afford the opportunity to include hyperlinks to examples of correctly filled-out forms or to further help and provide examples.

Form input for displays can be simplified by supplying default values for fields and then allowing users to modify default information if necessary. For example, a database management system designed to show a form for inputting checks may supply the next sequential check number as a default when a new check form is exhibited. If checks are missing, the user changes the check number to reflect the actual check being input.

Input for display screen fields can be alphanumerically restricted so that, for example, users can enter only numbers in a field requesting a Social Security number, or they can input only letters where a person's name is required. If numbers are input where only letters are allowed, the computer may alert the user via audio output that the field was filled out incorrectly.

The chief advantage of the input/output form interface is that the printed version of the filled-in form provides excellent documentation. It shows field labels as well as the context for entries. In addition, Web forms can return incomplete forms to the user with an explanation of what data must be entered to complete the transaction. Often, fields with missing data are marked with a red asterisk. Web-based documents can be sent directly to billing if a transaction is involved, or they can go directly to a real-time database if a survey is being submitted. Web-based forms push the responsibility for accuracy to the user and make the form available for completion and submission on a 24-hour, 7-day-a-week, worldwide basis.

There are few disadvantages to input/output forms. The main drawback is that users experienced with the system or application might become impatient with input/output forms and might want more efficient ways to enter data.

Command-language Interfaces

A command-language interface allows the user to control the application with a series of keystrokes, commands, phrases, or some sequence of these three methods. The simple syntaxes of command languages are considered to be close to natural language.

Two application examples of command language are shown in the figure. The first shows a user who asks to use a file containing data on all salespeople, then asks the computer to display all last names and first names for all salespeople whose current sales (CURSALES) are greater than their quotas. In the second example, a user asks to use a file called GROCER, and then directs the computer to calculate the spoilage (SPOILS) by subtracting produce sold from produce bought. After that is done, the user asks to go back to the top of the file and to print out (LIST) the file.

```
USE SALESPPL

DISPLAY ALL LNAME, FNAME FOR CURSALES > QUOTA


USE GROCER

REPLACE ALL SPOILS WITH PBOUGHT - PSOLD

GOTO TOP

LIST
```

Command-language interfaces.

The command language has no inherent meaning for the user, and that fact makes it dissimilar to the other interfaces. Command languages manipulate the computer as a tool by allowing the user to control the dialog. Command language affords the user more overall flexibility and control. When the user employs command language, the command is executed by the system immediately. Then the user may proceed to give it another command.

Command languages require memorization of syntax rules that may prove to be obstacles for inexperienced users. Experienced users tend to prefer command languages, possibly because of their faster completion time.

Graphical User Interfaces

The key to graphical user interfaces (GUIs) is the constant feedback on task accomplishment that they provide to users. Continuous feedback on the manipulated object means that changes or reversals in operations can be made quickly, without incurring error messages.

The creation of GUIs poses a challenge, because an appropriate model of reality or an acceptable conceptual model of the representation must be invented. Designing GUIs for use on intranets, extranets, and on the Web requires even more careful planning. Most users of Web sites are unknown to the developer, so design must be clear-cut. The choice of icons, language, and hyperlinks becomes an entire set of decisions and assumptions about what kinds of users the Web site is hoping to attract. The designer must also adhere to conventions that users now expect to encounter on Web sites.

Other User Interfaces

Other less common user interfaces are growing in popularity. They include pointing devices such as the stylus, touch-sensitive screens, and speech recognition and synthesis. Each of these interfaces has its own special attributes that uniquely suit it to particular applications.

The stylus (a small pointed stick that resembles a pen) is used with handwriting recognition software for mobile phones (acting as PDAs—personal digital assistants) and PC devices. They have been a success because they integrate many functions and are easy to use. Additionally, they are portable and sell for a comparatively low price. There has been an explosion of fun and useful applications written for these mobile devices, including popular programs for restaurant reviews such as Zagat, popular utilities such as "To Do" lists for work and personal use, and for popular games such as Sudoku. Data entry is also facilitated with a docking cradle so that data can be synchronized with your PC.

A tablet PC is a notebook computer with a stylus or touch-sensitive display. It can be equipped with built-in Wi-Fi or Bluetooth communication. Touch-sensitive displays allow a user to use a finger to activate the display. Touch-sensitive displays are useful in public information displays, such as maps of cities and their sights posted in hotel lobbies or car rental facilities. They can also be used to explain dioramas in museums and to locate camping facilities in state parks. Touch-sensitive displays require no special expertise from users, and the screen is self-contained, requiring no special input device that might be broken or stolen. Touch sensitive screens (also called simply touch screens or touch pads) for mobile phones such as the iPhone and the BlackBerry are making this alternative user interface familiar to users and widely used. Current research is examining how to make pressure-sensitive touch pads commercially viable. These interfaces can be used with both large and small touch screens and are practical for applications such as virtual painting or sculpting, a simulated mouse, and for musical instruments such as a piano keyboard where the intensity of the pressure applied is critical to the output.

With voice recognition, the user speaks to the computer, and the system is able to recognize an individual's vocal signals, convert them, and store the input. Voice recognition inventory systems are already in operation, and automobiles now feature voice input systems that respond to a driver's voice commands to navigate, change the radio station, or use the Bluetooth phone that has been paired with the vehicle.

An advantage of voice recognition systems is that they can speed data entry enormously, and free the user's hands for other tasks (for example, driving). Speech input adds still another dimension to the PC. It is now possible to add equipment and software that allows a PC user to speak commands such as "open file" or "save file" to avoid using the keyboard or mouse. Users with limited mobility or impaired sight can benefit from voice recognition systems. In the example shown in the figure, the user corrects a word by pulling down a menu of alternative words that sound the same.

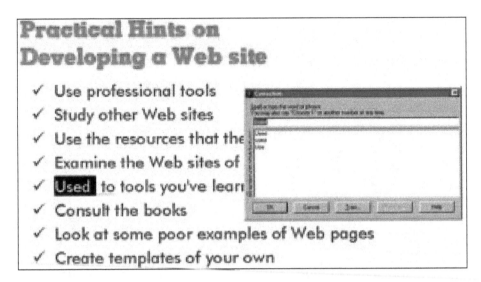

Using software a user can speak commands to their computer. In this example, the user corrects a word by pulling up a menu of alternative words that sound the same.

When evaluating interfaces, keep some standards in mind:

1. The necessary training period for users should be acceptably short.

2. Early in their training, users should be able to enter commands without thinking about them or without referring to a help menu or manual. Keeping interfaces consistent throughout applications can help in this regard.

3. The interface should be seamless so that errors are few and those that do occur are not occurring because of poor design.

4. The time that users and the system need to bounce back from errors should be short.

5. Infrequent users should be able to relearn the system quickly.

Many different interfaces are available, and it is important to realize that an effective interface goes a long way toward addressing key HCI concerns. Users should want to use the system, and they should find it attractive, effective, and pleasing to use.

User Interface Layer

The user interface layer consists of a Flex application, called the container application, that serves as a framework for a set of modular Flex elements. The container application supplies the structural components of the vSphere Web Client user interface, such as major navigation controls, window frames, and menus. The container application manages and renders each of the Flex GUI elements that it contains. Together, the collected Flex GUI elements and the container application make up the vSphere Web Client user interface.

Each Flex GUI element inside the container application is a self-contained object that communicates directly with the vSphere environment. Each element can retrieve data for display, or send commands or make changes to the virtual infrastructure. Each GUI element implements a version of the MVC architecture to manage communication with the vSphere environment.

The container application uses a metadata framework to determine where to place each GUI element in the interface, and how that element looks. Each GUI element has a metadata definition that you create using an XML schema that is defined in the vSphere Web Client SDK. The container application uses the values in the metadata definition to render the element at the appropriate place in the interface.

User Interface Plug-in Modules

A user interface plug-in module is a Web Application Archive (WAR) bundle. The WAR bundle contains all of the resources and Flex classes required for each GUI element the module adds to the vSphere Web Client interface. In a user interface plug-in module, the GUI elements you add to the interface are called extensions.

In the root folder of the WAR bundle, you must create a manifest file called plugin.xml. The `plugin.xml` manifest file uses metadata to define the plug-in module's extensions and resources.

Creating the Plug-in Module Manifest

The plug-in module manifest file, `plugin.xml`, is a metadata file that the vSphere Web Client container application uses to integrate the extensions in the plug-in module with the rest of the interface. The `plugin.xmlfile fulfills` the following functions.

- The manifest defines each individual extension in the user interface plug-in module.

- The manifest specifies the SWF file containing the Flex or ActionScript classes you have created for the module extensions.

- The manifest specifies the location of any included runtime resources in the module, such as localization data.

- If the user interface plug-in module hosts any extension points, manifest declares those extension points.

XML Elements in the Manifest File

The metadata in the manifest file follows a specific XML schema. The major XML elements of a user interface plug-in module manifest include the `<plugin>` element, the `<resources>` element, and one or more `<resources>` elements. The vSphere Web Client SDK contains several examples of user interface plug-in modules with complete `plugin.xml` manifest files.

`<plugin>` Element

The `<plugin>` element is the root element of any plug-in module manifest file. All other elements are contained within the `<plugin>` element. The attributes of the `<plugin>` element contain information about the entire plug-in module:

- id: The unique identifier that you choose for the plug-in module.

- moduleUri: A Uniform Resource Identifier (URI) for the SWF file in the plug-in module. The SWF file contains the Flex or ActionScript classes used by the extensions in the plug-in module. The URI should be specified relative to the root directory of the plug-in module WAR bundle.

- securityPolicyUri: A URI for a standard cross-domain security policy file. This optional element is used when the plug-in module is hosted remotely (and the domain of the plug-in module URL is different from the domain vSphere Web Client application server).

- defaultBundle: The name of the default resource bundle for the plug-in module. The bundle name must be unique to your plug-in module to avoid name clashing issues with other plug-in modules. Resources, such as localization data and icons, can be dynamically loaded at runtime.

The following XML fragment shows how the `<plugin>` element might appear in the plug-in module manifest file.

```
<plugin id="com.acme.sampleplugin"

moduleUri="SampleModule.swf"     defaultBundle="com_acme_sample-
plugin">

. . .

<!-- additional plugin data -->

. . .

</plugin>
```

<Resources> Element

The <resources> element is used to specify the location of the plug-in module's run-time resources, such as localization data. In general, resources are bundled in separate SWF files from the SWF file that contains the plug-in module Flex classes.

The vSphere Web Client supports the same set of locales as vCenter server. The default locale is the locale set the by the user's web browser. If the user's web browser is not set to a locale that the vSphere Web Client supports, the vSphere Web Client will default to the English (United States) locale.

It is a best practice to set the locale attribute in the <resources> element to the value locale, rather than hard-coding a specific locale, in your plugin.xml manifest. Using the locale value instructs the vSphere Web Client to use the locale specified by the user's Web browser at runtime.

For the vSphere Web Client to properly import the resource locale at runtime, resource bundles for all supported locales must be included in the plug-in module. Currently supported locales include English (United States) (en_US), French (fr_FR), German (de_DE), Japanese (ja_JP), Korean (ko_KR), and Mandarin Chinese (zh_CN) locales. For testing purposes, you can make simple copies of the default locale for any languages for which you do not have resources available. The sample plug-in modules included with the vSphere Web Client SDK demonstrate this method.

The following XML fragment shows how the <resources> element might appear in the plug-in module manifest file.

```
<resources>

<resource locale={locale}>

<module uri="locales/sample-plugin-{locale}.swf"/>

</resource>

</resources>
```

In the preceding example, the {locale} placeholder corresponds to a particular locale, such as en_US for English. Your plug-in module must contain a separate .SWF resource bundle for each of the supported locales, using the relative path in the preceding example.

Specifying Dynamic Resources

Your extension definitions can use the dynamic resource loader to load resources or localization data at runtime. When you have specified a <resources>bundle in the manifest file, the <extension> elements in the manifest file can specify that bundle by reference. Resource specifications in the `<extension>` elements should use the expression #{bundle:key} when specifying resources, where bundle indicates the name of the resource bundle, and key indicates the resource to use.

For example, within an <extension> element in the plugin.xml file, you can specify an icon resource to be loaded dynamically at runtime by using following the expression.

```
<icon>#{MyResourceBundle:MyIconImage}</icon>
```

Specifying a dynamic resources allows you to avoid using a static value for the icon resource. The bundle name must specify a resource bundle that you have made available in the `<resources>` element of plugin.xml.

You can also omit the bundle name from a resource expression:

```
<icon>#{MyIconImage}</icon>
```

Omitting the bundle name will cause the vSphere Web Client to use the bundle name specified by the defaultBundle attribute in the `<plugin>` element.

<Extension> Element

The plug-in module manifest file must define each individual extension that the plug-in module adds to the vSphere Web Client. Each extension is defined using the `<extension>` element. The `<extension>` element contains information about each feature, and its exact composition varies depending on the kind of user interface element your plug-in module is adding.

Extensions Ordering

You can use the `<precedingExtension>` element to specify the order in which the vSphere Web Client renders the extensions in your plug-in module.

Within each `<extension>` element, you can specify a `<precedingExtension>` element that contains the ID of another extension that is to be rendered before the current extension. Setting the value of `<precedingExtension>` to NULL will cause that extension to be rendered first.

If no `<precedingExtension>` value is specified, the extensions are rendered in the order they appear in the plugin.xml module manifest file. If multiple extensions specify the same value for `<precedingExtension>`, they will be rendered after that specified extension in the order in which they appear in the manifest.

The following XML fragment shows how the `<precedingExtension>` element might appear in the extension definitions in the plug-in module manifest file.

```
<extension id = "com.MyPluginPackage.MyPlugin.PerformanceView">
```

```
<extendedPoint>vsphere.core.vm.views</extendedPoint>

<precedingExtension>NULL</precedingExtension>

...(extension data)...

</extension>

<extension id = "UtilityView">

<extendedPoint>vsphere.core.vm.views</extendedPoint>

<precedingExtension>PerformanceView</precedingExtension>

...(extension data)...

</extension>
```

The `<precedingExtension>` elements in the example ensures that the Performance-View extension is rendered first, followed by the UtilityView extension.

Creating the WAR Bundle

The plug-in module WAR bundle is a standard web application bundle that packages the necessary Flex classes and resources in your plug-in module into SWF files.

In the SWF file that contains the Flex classes that make up the UI components of the plug-in module extensions, the main class must be an MXML class that extends the mx.modules.Module.

Events and Event Handlers

Change in the state of an object is known as event i.e. event describes the change in state of source. Events are generated as result of user interaction with the graphical user interface components. For example, clicking on a button, moving the mouse, entering a character through keyboard, selecting an item from list, scrolling the page are the activities that causes an event to happen.

Types of Event

The events can be broadly classified into two categories:

- Foreground Events - Those events which require the direct interaction of user. They are generated as consequences of a person interacting with the graphical components in Graphical User Interface. For example, clicking on a button, moving the mouse, entering a character through keyboard, selecting an item from list, scrolling the page etc.

- Background Events - Those events that require the interaction of end user are known as background events. Operating system interrupts, hardware or software failure, timer expires, an operation completion are the example of background events.

Event Handling

Event Handling is the mechanism that controls the event and decides what should happen if an event occurs. This mechanism have the code which is known as event handler that is executed when an event occurs. Java Uses the Delegation Event Model to handle the events. This model defines the standard mechanism to generate and handle the events.

The Delegation Event Model has the following key participants namely:

- Source - The source is an object on which event occurs. Source is responsible for providing information of the occurred event to its handler. Java provide as with classes for source object.

- Listener - It is also known as event handler. Listener is responsible for generating response to an event. From java implementation point of view the listener is also an object. Listener waits until it receives an event. Once the event is received , the listener process the event an then returns.

The benefit of this approach is that the user interface logic is completely separated from the logic that generates the event. The user interface element is able to delegate the processing of an event to the separate piece of code. In this model, Listener needs to be registered with the source object so that the listener can receive the event notification. This is an efficient way of handling the event because the event notifications are sent only to those listener that want to receive them.

Steps Involved in Event Handling

- The User clicks the button and the event is generated.

- Now the object of concerned event class is created automatically and information about the source and the event get populated with in same object.

- Event object is forwarded to the method of registered listener class.

- The method is now get executed and returns.

Points to Remember about Listener

- In order to design a listener class we have to develop some listener interfaces. These Listener interfaces forecast some public abstract call back methods which must be implemented by the listener class.

- If you do not implement the any if the predefined interfaces then your class can not act as a listener class for a source object.

Call Back Methods

These are the methods that are provided by API provider and are defined by the application programmer and invoked by the application developer. Here the call back methods represents an event method. In response to an event java jre will fire call back method. All such call back methods are provided in listener interfaces.

If a component wants some listener will listen to it's events the the source must register itself to the listener.

Event Handling Example

Create the following java program using any editor of your choice in say D:

```
import java.awt.*; import java.awt.event.*;

public class AwtControlDemo {

private Frame mainFrame;

private Label headerLabel;

private Label statusLabel;

private Panel controlPanel;

public AwtControlDemo(){

  prepareGUI();

}

public static void main(String[] args){

AwtControlDemo        awtControlDemonewAwtControlDemo();awt-
ControlDemo.shown EventDemo();

}

private void prepareGUI(){
```

```
mainFrame = new Frame("Java AWT Examples"); mainFrame.set-
Size(400,400); mainFrame.setLayout(new GridLayout(3, 1)); main-
Frame.addWindowListener(new WindowAdapter() {

public void windowClosing(WindowEvent windowEvent){ System.
exit(0);

}

});

headerLabel = new Label(); headerLabel.setAlignment(Label.CEN-
TER); statusLabel = new Label(); statusLabel.setAlignment(La-
bel.CENTER); statusLabel.setSize(350,100);

controlPanel = new Panel(); controlPanel.setLayout(new FlowLay-
out());

mainFrame.add(headerLabel); mainFrame.add(controlPanel); main-
Frame.add(statusLabel); mainFrame.setVisible(true);}

private void showEventDemo(){ headerLabel.setText("Control in
action: Button");

Button okButton = new Button("OK");

Button submitButton = new Button("Submit"); Button cancelButton
= new Button("Cancel");

okButton.setActionCommand("OK");    submitButton.setActionCom-
mand("Submit"); cancelButton.setActionCommand("Cancel");

okButton.addActionListener(new  ButtonClickListener()); sub-
mitButton.addActionListener(new ButtonClickListener()); cancel-
Button.addActionListener(new ButtonClickListener());

controlPanel.add(okButton);    controlPanel.add(submitButton);
controlPanel.add(cancelButton);

mainFrame.setVisible(true);

}

private class ButtonClickListener implements ActionListener{
public void actionPerformed(ActionEvent e) {

String    command    =    e.getActionCommand();    if(command.
equals("OK"))                          {
```

```
statusLabel.setText("Ok Button clicked.");

}

else if(command.equals("Submit"))              {      statusLabel.set-
Text("Submit Button clicked.");

}

else              {

statusLabel.setText("Cancel Button clicked.");

}

}}}
```

Compile the program using command prompt. Go to D:/ > AWT and type the following command.

```
D:\AWT>javac com\tutorialspoint\gui\AwtControlDemo.java
```

If no error comes that means compilation is successful. Run the program using following command.

```
D:\AWT>java com.tutorialspoint.gui.AwtControlDemo
```

Every event handler requires three bits of code:

1. In the declaration for the event handler class, code that specifies that the class either implements a listener interface or extends a class that implements a listener interface. For example:

```
public class MyButtonHandler implements ActionListener {

        // class members...

        // constructor ... ...

          ......

        }
```

2. Code that registers an instance of the event handler class as a listener upon one or more components. For example:

```
public class MyButtonHandler implements ActionListener {

        // class members ...

        //constructor...                                    //
```

```
someComponent.addActionListener(instanceOfMyClass);    button.
addActionListener(this);
```

...

}

3. Code that implements the methods in the listener interface. For example:

```
public class MyButtonHandler implements ActionListener {
          // class members ...
          // constructor ...
```

...

```
//someComponent.addActionListener(instanceOfMyClass);

button.addActionListener(this);
```

...

```
public void actionPerformed(ActionEvent e) {
// handle the event
// code that reacts to the action...
}
}
```

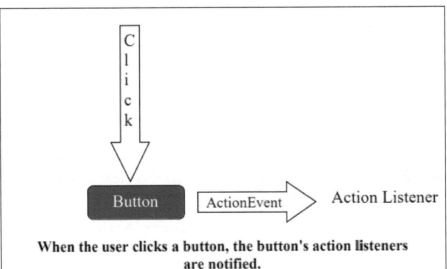

**When the user clicks a button, the button's action listeners
are notified.**

Some Event Classes

- KeyEvent: For keyboard input.

- MouseEvent: For all sorts of mouse events: press, release, move, drag.

- ActionEvent: For GUI actions like clicking on a button, selecting a menu item.

Some Event Listener Interfaces:

- MouseListener:

    ◦ Methods:

        void mouseClicked(MouseEvent me)

        void mouseEntered(MouseEvent me)

        void mouseExited(MouseEvent me)

        void mousePressed(MouseEvent me)

        void mouseReleased(MouseEvent me)

    ◦ Registered with some event source by calling: void addMouseListener (MouseListener ml).

- Mouse Motion Listener:

    ◦ Methods:

        void mouseDragged(MouseEvent me)

        void mouseMoved(MouseEvent me)

    ◦ Registered with some event source by calling:

        void addMouseMotionListener(MouseMotionListener mml)

- KeyListener:

    ◦ Methods:

        void keyPressed(KeyEvent ke)

        void keyReleased(KeyEvent ke)

        void keyTyped(KeyEvent ke)

    ◦ Registered with some event source by calling:

        void addKeyListener(KeyListener kl)

- ActionListener:

  ◦ Methods:

      void actionPerformed(ActionEvent ae)

  ◦ Registered with some event source by calling:

      void addActionListener(ActionListener al).

Event Driven Programming

Event-driven programming is a programming paradigm in which the flow of program execution is determined by events - for example a user action such as a mouse click, key press, or a message from the operating system or another program. An event-driven application is designed to detect events as they occur, and then deal with them using an appropriate event-handling procedure. The idea is an extension of interrupt-driven programming of the kind found in early command-line environments such as DOS, and in embedded systems (where the application is implemented as firmware).

Event-driven programs can be written in any programming language, although some languages(Visual Basic for example) are specifically designed to facilitate event-driven programming, and provide an *integrated development environment* (IDE) that partially automates the production of code, and provides a comprehensive selection of built-in objects and controls, each of which can respond to a range of events. Virtually all object-oriented and visual languages support event-driven programming. Visual Basic, Visual C++ and Java are examples of such languages.

A visual programming IDE such as VB.Net provides much of the code for detecting events automatically when a new application is created. The programmer can therefore concentrate on issues such as interface design, which involves adding controls such as command buttons, text boxes, and labels to standard *forms* (a form represents an application's workspace or *window*). Once the user interface is substantially complete, the programmer can add event-handling code to each control as required.

Many visual programming environments will even provide code templates for event-handlers, so the programmer only needs to provide the code that defines the action the program should take when the event occurs. Each event-handler is usually bound to a specific object or control on a form. Any additional subroutines, methods, or function procedures required are usually placed in a separate code module, and can be called from other parts of the program as and when needed.

Before the arrival of object-oriented programming languages, event handlers would have been implemented as subroutines within a procedural program. The flow of program execution was determined by the programmer, and controlled from within the application's main routine. The complexity of the logic involved required the implementation of a highly structured program. All of the program's code would be written by the programmer, including the code required to ensure that events and exceptions were handled, as well as the code required to manage the flow of program execution.

In a typical modern event-driven program, there is no discernible flow of control. The main routine is an event-loop that waits for an event to occur, and then invokes the appropriate event-handling routine. Since the code for this event loop is usually provided by the event-driven development environment or framework, and largely invisible to the programmer, the programmer's perception of the application is that of a collection of event handling routines. Programmers used to working with procedural programming languages sometimes find that the transition to an event-driven environment requires a considerable mental adjustment.

The change in emphasis from procedural to event-driven programming has been accelerated by the introduction of the *Graphical User Interface* (GUI) which has been widely adopted for use in operating systems and end-user applications. It really began, however, with the introduction of *object-oriented* (OO) programming languages and development methodologies in the late 1970s. By the 1990s, object-oriented technologies had largely supplanted the procedural programming languages and structured development methods that were popular during the 70s and 80s.

One of the drivers behind the object oriented approach to programming that emerged during this era was the speed with which database technology developed and was adopted for commercial use. Information system designers increasingly saw the database itself, rather than the software that was used to access it, as the central component of a computerised information system. The software simply provided a user interface to the database, and a set of event handling procedures to deal with database queries and updates.

One of the fundamental ideas behind object-oriented programming is that of representing programmable entities as objects. An entity in this context could be literally anything with which the application is concerned. A program dealing with tracking the progress of customer orders for a manufacturing company, for example, might involve objects such as "customer", "order", and "order item".

An object encompasses both the data (attributes) that can be stored about an entity, the actions (methods) that can be used to access or modify the entity's attributes, and the events that can cause the entity's methods to be invoked. The basic structure of an object, and its relationship to the application to which it belongs, is illustrated in the following diagram.

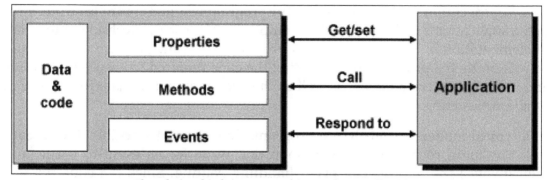

The relationship between an object and an application.

Before going any further, it is worth drawing the distinction between objects and class-es. A class, in very general terms, is an object template that defines the attributes, meth-ods and events that will be implemented in any object created with it. An object is an instance of a class. An analogy would be to say that Dog is a class, of which Fido is a specific instance. Fido has all of the generic characteristics and behaviours of the class "Dog", and responds to the same external stimuli.

The link between object-oriented programming and event-driven programming is fairly obvious. For example, objects on a Visual Basic form (usually referred to as *controls*) can be categorised into classes (e.g. "Button", "TextBox" etc.), and many instances of each can appear on a single form. Each class will have attributes (usu-ally referred to as *properties*) that will be common to all objects of that type (e.g. "BackgroundColour", "Width" etc.), and each class will define a list of events to which an object of that type will respond. The methods (*event-handlers*) to handle specific events are usually provided as templates to which the programmer simply has to add the code that carries out the required action.

Workings of Event-driven Programming

The central element of an event-driven application is a scheduler that receives a stream of events and passes each event to the relevant event-handler. The schedul-er will continue to remain active until it encounters an event (e.g. "End_Program") that causes it to terminate the application. Under certain circumstances, the sched-uler may encounter an event for which it cannot assign an appropriate event han-dler. Depending on the nature of the event, the scheduler can either ignore it or raise an *exception* (this is sometimes referred to as throwing an exception).

Within an event-driven programming environment, standard events are usual-ly identified using the ID of the object affected by the event (e.g. the name of a command button on a form), and the event ID (e.g. "left-click"). The information passed to the event-handler may include additional information, such as the *x* and *y* coordinates of the mouse pointer at the time the event occurred, or the state of the *Shift* key (if the event in question is a key-press).

Events are often actions performed by the user during the execution of a program, but can also be messages generated by the operating system or another application, or an interrupt generated by a peripheral device or system hardware. If the user clicks on a button with the mouse or hits the *Enter* key, it generates an event. If a file download completes, it generates an event. And if there is a hardware or software error, it generates an event.

The events are dealt with by a central event-handler (usually called a *dispatcher* or *scheduler*) that runs continuously in the background and waits for an even to occur. When an event *does* occur, the scheduler must determine the type of event and call the appropriate event-handler to deal with it. The information passed to the event handler by the scheduler will vary, but will include sufficient information to allow the event-handler to take any action necessary.

Event-handlers can be seen as small blocks of procedural code that deal with a very specific occurrence. They will usually produce a visual response to inform or direct the user, and will often change the system's *state*. The state of the system encompasses both the data used by the system (e.g. the value stored in a database field), and the state of the user interface itself (for example, which on-screen object currently has the focus, or the background colour of a text box).

An event handler may even trigger another event too occur that will cause a second event-handler to be called (note that care should be taken when writing event handlers that invoke other event-handlers, in order to avoid the possibility of putting the application into an infinite loop). Similarly, an event-handler may cause any queued events to be discarded (for example, when the user clicks on the *Quit* button to terminate the program). The diagram below illustrates the relationship between events, the scheduler, and the application's event-handlers.

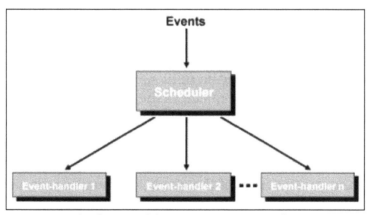

A simple event-driven programming paradigm.

The pseudo-code routine below shows how a (very simple) scheduler might work. It consists of a main loop that runs continuously until some terminating condition occurs. When an event occurs, the scheduler must determine the event type, and select an appropriate event-handler (or deal with the event, if no suitable event-handler exists).

```
do forever: // the main scheduler loop

    get event from input stream

    if event type == EndProgram:

        quit // break out of event loop

    else if event type == event_01:

        call event-handler for event_01 with event
parameters

    else if event type == event_02:

        call event-handler for event_02 with event parameters

    else if event type == event_nn:

        call event-handler for event_nn with event parameters

    else handle unrecognized event // ignore or raise
exception

end loop.
```

The Event Queue

In an event-driven system, a number of events can occur in a relatively short space of time. The scheduler, and the event-handlers at its disposal, may not be able to handle all of the events immediately they occur. The obvious solution is to place unhandled events into an event queue until such time as they can be dealt with. Events are added to the end of the queue as they arrive, and are dealt with by the scheduler once they reach the front of the queue.

There may well also be a priority scheme in operation in which certain types of event take priority over others. Such events may be fast-tracked through the scheduler by moving them to the head of the queue, or there may be a separate queue for priority events. The existence of the queue guarantees that all events will be handled at some point, and in some semblance of order.

The length of the queue, and the time taken to process events, will probably depend on factors such as the speed of the processor, the amount of installed RAM, and the number of other applications that are running at the same time (which will obviously be competing for the same system resources). Much of the time, however, the queue will be empty, and the scheduler will be in an idle state waiting for the next event.

GUI Programming

It should not be assumed that because most popular modern software applications have a graphical user interface (GUI) that event driven programming is the right solution for every programming requirement. Some software systems have a very specific role that involves them carrying out some task to completion with little or no user intervention (a C compiler, for example). Such applications are probably better served by a procedural programming paradigm. Having said that, most mainstream commercial software relies heavily on the availability of a GUI, and most GUI software is designed to be event-driven.

A visual programming language such as Visual Basic and Visual C/C++ now comes with an Integrated Development Environment (IDE) that provides an extensive array of standard controls, each with its own set of events and event-handler code templates. The task of the GUI programmer is thus twofold – to create the user interface, and to write the event-handler code (and any additional code modules that might be required).

The IDE provides the scheduler and the event queue, and to a large extent takes care of the flow of program execution. The GUI programmer is thus free to concentrate on the application-specific code. They will write the code required by each control or object to allow it to respond to a specific event, but do not need to know how to create the objects themselves.

The basic idea of event-driven programming is simply to create objects with methods that handle the appropriate events or circumstances, without explicit attention to how or when these methods will be called. These helper methods provide answers to questions of the form, What should you do when xxx happens? Because xxx is a thing that happens, or an event, these methods are sometimes called event handlers. As the writer of event handler methods, you expect that the event handlers will somehow (automatically) be invoked whenever the appropriate thing needs dealing with, i.e., whenever the appropriate event arises.

The result of this transformation is that your code focuses on the occasions when something of interest happens - instead of the times when nothing much is going on - and on how it should respond to these circumstances. An event is, after all, simply something (significant) that happens. This style of programming is called event-driven because the methods that you write - the event handlers - are the instructions for how to respond to events. The dispatcher - whether central control loop or otherwise - is a part of the background; the event handlers drive the code.

Dispatch Revisited

Consider the case of an Alarm, such as might be part of an AlarmClock system. The Alarm receives two kinds of signals: SIGNAL_TIMEOUT, which indicates that it is time for the Alarm to start ringing, and SIGNAL_RESET, which indicates that it is time for the Alarm to stop. We might implement this using two methods, handle-Timeout() and handleReset().

```
public class Alarm

   {

   Buzzer bzzz =  new Buzzer();


   public void handleTimeout()

   {

        this.bzzz.startRinging();

   }
 public void handleReset()

   {

     this.bzzz.stopRinging();

   }

}
```

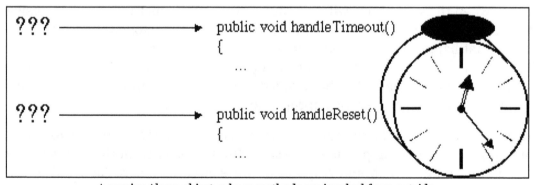

A passive Alarm object, whose methods are invoked from outside.

How do these methods get called? In a traditional control loop architecture, this might be accomplished using a dispatch loop. For example, we might make Alarm an Animate and give it its own AnimatorThread. The job of the dispatch loop would be to wait for and processes incoming (timeout and reset) signals. This AnimateAlarm's act() method might say:

```
public class AnimateAlarm extends AnimateObject

    {

    Buzzer bzzz =   new Buzzer();

    public void handleTimeout()

{

    this.bzzz.startRinging();

}

public void handleReset()

{

    this.bzzz.stopRinging();

}

    public void act()

{

    int signal = getNextSignal();

switch (signal)

:{

                        case SIGNAL_TIMEOUT:

                                this.handleTimeout();

                                break;

                        case SIGNAL_RESET:

                                this.handleReset();

                                break;

                                // Maybe other signals, too....

            }

}

}
```

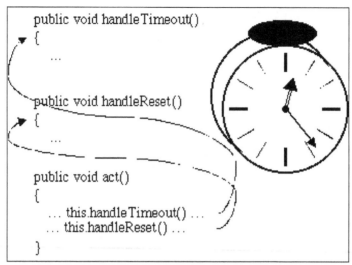

An active Alarm object, invoking its own methods.

Of course, the real work is still done by the handleTimeout() and handleReset() methods. The job of the dispatch loop (or other calling code) is simply to decide which helper (handler) method needs to be called. The dispatcher - this act() method - is only there to make sure that handleTimeout() and handleReset() are called appropriately.

Simple Event Handling

What would happen if we shifted the focus to the helper procedures? What if we made the dispatch code invisible? Imagine writing code (such as this Alarm) in which you could be sure that the helper methods would be called automatically whenever the appropriate condition arose. In the case of the Alarm, we would not have to write the act method or switch statement above at all. We would simply equip our Alarm with the appropriate helper methods - handleTimeout() and handleReset() - and then make sure that the notifier mechanism knew to call these methods when the appropriate circumstances arose. This is precisely what event-driven programming does.

Handler Interface

We have said that event-driven programming is a style of programming in which your code provides event handlers and some (as yet unexplained) event dispatcher invokes these event hander methods at the appropriate time. This means that the event dispatcher and the object with the event hander methods will need a way to communicate. To specify the contract between the event dispatcher and the event handler, we generally use an interface specifying the signatures of the event handler methods. This way, the event dispatcher doesn't need to know anything about the event handlers except that they exist and satisfy the appropriate contract.

In the case of the alarm, this interface might specify the two methods, `handleTim-eout()` and `handleReset()`:

```
public interface TimeoutResettable

{

    public abstract void handleTimeout();


    public abstract void handleReset();

}
```

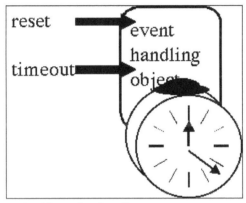

An Alarm that handles two event types.

Of course, we'll have to modify our definition of Alarm to say that it implements TimeoutResettable:

```
public class Alarm implements TimeoutResettable

    {

    Buzzer bzzz =  new Buzzer();


    public void handleTimeout()

{

    this.bzzz.startRinging();

}


public void handleReset()
```

```
{

    this.bzzz.stopRinging();

}

}
```

This is a modification of our original Alarm, not of the Animate Alarm class. The Time out Resettable Alarm need not be Animate. In fact, if it is truly event-driven, it will not be.

This Time out Resettable Alarm definition works as long as some mechanism - which we will not worry about just yet - takes responsibility for dispatching handle Time out() and handle Reset() calls as appropriate. That dispatcher mechanism can rely on the fact that our Alarm is a Time out Resettable, i.e., that it provides implementations for these methods. The dispatcher that invokes handle Timeout() and handle Reset() need not know anything about the Alarm other than that it is a Time out Resettable.

Unrealistic Dispatcher

How might our Time out Resettable Alarm be invoked? There are many answers, and we will see a few later. For now, though, it is worth looking at one simple answer to get the sense that this really can be done.

A simple - and not very realistic - event dispatcher might look a lot like the act method of Animate Alarm. To make it more generic, we will separate that method and encapsulate it inside its own object. We will also give that object access to its event handler using the Time out Resettable interface. Major differences between this code and Animate Alarm are highlighted. Of course, the dispatcher doesn't have its own handler methods; its constructor requires a Time out Resettable to provide those.

```
public class TimeoutResetDispatcher extends AnimateObject

{

    private TimeoutResettable eventHandler;


public TimeoutResetDispatcher(TimeoutResettable eventHandler)

{

        this.eventHandler = eventHandler;
```

```
}


public void act()

{

int signal = getNextSignal();

switch (signal)

{

    case SIGNAL_TIMEOUT:

            this.eventHandler.handleTimeout();

            break;

    case SIGNAL_RESET:

            this.eventHandler.handleReset();

            break;

}

}

}
```

The details of this dispatcher are rather unrealistic. For one thing, it is extremely specific to the type of event, and extremely general to its event handler dispatchees. More importantly, in event-driven programming it is quite common not to actually see the dispatcher.

But dispatchers in real event-driven programs play the same role that this piece of code does in many ways. For example, the dispatcher doesn't know much about the object that will actually be handling the events, beyond the fact that it implements the specified event-handling contract. This dispatcher can invoke handle Time out() and handle Reset() methods for any Time out Resettable, provided that the appropriate Time out Reset table is provided at construction time. Different dispatchers might dispatch to different Alarms. In fact, timeout and reset are sufficiently general events that other types of objects might rely on them.

Sharing the Interface

Another object that might be an event-driven user of timeouts and resets - and be controlled by the Time out Reset Dispatcher - is an image animation. An image animation is a series of images, displayed one after the other, that give the impression of motion. In this case, we use the timeout event to cause the next image to be displayed, while reset restores the image sequence to the beginning. Image Animation simply provides implementations of these methods without worrying about how or when they will be invoked.

An Image Animation is a single component that displays a sequence of images, one at a time.

```
public class ImageAnimation implements TimeoutResettable

{

    private Image[] frames;

    private int currentFrameIndex = 0;


    // To be continued...
```

The image array frames will hold the sequence of images to be displayed during the animation. When the Image Animation is asked to paint (or display) itself, it will draw the Image labeled by this.frames[this.currentFrameIndex]. By changing this.currentFrameIndex, we can change what is currently displayed. When we do change this.currentFrameIndex, we can make that change apparent by invoking the ImageAnimation's repaint() method, which causes the ImageAnimation to display the image associated with this.frames[this.currentFrameIndex].

The next segment of code is the timeout event handler, the helper method that is called when a timeout occurs. What should the ImageAnimation do when a timeout is received? Note that the question is not how to determine whether a timeout has occurred, but what to do when it has. This is the fundamental premise behind event-driven programming: the event handler method will be called when appropriate. The event handler simply provides the instructions for what to do when the event happens. When a timeout occurs, it is time to advance to the next frame of the animation:

```
public void handleTimeout()

    {
```

```
      if (this.currentFrameIndex < (this.frames.length - 1))

      {

          this.currentFrameIndex = this.currentFrameIndex + 1;

          this.repaint();

      }

  }
```

This code checks to see whether there are any frames left. If the animation is already at the end of the sequence, the execution skips the if clause and - since there is no else clause - does nothing. Otherwise - if there's a next frame - the execution increments the current frame counter, setting up the next frame to be drawn. Then, it calls this.repaint(), the method that causes the ImageAnimation to be redrawn. Recall that the Image Animation paints itself using the image that is associated with this.frames[this.currentFrameIndex].

What about a reset? What should the Image Animation do when it receives the signal to reset? Handling a reset event is much like handling a timeout, but even simpler. The Image Animation simply returns to the first image in the sequence:

```
public void handleReset()

    {

        this.currentFrameIndex = 0;

        this.repaint();

    }
```

No matter what, we reset the current frame index to 0, then repaint the image animation with the new frame. Note also that the next timeout will cause the frame to begin advancing again.

The code to actually repaint the image, makes this.frames[this.currentFrameIndex] appear. As a result, handleTimeout() works by changing the index to the next frame (until the end of the animation is reached); handleReset() restarts the image animation by restoring the index to the beginning index of this.frames once more.

Both Alarm and Image Animation are objects written in event-driven style. That is, they implement a contract that says "If you invoke my event handler method whenever the appropriate event arises, you will take care of responding to that event." Alternately, we think of the contract as saying "When the event in question happens, just let me know." When building both Alarm and Image Animation, the question to ask is, "What should you do when the specified event happens?"

Real Event-driven Programming

We briefly review these and recast them in light of event-driven programming's central question, "What should you do when xxx happens?" After reviewing these examples, we turn to look at the relationship of event providers to event handlers.

We saw how an Animate's act() method is repeatedly invoked by an Animator-Thread. This act() method is in effect an event handler. It answers the question, "What should I do when it is time for me to act?" The Animate doesn't know who is invoking its act() method or how that invoker decided that it was time to act. It simply knows that it is, and how to respond to that knowledge, i.e., how to act(). The act() method may be invoked by an AnimatorThread instruction follower, executing at the same time as other parts of the system. It might equally well be invoked by a Turn Taker Animator that controls a group of Animates and gives one Animate at a time a turn to act(). This latter approach might make sense, for example, in a board game where each player could move only when it was that player's turn.

Similarly, we saw how a Runnable object has a run() method that can be invoked in an event-driven style. This is commonly done when the run() method is invoked by starting up a new Thread. In this case, the Runnable's run() method is invoked when the Thread is start()ed. From the perspective of the Runnable, its run() method is automatically invoked whenever it is time for the Runnable to "do its thing". In a self-animating object like a Clock, run() might be an event-handler-like method that is called by something "outside" (in this case, the Thread) when it is time for the Clock to begin execution.

The String Transformer's transform methods of Interlude 1 were yet other examples of an event-driven style. These event handler methods simply answer the question, "What should you do when this String Transformer is presented with a String to transform?" or "How do you respond to such a request?" These objects provide customized implementations for transforming strings. The decision of when to invoke these methods are outside the control of their owning objects.

In each of the cases the event producer - the thing that knows that it is time for a handler method to be invoked - and the event handler - which responds to the occurrence - communicate fairly directly. For example, the Time out Reset Dispatcher polls (or explicitly asks) for signals and then directly invokes the event handler methods of its Time out Resettable.

The Idea of an Event Queue

Event-driven programming by its very nature allows a more distant relationship between event producers and event consumers. Since the producer disavows responsibility for handling the event, it doesn't need to know or care who is taking on that responsibility; it merely needs to indicate that the event has arisen. The event handler doesn't really care where the event came from; it just need to know that it will be invoked whenever the event has happened. This dissociation between event producers and event consumers is one of the potential benefits of programming in an event driven style.

Systems that take advantage of this opportunity to separate event producers from event handlers generally contain an additional component, called the event queue, that serves as an intermediary. It is important to understand how the event queue can be used and the role that it plays as an intermediary between event producers and event handlers. Unless you are building your own event-driven system from the ground up, it is not important that you be able to build it. Generally, an event queue is provided as a part of any event-based system, and the major event-based systems in Java are no exception.

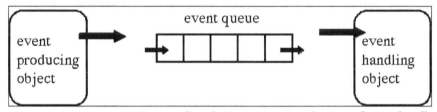

An event queue serves as an intermediary between event producers and event handlers.

The role of the event queue is to serve as a drop-off place for events that need to be handled, sort-of like a To Do list. When an object produces behavior that constitutes an event, it reports that event to the event queue, which holds on to the event. The report of the event may be as simple as an indication that something happened ("Timeout!") or as complex as a complete description of the state of the world at the time that the event happened. What is important is that the event queue stores (remembers) this event report.

In addition to receiving event reports, the event queue also has an active instruction-follower that removes an event (typically the oldest one) from the queue and notifies any interested event handler methods. This is the queue-checker/dispatcher. An event queue also needs some way to figure out who to notify when an event has happened.

Consider the Time out Resettable event handlers. A timer might generate the timeout events and deposit them into the queue. It would then return to its own business, keeping time and paying no more attention to the event queue. A separate instruction follower, the event dispatcher, would discover the timeout event in the queue and invoke the handle Time out() method of the relevant party. The structure of this "queue cleaner" would be very similar to the Time out Reset Dispatcher.

Properties of Event Queues

This mechanism allows for a separation between the event producer and the event handler. The instruction-follower that puts an event into the queue - the one who generates the event - is not necessarily the instruction follower who performs the handler method (i.e., handles the event). Instead, one or more dedicated instruction followers have the task of processing events deposited into the queue, invoking the event handler method(s) as needed. Event suppliers need to know only about the event queue, not about the event handler methods.

Note that it is the event queue dispatcher's Thread (or instruction follower) that actually executes the steps of the event handler method. (Method invocation does not change which instruction follower is executing.) As a result, when you are writing event handlers, it is important that the event handler code complete and return (relatively) quickly; for example, it should not go into an infinite loop. If the event dispatcher invoked an event handler that did not return, the dispatcher would be unable to process other events waiting in the queue.

You will almost never have to deal with an event queue explicitly unless you write your own event-driven system from scratch. Most programmers who write event-driven programs do not ever touch the event queue that underlies their systems. Instead, like many other aspects of event-driven programming, event queueing is generally a part of the hidden behavior of a system. However, there's nothing particularly mysterious about it. An event queue's contract provides an enqueue (add to the queue) operation and a dispatcher that actually invokes the event handler methods.

In Java, the graphical user interface toolkit provides an event queue to handle screen events such as mouse clicking and button pressing. That event queue is fairly well hidden under the abstractions of the toolkit, so that you may not realize that it is an event queue at all,

Graphical User Interfaces: An Extended Example

So far, we have left open the question of where and how events get generated. This is because in the most common kind of event system that you are likely to encounter - a windowing system for a graphical user interface - you do not deal with event generation directly. Instead, Java takes care of notifying the appropriate objects that an event of interest has occurred. When you are writing graphical user interfaces in Java, you will write event handlers without ever having to worry about when, where, and how the appropriate events are produced.

Before we can begin to talk about event handling in graphical user interfaces, we need to look briefly at what graphical user interfaces are and how they are built in Java. A graphical user interface - sometimes called a GUI, pronounced "gooey" - is a visual display containing windows, buttons, text boxes, and other "widgets". It is common to interact with a graphical user interface using a mouse, though a keyboard is often a useful adjunct. Graphical user interfaces became the standard interface for personal computers in the 1980s, though they were invented much earlier.

A sample graphical user interface.

Java.awt

Java provides a few different ways of making graphical user interfaces. We will take a look at the package java.awt. This package contains three major kinds of classes that are useful for making GUIs. The first of these is java.awt.Component and its subclasses. These are things that appear on your screen, like windows and buttons. The immediately following subsection explores this component hierarchy. The second major GUI class is the class java.awt.Graphics, which is involved in special kinds of drawing.

The event that we will be concerned with here is painting. That is, this is the event that occurs when a window or other user interface object becomes visible, is resized, or for other reasons needs to be redrawn. This event happens to a Component. In order to handle this event you need to know what the current state of the drawing is, including both its coordinate system and what if anything is currently visible. That information is held by a Graphics. So when the event happens, it takes a form roughly paraphrased as "paint yourself on this screen". The event handler belongs to a Component - the "self" to paint - and it takes a single argument, a Graphics - the "screen" on which to paint.

Components

A component is a thing that can appear on your screen, like a window or a button. The parent of all component classes is java.awt.Component. The Component class embodies a screen presence. You can't have a vanilla Component, though; you can only have an instance of one of its subclasses.

Although you can't instantiate Component directly, Component has several useful subclasses. One group of these is the set of stand-alone widgets that let you interact with your screen in stereotyped ways. There are many GUI widgets built in to java. awt. These include Checkbox, Choice, List, Button, Label, and Scrollbar. In addition, there are several Menu variants that don't extend Component directly, but also provide useful widgets. Each of these widgets is pretty well able to handle its GUI behavior - showing up, disappearing, allowing selections to be made, etc.

Another set of components are called Containers. These Components extend java. awt.Container (which itself is an abstract class extending java.awt.Component.) Containers are components that can have other components inside them. For example, a java.awt.Window (which is a kind of component) can have a java.awt.Scrollbar.

We will confine ourselves to one simple component behavior: painting itself. To do this, we will use a generic Component, called Canvas, that you can instantiate. The java.awt.anvas class doesn't do anything special, but you can either use it as a generic component or extend it to get specialized behavior. We will make a Canvas that paints itself with a special picture.

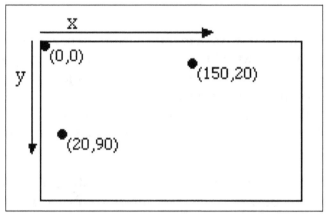

Standard screen coordinates, showing the origin, directions of
increasing horizontal (x) and vertical (y) coordinates, and two other sample points.

Graphics

A java.awt.Graphics (sometimes called a "graphics context") is a special kind of object that knows how to make pictures appear. A Graphics uses a coordinate system to keep track of locations within it. The origin of this coordinate system - the point (0,0) - is in the upper left-hand corner. Moving right from this point involves increasing the first (x) coordinate, so (100, 0) is 100 pixels to the right of the origin, along the top edge of the Graphics. Moving down increases the second (y) coordinate, so (0,50) is 50 pixels below the top of the Graphics, along its left-hand side. (100,50) is a point that is not on either the top or left edge; it is 100 pixels to the right and 50 pixels down.

Each Graphics has methods such as drawLine, fillOval, and setColor that allow you to create pictures. For example, if you had a Graphics named g, g.fillOval(100,100,10,10) would make it display a 10-pixel by 10-pixel circle with its upper left-hand corner at position 100, 100. If you called g.setColor(Color.red) first, the circle would be red.

A Graphics is not the kind of object that you are likely to create or have hanging around. You will probably never run into the Graphics associated with GUI widgets or containers. However, each time that your Canvas needs to redisplay itself, it will be handed a Graphics context with which to do that redisplaying. So there will be times when your code will be given a Graphics to use.

The Story of Paint

Painting (itself) is what a GUI component does when it becomes visible. For example, if a window is (partially) covering a component and then the window is moved, the component needs to make itself look right again. Java takes care of automatically determining that this should happen and asks the component to paint itself.

Every java.awt.Component has an event-driven paint method. This method does not say when the component should be painted, nor why, nor on what. This method has nothing to do with determining that painting is necessary. Instead, this method is the set of instructions that describe how to paint the Component. It is the answer to the question, "What should you do when it is time to paint myself (on the provided Graphics screen)?" It is the job of whatever calls the paint method to determine whether and when the Component needs to be painted.

The paint method of a Component is passed a Graphics object. This is the Graphics which contains, among other things, the coordinate frame within which drawing on this Component should take place. It also contains a variety of utilities that will make things actually appear within the Component. Just as you don't have to determine when or whether paint should be invoked, you don't need to provide the Graphics object. Like magic, when paint is invoked, the Graphics object will be there.

Each paint method contains the specific instructions that that component needs to make itself appear. For example, a Button's paint method makes the button label appear on the button. A Window's paint method not only makes the Window appear, it also makes sure that the paint method of each of the components contained in the Window gets called as well.

When the paint method is invoked, it is equipped with a single argument, a Graphics. If what the Component does to display itself is, for example, to draw shapes, this Graphics (the argument passed in to the Component's paint method) is what actually does the drawing.

Your job, when implementing a paint method, is to make use of this provided Graphics (and any other information that the object may have) in order to make the correct picture appear. You supply the instructions to be executed. To paint me, make a big red dot. Or, to paint me, print my name. Or, to paint me, paint each of the Components that appear inside me.

Suppose that you want to have your Component contain a rectangle in the upper left-hand corner. A Graphics has a drawRect method which does just that. When your component's paint method is called, it should ask whatever Graphics object is supplied to it to drawRect int x, int y, int width, int height.

For example, if paint were called with a Graphics named g, the instructions might read:

```
g.fillRect(0,0,20,20);
```

to draw a square in the upper left-hand corner of the Component. The whole method would read:

```
public void paint(Graphics g)

{

    g.fillRect(0,0,20,20);

}
```

A Component's paint method is an event handler. This means that the Component's paint method is the set of instructions describing the Component's response to a request to redisplay itself. It triggers whenever Java finds that something has happened that requires the component to redisplay itself.

Painting on Demand

When we say that paint is an event handler method, what we mean in part is that your code doesn't call paint directly. Instead, paint is called automatically by the Java runtime system any time the Component needs to redisplay itself. This could happen, for example, if a window were covered up and then uncovered: when the uncovering event occurs, the window needs to repaint itself. Each of the components, containers, and widgets in java.awt has an event-driven paint method. Note, however, that there's no Paintable interface; paint is a method of Component and is inherited by every class that extends Component.

The paint method takes a Graphics context as an argument. You cannot, in general, supply the appropriate Graphics context to a Component; but since you don't call paint, you don't need to supply the Graphics. Instead, Java's behind the scenes bookkeeping takes care of this. (Remember, paint(Graphics g) is used in event-driven style; that is, it is called by Java, not by your program.)

Your code cannot call paint directly. It is an event handler method and it uses an event queue; only the queue manager can call paint. But sometimes you will know that it is necessary for a GUI object to repaint itself. For example, in the code above the image animation needed to repaint itself each time the currentFrameIndex changed. Since you can't call the component's event handler directly, each Component provides another method, called repaint(), that you can call. If you call the component's repaint() method, it will ask Java to send it a new paint event.

If you do ever need to tell the system that you want your component to be painted, you need to arrange for Java to provide the appropriate information to your class. You can do this by calling the component's repaint() method. Unlike paint, which takes a Graphics as an argument, repaint takes no parameters. (This is good, because you don't generally have a Graphics around to give paint. This is another thing that Java keeps track of automatically.) You don't have to implement repaint(); java.awt.Component.repaint(), which you will inherit, queues up a new paint(Graphics g) request (even supplying the appropriate Graphics) behind the scenes. Remember: You never call paint, and you never implement repaint. To cause a painting to happen, call repaint(); to explain how to paint your component, implement (override) the paint(Graphics g) method - and don't worry about the Graphics, it will be automatically supplied to you.

Events and Polymorphism

One advantage of using an event-driven style is that your code can focus on how to respond to things that happen. It does not have to spend a lot of time figuring out whether things happen or deciding what has happened and who should deal with it. (Of course, event-driven code relies on an event dispatcher, which does have to deal with these things, but often either one is available - as in the GUI case - or a fairly simple and generic one will do.)

A second advantage of the event-driven style is that, when used in concert with an event queue (as in Java's AWT), it separates the generator of the event (e.g., the window motion) from the handler of the event (the component that is uncovered). This means that these two pieces of the system can be designed independently. All they have to do is to agree on the event protocol that they will use (in this case, repaint() and paint(Graphics g)). How each one fulfills its side of the contract - how the component decides to paint itself, for example - is something that the rest of the system doesn't have to worry about.

A corollary benefit, then, is that different kinds of components can handle the same event in very different ways. the same pair of events - timeout and reset - were used to run both an alarm and an image animation. In these two objects, the timeout event meant very different things. The alarm handled a timeout by turning on its buzzer; the image animation switched to the next image each time a timeout occurred.

The GUI painting system that we have described uses this polymorphism to great advantage. When a component like a Canvas is asked to paint itself in a Graphics, it may draw a simple picture using the Graphics supplied. When a widget like a Button is asked to paint itself, it creates labeled region of the screen appropriate for clicking into. A Checkbox may paint itself as a square, with or without an X in it depending on whether the Checkbox is checked. A container such as a Window not only paints itself, it also asks each of the components contained inside it to paint themselves. The Window doesn't need to know anything about how these components appear; it simply asks them to paint themselves in the way that they know best.

UI Objects

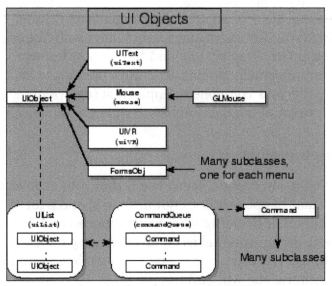

User interface objects used in VMD.

A major design point for VMD is to make it relatively easy to add completely different user interface (UI) methods, and allow for each interface to provide a means for accomplishing tasks that may also be accomplished by using the other interfaces as well. Figure illustrates the objects which are used to realize this design. There are four main or base-class level objects used in this category:

- Command objects, which each represent a single task which may be accomplished in VMD;

- CommandQueue, which maintains a queue of Command instances and which requests these Commands to be executed;

- UIObject objects, each of which represent one UI component.

Since there are to be several different UI components, there needs to be a way to avoid duplication of the code required to carry out the tasks requested by the user manipulating the user interface. This is the purpose of the Command object: each subclass of Command represents a single operation or tasks which the user may request to be done via a user interface of some form. These Command objects may take parameters to tell them exactly how to perform the task, but are designed to be rather specific about exactly what they should do. For example, CmdMolNew is the Command subclass which contains all the code necessary to create a new molecule via the algorithm, while the CmdRotate object knows how to apply a specified rotation to the current Scene. Each Command has a unique code, defined in the file Command.h, and requires derived classes to do the following things:

1. In the constuctor, the data necessary to perform the command must be given to the class and stored for the time when the command will be executed.

2. In a virtual function void Command::create_text(), use a streams output technique to place within the protected variable ostrstream *cmdText a string which is the text command equivalent of the requested operation. For example, for CmdRotate, if deg is the amount specified to rotate the scene, the function contains lines such as these:

```
*cmdText    rot    axis;

*cmdText    (byOrTo  ==  CmdRotate::BY ? " by " : " to ");

*cmdText    deg;

*cmdText    ends;
```

3. Provide a version of the protected virtual function int Command::do_execute(), which is called when the Command is requested to perform the actions it must do. More completely, to execute a Command the routine int Command::execute() is called, which then calls do_execute.

Since the Command will contain a text version of the requested action, it is relatively simple to create a text log of a VMD session: each time a Command is executed, the string for that command is simply written to a file.

There are many many actions which need to be done each time through the main execution loop of VMD. The CommandQueue object is used to queue and execute all the actions that need to be done. This is essentially a FIFO queue, and there is just one instance of this in VMD (stored in the global variable commandQueue). This object also contains routines for logging a VMD session. New Command objects are added to the queue via the routine void CommandQueue::append(Command *), and are appended to the end of the queue; the routine void CommandQueue::execute() then executes the top Command in the queue, and then deletes the Command instance. After the Command is executed, but before it is deleted, CommandQueue informs the UIObject's that the action was done. Since the Command is deleted after it is executed, an instance of the Command must be created via new, and then left to CommandQueue to be deleted. This is done because due to the asynchronous nature of this method of executing commands, it is not known exactly when the data in the Command will be needed, and thus it is unknown when the storage space may be freed up for other use. The only object which knows this is Command-Queue, and so it must be given new copies of these Command objects which it must delete when done.

The objects which create these Command objects are derived from the UIObject base class. This base class forms the heart of all the different types of UI components which VMD provides. For example, the text console UI (UIText), the mouse interface (Mouse), and all the GUI forms (FormsObj and derivations thereof) are derived from UIObject. All the UIObjects, when they are initialized, register with a CommandQueue object, which maintains the list of all UIObjects and can work with them as a group. The UIObject is given a unique ID code when it registers, which it uses to identify later if any actions being done were a result of a request from itself.

Each UIObject basically works with a subset of all the possible Command objects which VMD contains. Typically a UI component displays some graphical feedback or status of the current state of the program, such as displaying via a slider or lighted button what the value of some variable is. When an action is performed the UI components must be informed because this graphical status must be updated to reflect any changes. Any number of different UI components may require such an update, but since the number of Commands which can result in a change to the particular graphical display of each UIObject is much smaller than the total number of available actions, it would be very inefficient to have every UI component notified when each action is performed. Instead, the UIObjects each maintain a list of the integer codes for the Commands in which they are interested. When a Command is executed, the Commandqueue notifies only those UIObjects which have indicated they are interested in the Command. However, a UIObject can create any available Command instance, and give it to the CommandQueue to be executed. When a new Command is created, the ID of the UI which is creating it is also given to the Command, so that later when the UI components are notified of the action they can tell who requested the activity.

The purpose of each UIObject is to provide a means for the user to input commands, and to display to the user the current status of the program. The virtual routine int UIObject :check_event() is called once for each UI during the main execution loop to allow the UI component to check for user events (such as keyboard entries, mouse button presses, or manipulations of GUI components such as buttons or sliders). If such an event is found, a new Command is created for the event (events are simply derived from Command, and contain the data specifying the type of event) and put on the CommandQueue. After all UIObjects are checked for events, the CommandQueue is told to start executing its queued actions, continuing until the queue is empty. When an event action is processed, typically it results in some other form of Command to be requested, which is done by creating the proper special derivation of Command for the action and giving it to the Command-Queue. Eventually all events are processed, and the actions requested by them are then processed, and finally the queue is empty. As each Command is processed the requested action is done and all the UIObjects which expressed an interest in the action are notified, which allows them to update their display. When the queue is empty, VMD proceeds to then redraw the Scene.

It is relatively simple to create a new UIObject; each on-screen menu is a separate UIObject as is the mouse, the text console (which almost never needs to be updated due to a command being executed), and the 3D UI. Each UIObject can contain the ability to execute as many or as few actions as is desired. New UIObjects should be new'ed in the VMDinitUI routine, after the and CommandQueue global instance are created.

User Interface Toolkit

UI Toolkit is a set of routines and utility programs that gives you the tools you need to create user interfaces for your applications. Toolkit helps you provide a user interface that is easy to use and includes the following:

- Color.
- Drop-down menus.
- Cascading menus.
- Pop-up help.
- Ability to run in Windows environments.
- ActiveX controls.
- Tabbed dialogs.
- Composite windows (parent/child windows).

The UI Toolkit environment establishes and maintains input, prompts, messages, menus, help, and other user interface details—so you don't have to write such code yourself. Toolkit utilities handle the user-interface details for you and ensure consistency throughout your application.

UI Toolkit is structured to support large applications. Its design assumes that the major functions of your application will be supported by individual routines, while the main routine will consist primarily of a small decision apparatus that makes the appropriate calls to these routines. These routines and programs interact with window library files that UI Toolkit creates when it processes the script files you have written.

To use UI Toolkit, you first create a user interface window script file with Composer or a text editor. Next, you compile the script file with one of Toolkit's utility programs: Composer, Proto, or Script. These utility programs build the windows and store their definitions in a window library file. (Proto also allows you to preview your window script.) In the final step, you write a Synergy program that calls Toolkit routines. Figure illustrates this basic procedure.

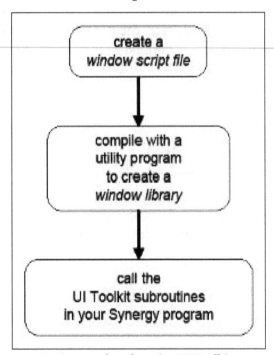

Basic procedure for using UI Toolkit.

UI Toolkit Components

Window Scripts

At the heart of the UI Toolkit windowing system are window script files, which enable you to quickly create general windows, input windows, menu columns, selection windows, and list classes from your own editable text files.

You provide the "script" to build a window, using script commands and arguments. The commands and arguments control the overall window characteristics and the items the window will contain.

You can create your script automatically with Composer, which enables you to interactively design windows, fields, buttons, and so on, in a graphical UI. Once your design looks exactly like you want it, you select the "Save script" option and Composer will translate your design into a script file.

Once your script file is created, you merely run a script processing utility or program (Script or Proto), or select "Compile Script" in Composer to build the window definitions. This processing also saves these definitions in a window library file.

Using UI Toolkit routines, your Synergy program can restore windows from the window library when they are needed. The routines and script files do not interact directly. Rather, at runtime, the routines open and use the window library that was created when the script file was processed.

Using window scripts has a distinct advantage. Each window is in a window library file, instead of being hard-coded into your programs. Because these libraries can be maintained outside your programs, you can modify window parameters and text without changing or recompiling your Synergy routines.

The UI Toolkit Utility Programs

UI Toolkit contains three utility programs: Composer, Script, and Proto.

Composer (Windows)

Composer creates and modifies window script files with a graphical user interface, enabling you to do the following:

- Interactively design windows and input windows.
- Save your design to a script file.
- Read and modify existing script files.
- Compile window scripts, storing the definitions into a window library.

Composer is available on Windows only.

Script

The Window Scripts program processes all forms of window script files, batch-style, to generate windows. In one step, it does the following for you:

- Reads and interprets the script.
- Converts window and column scripts into window and column definitions.
- Stores the definitions into a window library.

Proto

Proto performs all the actions that Script does, except that it also enables you to interactively process window scripts. Proto lets you display windows, too. Using it, you can do the following:

- Load (from a window library file) and view menu columns and windows.

- Test menu columns and windows.

- Create and update window libraries.

- Prototype display renditions.

- Edit key map definitions.

Figure illustrates how these utilities work together.

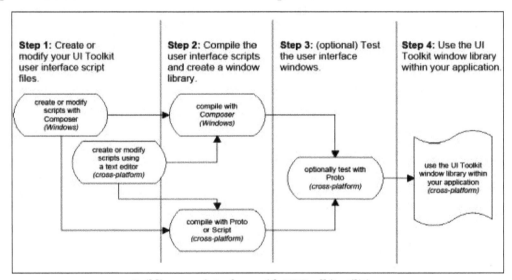

Building user interfaces with UI Toolkit utilities.

The UI Toolkit Routines

The main component of UI Toolkit is a set of routines. These routines link your application and the windowing system. They handle menu processing, input processing, text processing, selection processing, list processing, toolbar processing, tab set processing, environment maintenance, and more. These routines are based on a set of low-level Synergy windowing routines (the "W_" routines) that are part of the Synergy runtime.

The specific attributes of menus, input windows, and other window elements are defined in window script files and stored in window libraries, external to your application. You can also set display renditions, and define control and function key sequences externally.

Window Debugger

The UI Toolkit window debugger gives you information and the current status of the windowing environment. Using the debugger you can view the following:

- Any loaded window.

- Any environment level.

- General information about loaded windows and open channels.

- List and file-stack information.

- Detailed information about a specific window.

Abstract Window Toolkit

In today's world the most important interface is the graphical interface which provides the facilities for the user to create their applications which contains all the graphical elements. So that JAVA provides various GUI Classes and their methods those are organized in the form of packages. The most important packages are the java's awt packaged which contains 63 classes and 14 interface which provides various functions for a user to create his application.

Window Fundamentals

Java Abstract window tool kit package is used for displaying the data within a GUI Environment. Features of AW T Package are as Followings:

- It provides us a set of user interface components including windows buttons text fields scrolling list etc.

- It provides us the way to laying out these above components.

- It provides to create the events upon these components.

The main purpose for using the AWT is using for all the components displaying on the screen. Awt defines all the windows according to a class hierarchy those are useful at a specific level or we can say arranged according to their functionality.

The most commonly used interface is the panels those are used by applets and those are derived from frame which creates a standard window.

As you see in figure this Hierarchical view display all the classes and also their Sub Classes. All the Classes are Contained as a Multi-level inheritance, As You see that Component Class contains a Panel Class which again Contains a Applet Class so that in the AWT Package are Stored in the form of Multi-values inheritance.

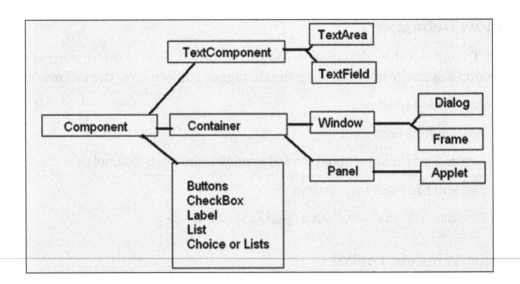

Component Class

This is the super class which defines all the methods for developing the methods those are related with the components and the methods those are related with the Actual Position of the Control and this also provides the various methods to Setup the Sized, Colors either this may a Background or a Foreground Color. It includes all the components those are displayed on the screen and it also defines various types of public methods for managing events such as mouse and keyboard window etc. the Various Methods those are Contained in the Component Class are:

- Void SetSize(int Width, int Height): This Method is used to Set the Size by taking the height and width of a Control for Example height of Textbox and width of Textbox. With this Method we Can set height and width of any Control.

- Void SetLocation (int x,int y): Used to Set the location on the Applet and this will take the Coordinates in the Form of x and y.

- Void setBounds(int x,int y,int width,int height): This Method will also set the Acual Loction in the Applet by Specifying the X and y Coordinate and also Specify the Width and Height of the Control.

- Void setForeground(Color c): This Method is used to set the Font Color or Text Color of a Control.

- Void setBackground(Color c): This Method is used to set the Background Color of a Control whether this may a Control or any Window Like an Applet,Panel etc.

Container

It is subclass of components which Inherits the various Properties from that Class and it provides to laying out the component , that are contains by using the various layout managers. Means how the Components will be displayed in the applet and in which Manner the Components will be displayed in the window or Position of the Controls without setting the X and y Axis is determined by the Layout Manager and. The Container Provides very important Methods to add or Remove the Components from the Applet or from any other Window. The various Methods those are Contained in the Container class are:

- Void add (object o): This Method id used to Add a Control in the Applet of in any Container.

- Void remove(object o): This is used if a user wants to Remove an Control from a Container For Example if a user wants to Remove the Control from a Applet then he may uses this Method.

- Void removeAll(): This Method does not take any argument and this will remove all the Controls from the Container.

Panel

It is a subclass of container and it is the super class of Applet. It is a window that does not have a title bar menu bar or border. Generally a Panel is used for displaying Multiple Windows in a Single Window and a Panel may have any Layout. And for Adding any Control in the Panel we have to use the Add Method and there are also some important Methods those are Provided by the Panel Class those are Explained below:

- Panel(): This is the name of class for using you have to create the object first.

- Void setLocation: Method is used to set the Location of a control in the Panel.

- Void setSize(): This will takes two Arguments and those Arguments will Specify the Width and Height of the Panel.

- Void setBounds: This Mcthod is used to set the Bounds of an Control in the Panel for example X and y Axis and Width and Height of a Control.

Window

Window is also a Sub Class of a Container and window class creates a top level window. These are not directly created, for this the subclass of window name frame is used and dialogs are used . This is used for displaying a Sub Windows from a Main Window and the various Methods of Window are as follows:

- Void Pack(): This Method is used for adjusting the Size of Window according to the number of Controls in the Container or in the Applet or in the other window.

- Void show(): This Method is used for displaying a Window.

- Void dispose(): This Method is used for de-allocate the Memory Space which is Consumed by the Controls of the Window.

Working with Frames

Frame class is also a sub class of window class and frame class allows to create a pop-menus. And frame class provides a special type of window which has a title bar, menu bar, border. Resizing corners and it is a subclass of window class when we creates A frame object within a applet, will display a warning message that a frame window is created by an applet not by any software. But when a frame window is created by a program other than an applet then a normal window is created. The Various Methods those are Provided by the Frame Class are as follows:

- Frame(): This is name of Class and used for Creating an object of this Class and this will not display any title on the title bar of Frame.

- Frame(String Title): This will also create an object of Frame Class and this will also Display a Title on the Title bar of the Window.

- Void setsize(): This is Method of Frame Class which will be Accessed by the object of Frame Class and this will takes two Arguments to set the Size in the Form of width and Height.

- Void show(): This is used for displaying or showing a Frame from a Main Window.

- Void setBackground(Color c): This is used to set the background color of the frame.

- Void setLocation(int x,int y): This Method will display the frame on the window according to the values of x and y coordinates those are Specified Always Remember that for displaying a frame you have to set the Layout and the default Layout of the Frame is Border Layout.

Creating a Frame

An instance of frame can be created using any of the constructors. You can use the frame objects unique methods as well as its inherited method by specifying the frame object name with the method name. The syntax to invoke a method is:

Frame1.show();

The following program code show how to create a frame window:

```
/*

=================================================================

File Name : Framed1.java
```

: http://javaproglang.blogspot.in/

Facebook : https://www.facebook.com/AdvanceJavaProgramming

Created By :

==

```
*/

import java.awt.*;

public class Framed1 extends Frame

{

     public static void main(String args[])

     {

          /* Creating a frame object */

               Frame frmobj=new Frame("My First Frame");

               frmobj.setSize(400,450);

               frmobj.setVisible(true);

     }

}
```

The above code shows how to create an empty frame. The java.awt.* package should be included in the java programs to implement the functions of AWT classes in your program. Saved file with Framed1.java and follow below commands:

```
C:\>jdk1.4\bin>javac Framed1.java

C:\>jdk1.4\bin>java Framed1
```

Setting Frame Properties

Frame class inherits all the methods of its super class. The inherited methods such as set Size() and set Visible() enable you to set the propertied for a frame window. The dfault size of frame 0,0 in terms of width and height. You can set the size of a frame at any time in your program using the set Size() method. The syntax to implement the set Size() method is:

```
Void Set Size(Int Width, Int Height)

Void Set Size(Dimension Size)
```

In the above syntax, you can specify the width and height of frame window as arguments in the set Size() methods. In addition, you can also specify the dimension for frame window by passing an object of the Dimension class size is the object of the Dimension class that has width and height fields, which set the size of frame in terms of pixels. These are the two ways of setting frame window size property. You can use the get Size() method to obtain the current size of the frame. The syntax obtain the current size of the frame window is:

```
Dimension get Size()
```

This method returns an object of dimension type. This object has width and height fields that store the current size of the frame window, which is displayed on the screen.

Specifying the frame named followed by the method name sets properties for a frame. The following program code shows how to set the properties of a frame window:

Setting the Properties of a Frame:

```
/*

================================================================

File Name : Framed.java

: http://javaproglang.blogspot.in/

Facebook : https://www.facebook.com/AdvanceJavaProgramming

Created By :

================================================================

*/

import java.awt.*;
```

```
import java.awt.event.*;

public class Framed extends Frame

{

    public static void main(String args[])

    {

        /* Creating a frame object */

            Framed frmobj=new Framed();

            Framec fc=new Framec(frmobj);

            /*Set frame properties*/

            frmobj.setSize(400,450);

            frmobj.setVisible(true);

            frmobj.setTitle("Demo");


            /*Setting the Background color for frame
using color object.*/

            Color col = new Color(178,185,255);

            frmobj.setBackground(col);


            /*Add windowListener method to provide window
functionality*/

            frmobj.addWindowListener(fc);

    }

}

/*Subclass of the windowadapter class is created to

provide window events such as closing a frame or minimizing
a frame.*/


class Framec extends WindowAdapter
```

```
{

    /*Object of the frame subclass is created*/


    Framed fd;


    /*Object of frame subclass is passed as arguments in the
windowadpter method*/


    Framec(Framed f)

    {

        fd = f;

    }

    /* Closing event is defined for frame.*/

    public void windowClosing(WindowEvent we)

    {

        System.exit(0);

    }

}
```

Saved file with Framed.java and follow below commands:

```
C:\>jdk1.4\bin>javac Framed.java

C:\>jdk1.4\bin>java Framed
```

Canvas

This is also a Special type of Class which is also derived from a Windows Class and this is not a part of AWT hierarchy class and this is one another type of window which is used for creating a blank Area and this will Creates an Empty Area for doing drawing. It provides us a blank window which can be drawn upon it. And it inherits the Properties from the Paint Method from the Graphics Class which is Located in the Component Class.

Java Awi Ui Toolkit

Java AWT is also known as Abstract Window Toolkit is an API that is used to develop either GUI or window-based applications in Java. Java AWT components are platform-dependent which implies that they are displayed according to the view of the operating system. It is also heavyweight implying that its components are using the resources of the Operating System. java. awt package provides classes for AWT api. For example, TextField, CheckBox, Choice, Label, TextArea, Radio Button, List, etc.

AWT Hierarchy

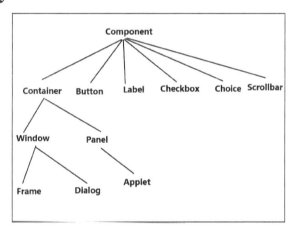

Container

The Container is one of the components in AWT that contains other components like buttons, text fields, labels, etc. The classes that extend Container class are known as containers such as Frame, Dialog, and Panel as shown in the hierarchy.

Types of Containers

The container refers to the location where components can be added like text field, button, checkbox, etc. There are in total, four types of containers available in AW, that is, Window, Frame, Dialog, and Panel. As shown in the hierarchy above, Frame and Dialog are subclasses of Window class.

Window

The window is a container which does not have borders and menu bars. In order to create a window, you can use frame, dialog or another window.

Panel

The Panel is the container/class that doesn't contain the title bar and menu bars. It has other components like button, text field, etc.

Dialog

The Dialog is the container or class having border and title. We cannot create an instance of the Dialog class without an associated instance of the respective Frame class.

Trim

The Frame is the container or class containing the title bar and might also have menu bars. It can also have other components like text field, button, etc.

Why AWT is Platform Dependent?

Java Abstract Window Toolkit calls native platform i.e., Operating system's subroutine in order to create components like text box, checkbox, button, etc. For example, an AWT GUI containing a button would be having varied look-and-feel in various platforms like Windows, Mac OS, and Unix, etc. since these platforms have different look and feel for their respective native buttons and then AWT would directly call their native subroutine that is going to create the button. In simple words, an application build on AWT would look more like a windows application when being run on Windows, however, that same application would look like a Mac application when being run on Mac Operating System.

Basic Methods of Component Class

- Public void add(Component c): This method would insert a component on this component.

- Public void setSize(int width, int height): This method would set size (width and height) of the particular component.

- Public void setVisible(boolean status): This method would change the visibility of the component, which is by default false.

- Public void setLayout(LayoutManager m): This method would define the layout manager for the particular component.

Java AWT Example

We can create a GUI using Frame in two ways:

Either by extending Frame class or by creating the instance of Frame class.

Let's show this by both examples, first extending Frame Class:

```java
import java.awt.*;/* Extend the Frame class here,
*thus our class "Example" would behave
*like a Frame
*/public class Example extends Frame
{Example()
{Button b=new Button("Button!!");
//setting button position on screen
b.setBounds(50,50,50,50);
//adding button into frame
add(b);
//Setting  width and height
setSize(500,300);
//Setting title of Frame
setTitle("This is First AWT example");
//Setting the layout for the Frame
setLayout(new FlowLayout());
/*By default frame is not visible so
*we are setting the visibility to true*to make it visible.
*/
setVisible(true);}public static void main(String args[]){
//Creating the instance of Frame
Example fr=new Example();
```

```
}

}
```

Creating an Instance of Frame Class

```
import java.awt.*;

public class Example {

Example()

{//Creating Frame

Frame f=new Frame();

//Creating a label

Label l = new Label("User: ");

//adding label to the frame

f.add(l);

//Creating Text Field

TextField t = new TextField();

//adding text field to the frame

f.add(t);

//setting frame size

f.setSize(500, 300);

//Setting the layout for the Frame

f.setLayout(new FlowLayout());

f.setVisible(true);

}public static void main(String args[])

{Example ex = new Example();

}

}
```

Layouts in AWT

There are 2 layouts in AWT which are as follows:

- Flow layout is default layout, which implies when you don't set any layout in your code then the particular layout would be set to Flow by default. Flow layout would put components like text fields, buttons, labels, etc in a row form and if horizontal space is not long enough to hold all components then it would add them in a next row and cycle goes on. Few points about Flow Layout:

  ○ All the rows in Flow layout are aligned center by default. But, if required we can set the alignment from left or right.

  ○ The horizontal and vertical gap between all components is 5 pixels by default.

  ○ By default, the orientation of the components is left to right, which implies that the components would be added from left to right as required, but we can change it from right to left when needed.

- Border layout wherein we can add components like text fields, buttons, labels, etc to specific five. These regions are known as PAGE_START, LINE_START, CENTER, LINE_END, PAGE_END.

Method for border layout is:

```
public BorderLayout(int hgap,int vgap)
```

It would construct a border layout with the gaps specified between components. The horizontal gap is specified by hgap and the vertical gap is specified by vgap.

Parameters are:

- Hgap – The horizontal gap.
- Vgap – The vertical gap.

We can also achieve the same by using setHgap(int hgap) method for the horizontal gap between components and setVgap(int vgap) method for the vertical gap.

Visual Design in HCI

For every system to be widely accepted and used effective they need to be well designed. This is not to say that all systems have to be designed to accommodate everyone, but that they should be designed for the needs and capabilities of the people, for whom, they are intended. Donald Norman wrote that many examples of everyday things that do not present a clear and obvious image to their users. In this case, with the complexity of most computer systems, it is clearly to see that the potential of poorly designed is very high.

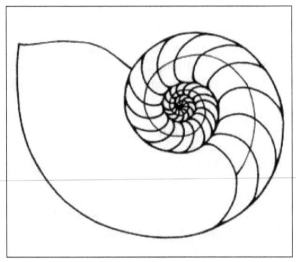

The nautilus shell.

For this reason, a study of visual design is needed. As written by Davis, Hawley, McMullan, and Spilka, the nautilus shell is an example of synthesis between form and function found in nature; its form is the result of evolution, which is both transparent and beautiful. The nautilus shell is a perfect analogy for design and the design process because it creates valuable user experiences and usable interfaces.

The word design functions as both a noun and a verb. Many people use it to refer to the outward appearance or style of a product. However, design also refers to a process that of intentionally establishing a plan or system by which a task can be accomplished or a goal reached. It includes tangible and intangible systems in which objects or processes are coherent organized to include the environment in which these objects and processes function. Consequently, design can affect all people in every aspect of what they do. A good design performs for people; it is concerned with economics and the transmission of ideas. Thus, the challenge presented to a design team is to plan a prototype with a clear purpose that is easy to use, meet user needs, addresses commercial considerations, and can be mass-produced. Its visual form, whether two or three dimensional, digital or analog, logically explains its purpose and efficiently leads the user through its function.

Moreover, design is not a series of subjective choices based on personal preference, at best a cosmetic afterthought considered if time and money are leftover. Good design is the tangible representation of product goals. An iterative and interactive proves that requires active learning, design unifies a wide range of disciplines. Good design is a significant activity that reveals multiple solutions to each problem. Design equally values different ways of thinking. It allows people with a variety of skills and learning abilities to work cooperatively to bring insights and expertise to problems and opportunities in order to better develop new and innovative solutions.

Understanding the fundamentals of visual design is clearly an effective way responds to human problems. For this reason, the design processes/steps are required, and will be described using the following table:

Table: Visual Design Step.

Steps	Description
Problem identification and definition	A need or problem is identified, research, and defined.
Gathering and analysing information	The focus is on learning what is not known. Assumptions are questioned. Wide and broad research is used to located information and general ideas.
Determining performance criteria for a successful solution	Research continues as imagery is selected. Rules are declared and what is known is specified.
Generating alternative solutions and building prototypes	Multiple solutions are generated. A variety of methods for analysis, such as drawing, inter- viewing, modeling or evaluating statistics, are used.
Implementing choices	Project content, scope, and intent are formally established. Initial possibilities are represented and presented as prototypes.
Evaluating outcomes	Prototypes are assessed, tested, evaluated, and judged. The knowledge gained is incorporated into further studies and refinements.
Production	A prototype, which is synthesis of the initial solutions made using this process, and specifications are released for making multiples to manufacture.

The visual design decisions are based on project goals, user perspective, and informed decision-making. These are the responsibilities of the role of the Designer. While many aspects of design are quantifiable, there are visual principles that are measurable but equally important. In fact, nowadays, the Designers face great challenges. There are many questions such as: How products that are seen, read, understood, and acted upon can be created? Given increasing variety and complexity, how the power of new technologies can be harnessed? And how informed visual choice can be made? Consequently, the visual design principles will act as guidelines for the Designers on how to make informed design decisions – design that provides the best, most thoughtful and appropriate integration of both form and function.

There are no universal rules, only guidelines. If there were rules, everything would look the same and work perfectly according to these rules. Each situation is different with its own context and parameters.

1. Remember the audience: be a user advocate. It is necessary to think about audience needs first throughout the development process. Some possible questions require answers such as: Who is in the audience? What are their requirements? The evaluation criteria used in the design development process springs from answers to these and other questions. Therefore, Designers must understand and advocate for the user.

2. Structure the messages: The Designer needs to analyze content to create a clear visual hierarchy of major and minor elements that reflects the information hierarchy. This visual layering of information helps the user focus on context and priorities.

3. Test the reading sequence: It is essential to apply the squint test. How does the eye travel across the page, screen, or publishing medium? What is seen first, second, and third? Does this sequence support the objectives and priorities as defined in the audit (a critical step in determining the scope and parameters of an organization's corporate graphic standards)?

4. Form follows function: The Designer should be clear about the user and use environment first. An effective interface design represents and reinforces these goals.

5. Keep things simple: The Designer needs to remember the objective is to communicate a message efficiently and effectively, so that users can perform a task. Fewer words, type styles, and graphic elements mean less visual noise, and greater comprehension. An obvious metaphor enhances intuitive understanding and use. As the result, the goal is to transfer information, not show off features or graphic.

6. People don't have time to read: When there is text involves in the design, it must be written as clear and concise as possible. Design information in an economical, assessable, intuitive format that is enhanced by a combination of graphic and typography. Graphics are very powerful and can be efficiently and effectively provide explanations while saving space on page.

7. Be consistent: The design must be consistency in using of type; page structure and graphic and navigation elements can create a visual language that decreases the amount of effort it takes to read and understand a communication piece. Thus, the goal is to create a user experience that seem effortless and enjoyable throughout.

8. Start the design process early: The development team of Designers, usability professionals, engineers, researchers, writers, and user advocates should be assembled at beginning of the process. Successfully applying the principles of good design enables an organization to communicate more effectively with its audiences and customers, improving the worth of its products and services and adding value to its brand and identity.

9. Good design is not about luck: A good design for usable interfaces appropriately applies the fundamentals of visual design to interactive products. However, creating the most useful, successful design for an interactive product is difficult. For the reason, the design process is iterative and experiential. There are usually several possible ways to solve a problem, and the final design decision is dictated by the best choices that work within the parameters at any particular time. Advocate on behalf of the user. Users are the reason why Designers are here and have this work to do. Users are everywhere, often in places not yet imagined. As the world grows smaller and becomes even more connected, the opportunity lies in where and what has not been discovered.

User Interface Usability Testing and Evaluation Methods

Human-Machine Interface Also known as the user interface, it is the medium through which the system and user exchange and exchange information. The slogan "user-friendly" appeared in the mid-1980s. This slogan is translated into the concept of "usability" of the human interface. And become one of the key metrics for measuring the user interface.

The Usability has the following elements:

1. Easy to learn: Whether the product is easy to learn.

2. Interactive efficiency: How efficiently users use the product to accomplish specific tasks.

3. Easy-to-remember behavior: Operation.

4. The frequency and severity of the error: The frequency of operational errors, the severity.

5. The user satisfaction: the user is satisfied with the product.

Nigel Bevan believes that usability is the degree of effectiveness (Effectiveness), efficiency (Efficiency) and user satisfaction (Satisfaction) of a particular product when it is used for a particular purpose in a particular environment.

Usability refers to the effectiveness of the interaction process, interaction efficiency and user satisfaction when users use the product in a specific environment to accomplish specific tasks. "Effectiveness" as used herein refers to the correctness and completeness of a user's accomplishment of a particular task and its attainment of a particular goal: "Efficiency" refers to the degree to which a user accomplishes the correctness and completeness of the task and the resources used, eg, the ratio between time: "satisfied Degree "refers to the degree of subjective satisfaction and acceptance felt by the user in using the product.

Usability Testing and Evaluation of Indicators

Most studies typically use typical usability tests for subjective evaluation of task time, percentage of tasks completed, type and amount of errors, and satisfaction.

Usability Testing and Evaluation Methods

Traditional Usability Testing and Evaluation Methods

There are many traditional usability testing and evaluation methods, such as user testing, heuristic evaluation, cognitive walking, behavioral analysis, structured and unstructured interview, questionnaire, GOMS (Goals, Operators, and Methods, Selection rules) Probability rules grammar for interface usability assessment. These methods are now widely used in a variety of interface evaluation process. Suitable for different user interface design and development stages. Each has its own advantages and disadvantages.

Usability of Cognitive Physiology Assessment Method

Eye Tracking Technology

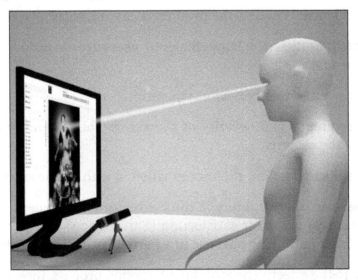

Visual is the direct way for users to interact with the interface. Visual Awareness (Eye-tracking) Physiological Assessment is a very effective method of evaluating the pros and cons of the interface, using line-of-sight tracking as an assessment technique to evaluate a range of website usability levels.

EEG Technology

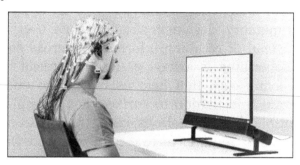

EEG can accurately analyze neuropsychological data in a small real-time window, with high sensitivity to task complexity. Is a very attractive way to measure cognitive workloads in the man-machine interface.

User Interface Design Guidelines

These are the Guidelines for User Interface Design:

- Visibility of system status: Users should always be informed of system operations with easy to understand and highly visible status displayed on the screen within a reasonable amount of time.

- Match between system and the real world: Designers should endeavor to mirror the language and concepts users would find in the real world based on who their target users are. Presenting information in logical order and piggybacking on user's expectations derived from their real-world experiences will reduce cognitive strain and make systems easier to use.

- User control and freedom: Offer users a digital space where backward steps are possible, including undoing and redoing previous actions.

- Consistency and standards: Interface designers should ensure that both the graphic elements and terminology are maintained across similar platforms. For example, an icon that represents one category or concept should not represent a different concept when used on a different screen.

- Error prevention: Whenever possible, design systems so that potential errors are kept to a minimum. Users do not like being called upon to detect and remedy problems, which may on occasion be beyond their level of expertise. Eliminating or flagging actions that may result in errors are two possible means of achieving error prevention.

- Recognition rather than recall: Minimize cognitive load by maintaining task-relevant information within the display while users explore the interface.

Human attention is limited and we are only capable of maintaining around five items in our short-term memory at one time. Due to the limitations of short-term memory, designers should ensure users can simply employ recognition instead of recalling information across parts of the dialogue. Recognizing something is always easier than recall because recognition involves perceiving cues that help us reach into our vast memory and allowing relevant information to surface. For example, we often find the format of multiple choice questions easier than short answer questions on a test because it only requires us to recognize the answer rather than recall it from our memory.

- Flexibility and efficiency of use: With increased use comes the demand for less interactions that allow faster navigation. This can be achieved by using abbreviations, function keys, hidden commands and macro facilities. Users should be able to customize or tailor the interface to suit their needs so that frequent actions can be achieved through more convenient means.

- Aesthetic and minimalist design: Keep clutter to a minimum. All unnecessary information competes for the user's limited attentional resources, which could inhibit user's memory retrieval of relevant information. Therefore, the display must be reduced to only the necessary components for the current tasks, whilst providing clearly visible and unambiguous means of navigating to other content.

- Help users recognize, diagnose and recover from errors: Designers should assume users are unable to understand technical terminology, therefore, error messages should almost always be expressed in plain language to ensure nothing gets lost in translation.

- Help and documentation: Ideally, we want users to navigate the system without having to resort to documentation. However, depending on the type of solution, documentation may be necessary. When users require help, ensure it is easily located, specific to the task at hand and worded in a way that will guide them through the necessary steps towards a solution to the issue they are facing.

Example of the Guidelines for User Interface Design

We will take a closer look at how Adobe Photoshop reflects each of these guidelines in order to inspire you to improve the usability, utility, and desirability of your own designs by incorporating the 10 rules of thumb into your own work.

Visibility of System Status

Photoshop does a great job of letting the user know what's happening with the program by visually showing the user what their actions have led to whenever possible.

For example, when users move layers around in the Layers palette, they can visually see the layer being represented as physically dragged within the space.

The cursor graphic goes from representing an open-hand to a gripped hand when the user drags a layer around within the Layers palette. This makes it easier to instantly understand the system status. Additionally, Adobe's choice of using a 'hand' is a great example of the second guideline where the system matches the real world.

System Match to the Real World

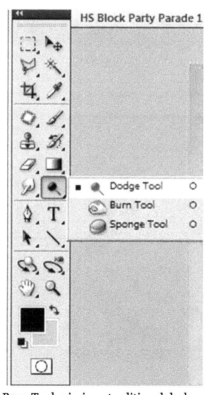

Photoshop's Dodge Tool and Burn Tool mimics a traditional darkroom technique for photographs.

An example of Photoshop mimicking the real world in terms and representations that their target users would understand, is where they design the information structure and terminology to mirror the same wording we would use in the world of photography or print media. Familiar concepts and terms like RGB, Hue/Saturation/Brightness and CMYK are used to represent color, while various tools like the dodge tool and the burn tool mimics a traditional darkroom technique for photographs.

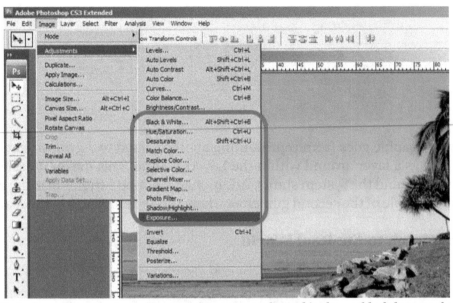

Photoshop utilizes the term, "Exposure", as commonly used in the world of photography.

User Control and Freedom

Photoshop is very good at providing users with control every step of the way. As the user makes changes to an image or adds various artistic effects, they are able to quickly and easily take a step backwards if they make an error, for instance.

The users are in control as they can take a Step Backward or Step Forward under the Edit menu, or alternatively they can use Photoshop's keyboard shortcuts like Alt+Ctrl+Z, for example.

Consistency and Standards

Photoshop maintains a standard layout and look & feel when it comes to the menu bar. They also utilize commonly known terminology such as "New...", "Open...", "Save As...", etc.

The File menu in Photoshop displays a variety of highly familiar options.

Error Prevention

To prevent users from making errors, photoshop provides a brief description or label of the tools when a user hovers over it to help make sure users are using the proper tool for the task at hand.

The user hovers over the eraser icon and Photoshop displays the "Eraser Tool" label.

Recognition rather than Recall

Whether it be making a selection from the artistic filters menu, or opening a new image file, photoshop provides a sample view for users to make the right choice. This allows for the user to visually recognize what they're looking for instead of having to recall the name or typing it in to search for it. Perhaps you have encountered other photo editing programs which ask you to recall and type the name of the file you want to work on. This can indeed be really difficult to recall as it is often something to the effect of: 29412_09342.JPG.

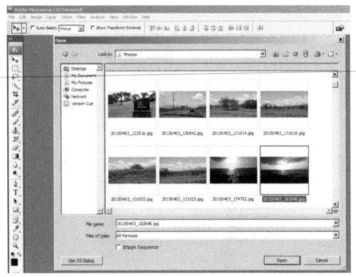

The user is able to visually recognize the sunset image by its thumbnail and select it.

Flexibility and Efficiency of Use

One of the many reasons for frequent users to love Photoshop is for its flexibility and efficiency. Users are able to utilize its flexibility by organizing and adding to their Workspace, as well as making things more efficient by saving it for future use.

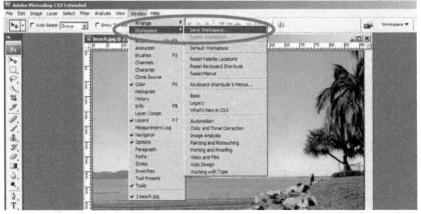

Photoshop gives frequent users the ability to save their preferred workspace-setup.

8. Aesthetic and Minimalist Design

The toolbar in Photoshop only displays the icons and is neatly tucked to the side to help keep clutter to a minimum, and maintain a minimalist aesthetic.

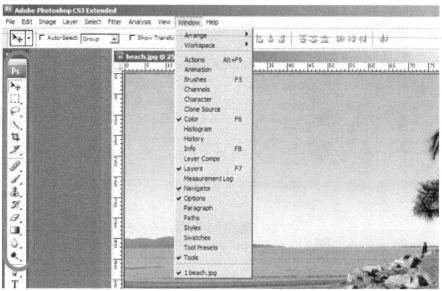

The Photoshop toolbar is minimalist and avoids clutter by representing the tools with icons only.

Help Users Recognize, Diagnose and Recover from Errors

Whenever there is an error, Photoshop provides dialogue that lets the user know what went wrong and how to fix it.

In this error message for the user's misuse of the clone stamp, Photoshop
explains what went wrong, the reason why and how the user should proceed from there.

Help and Documentation

Help and documentation can be accessed easily via the main menu bar. From there, you can find a wide variety of help topics and tutorials on how to make full use of the program.

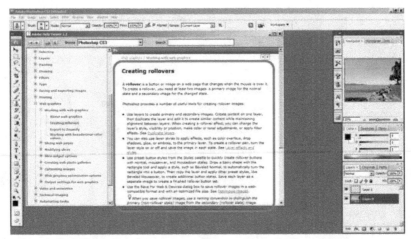

The window displays information on how to create rollovers in the context of web graphics. The user is also able to see a list of topics on the side menu.

Ethics of User Experience Design

New technologies have always produced unintended consequences. But user experience (UX) designers and engineers face a number of new ethical challenges today with the rise of technology and our interaction and dependence on it.

UX designers' primary job is to improve usability and extend productivity. But they also have a responsibility to address the unintended consequences of new technologies, some of them with a clear ethical dimension. Following is a look at some of the principle ethical quandaries that UX designers will run up against and must deal with responsibly.

Human Costs and De-valuing Work

So much of the UX discipline's early efforts were driven by the desire to improve human performance and productivity while reducing errors. Few questioned the value of these gains, achieved by optimizing system design, augmenting human ability, and automation, especially as it eliminated dangerous, repetitive, or tedious work — think of assembly line factory jobs that in past decades injured and maimed scores of people.

But some forms of automation come at the cost of diminishing the work's intellectual and emotional value. Consider the levels of automation found in fast-food restaurants or warehouse fulfillment centers, where work is de-humanized, worker growth is diminished, and the value of rewarding work is stripped away. Undoubtedly these issues were at play with the spate of protests and suicides by distraught Foxconn workers in recent years.

The question for the UX professional who designs these work experiences then is: at what point must efficiency and optimization yield to human concerns?

De-skilling

Over the past two decades, there have been tremendous advances in the development of powerful support systems that augment human intelligence in demanding environments. For example, some aircraft systems, such as the Boeing Dreamliner and the F-35 Lighting II, have become so complicated that they challenge the human capacity to fly them without assistance from an "intelligent" assistant. The positive benefits of this technology can reduce error and improve safety.

At the same time, UX researchers must examine the possibiliy that automation can create a situation where skilled operators can be replaced be less-skilled operators. On a mainstream level, that would include losing the ability to navigate without the aid of GPS, or more simply the ability to do math without using a calculator.

In some cases, the gains from technology will outweigh the loss of skills. In others, the level of support and automation might warrant reconsideration. Whatever the outcome, it is critical that UX designers initiate this conversation, so that users of technology can make informed choices about their extent and consequences.

Influencing User Behavior

We've gotten pretty good at being able to subconsciously influence and alter behavior (by nudging, for one), which creates a vexing ethical conundrum for UX designers. The UX professional must understand that for every product created with the "best intention," there will be another that deliberately nudges the user to ends not in the user's best interest. Thus on the one hand, they recognize that human behavior often results in sub-optimum choices and actions. On the other hand, they recognize that they have the potential, through design, to affect that behavior in other ways — positive and negative.

So how do UX professionals define their ethical responsibilities as they subconsciously influence users' decisions or actions? The case of producing negative outcomes is clear; less clear is who determines what is "positive." The line between the two is often not well defined. Take for instance the medicare prescription drug plan finder tool on the medicare.gove site which navigates this dilemma well. It guides and supports the user in an unbiased fashion to the plan that best aligns with their health needs — a great improvement over early support efforts on the site.

The Erosion of Privacy

With the best intentions, technologies have been developed to remotely monitor the activities of the elderly — what and how much they eat, where they're located, even when they take their prescriptions. Similarly, products like vuezone or Car Connection allow parents to monitor every movement of their children — what they're doing at home, how fast they are driving, where they are at 2 a.m.

The benefits of such technologies are real, for one allowing the elderly to live independently or for parents to be confident in the safety of their children. Yet such constant monitoring of the individual can also have the opposite effect, instead leaving one feeling the loss of highly valued privacy and dignity because of nonstop monitoring. With each new capability comes added consequences.

The Dangers of Distraction

The convergence of technologies can tax our attention spans in a way that threatens the limits of human capabilities. One case is the increased integration of communication, navigation, and entertainment technologies in automotive design. We now have GPS screens, entertainment monitors, handsfree cellphone use, and advanced stereo systems with various control mechanisms.

While these technologies deliver unquestionable value and pleasure to the driver and passengers, they indisputably divide the operator's attention, distracting him or her from the stated purpose of driving, leading to life-threatening situations (and that's not even including texting while driving). The problem has become so severe that the Highway Safety Administration has created a website to address this issue.

So what responsibility do UX professionals have in these situations? The likelihood of distraction and its consequences should become an area of intense focus in the UX discipline's research agenda.

At the end of the day, UX professionals must increasingly consider where their responsibilities lie — with the organization that reaps financial gains from the technology sold, or with the user who may possibly suffer negative or life-threatening consequences from these products.

References

- Types-user-interface, systemsanalysis: w3computing.com, Retrieved 23 July, 2019

- Awt-event-handling: tutorialspoint.com, Retrieved 28 March, 2019

- User-interface-design-guidelines-10-rules-of-thumb: interaction-design.org, Retrieved 15 May, 2019

- Ethics-user-experience: bentley.edu, Retrieved 02 February, 2019

- Apperley, T. 2006. Genres and Game Studies: Toward a Critical Approach to Video Game Genres. Retrieved 15.2.2012, from Academia.edu

4

Interactive System Development Framework

Computer systems characterized by notable amount of interactivity between humans and computer are referred to as interactive systems. This chapter delves into components of development framework such as model, view and controller, wimp interface, post-WIMP interface, multimodel interface and gestures and image recognitions to provide an extensive understanding of this subject.

Model, View and Controller (MVC)

MVC is an acronym for Model, View and Controller. It's a product development architecture. The traditional approach of programming works on Input -> Process -> Output approach while MVC works on Controller → Model -> View.

During, traditional approach of programming, the UI coding, business logic and applications data domain was written into a single file which creates lack of maintainability, testability as well as scalability of the application.

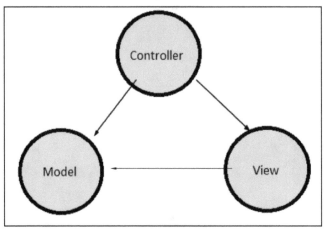

MVC Design diagram.

With the emerge of MVC approach, it helps one create applications that separate the different aspects of the application (input logic, business logic, and UI logic), while providing a loose coupling between these elements. The pattern specifies where each kind of logic should be located in the application. The UI logic belongs in the view. Input logic belongs in the controller. Business logic belongs in the model. This separation helps one manage complexity when one build an application, because it enables one to focus on one aspect of the implementation at a time. For example, one can focus on the view without depending on the business logic.

The MVC framework includes the following components:

- Models: Model objects are the parts of the application that implement the logic for the application's data domain. Often, model objects retrieve and store model state in a database. For example, a Customer object might retrieve information from a database, operate on it, and then write updated information back to a Customer table in a SQL Server database. In small applications, the model is often a conceptual separation instead of a physical one. For example, if the application only reads a dataset and sends it to the view, the application does not have a physical model layer and associated classes. In that case, the dataset takes on the role of a model object.

- Views: Views are the components that display the application's user interface (UI). Typically, this UI is created from the model data. An example would be an edit view of a Customer table that displays UI Controls based on the current state of a Customer object.

- Controllers: Controllers are the components that handle user interaction, work with the model, and ultimately select a view to render that displays UI. In an MVC application, the view only displays information; the controller handles and responds to user input and interaction. For example, the controller handles query-string values, and passes these values to the model, which in turn might use these values to query the database.

Below are few pros and cons of this architecture:

Pros

- Simultaneous development: Multiple developers can work simultaneously on the model, controller and views.

- High cohesion: MVC enables logical grouping of related actions on a controller together. The views for a specific model are also grouped together.

- Low coupling: The very nature of the MVC framework is such that there is low coupling among models, views or controllers.

- Ease of modification: Because of the separation of responsibilities, future development or modification is easier i.e. scalability of the product is increased.

- Multiple views for a model: Models can have multiple views.

Cons

- Code navigability: The framework navigation can be complex because it introduces new layers of abstraction and requires users to adapt to the decomposition criteria of MVC.

- Multiple Representations: Decomposing a feature into three artifacts causes scattering. Thus, requiring developers to maintain the consistency of multiple representations at once.

WIMP Interface

A graphical user interface is the most common type of user interface seen today. it is a very friendly way for people to interact with the computer because it makes use of pictures, graphics and icons - hence why it is called 'graphical'.

A GUI (pronounced gooey) is also known as a WIMP interface because it makes use of:

- Windows - A rectangular area on the screen where the commonly used applications run.

- Icons - A picture or symbol which is used to represent a software application or hardware device.

- Menus - A list of options from which the user can choose what they require.

- Pointers - A symbol such as an arrow which moves around the screen as you move your mouse. Helps you to select objects.

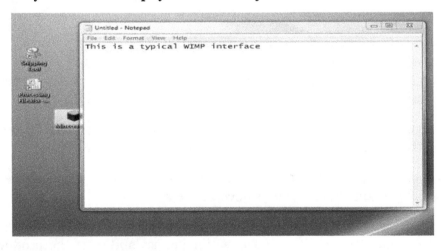

All modern operating systems have at least one type of GUI. For example Microsoft Windows is a GUI, Apple Macintosh has another. Linux has a number of Graphical User Interfaces available.

Many programs that run in Windows are known as WYSIWYG - this stands for What You See Is What You Get. In the early days of word-processors, you typed your essay or letter on the screen, but it could look completely different on the printer. A GUI normally tries to ensure that whatever you create on the screen will be very similar to what appears on the printer or the web.

Post-WIMP Interface

In computing, post-WIMP ("windows, icons, menus, pointer") comprises work on user interfaces, mostly graphical user interfaces, which attempt to go beyond the paradigm of windows, icons, menus and a pointing device, i.e. WIMP interfaces.

The reason WIMP interfaces have become so prevalent since their conception at Xerox PARC is that they are very good at abstracting work-spaces, documents, and their actions. Their analogous paradigm to documents as paper sheets or folders makes WIMP interfaces easy to introduce to other users. Furthermore their basic representations as rectangular regions on a 2D flat screen make them a good fit for system programmers, thus favoring the abundance of commercial widget toolkits in this style.

However, WIMP interfaces are not optimal for working with complex tasks such as computer-aided design, working on large amounts of data simultaneously, or interactive games. WIMPs are usually pixel-hungry, so given limited screen real estate they can distract attention from the task at hand. Thus, custom interfaces can better encapsulate workspaces, actions, and objects for specific complex tasks. Applications for which WIMP is not well suited include those requiring continuous input signals, showing 3D models, or simply portraying an interaction for which there is no defined standard widget.

Interfaces based on these considerations, now called "post-WIMP", have made their way to the general public. Examples include the interface of the classic Music player iPod and a bank's automated teller machine screen.

Meanwhile, average desktop computers are still based on WIMP interfaces, and have started undergoing major operational improvements to surpass the hurdles inherent to the classic WIMP interface. These include the exploration of virtual 3D space, interaction techniques for window/icon sorting, focus, and embellishment.

Multimodal Interface

Multimodal systems are computer systems endowed with multimodal capabilities for human/machine interaction and able to interpret information from various sensory and communication channels. Literally, multimodal interaction offers a set of "modalities" to users to allow them to interact with the machine. According to Oviatt, Multimodal interfaces process two or more combined user input modes (such as speech, pen, touch, manual gesture, gaze, and head and body movements) in a coordinated manner with multimedia system output. They are a new class of interfaces that aim to recognize naturally occurring forms of human language and behavior, and which incorporate one or more recognition-based technologies (e.g. speech, pen, vision). Two unique features of multimodal architectures and processing are: (1) the fusion of different types of data; and (2) real-time processing and temporal constraints imposed on information processing.

Thus, multimodal systems represent a new class of user-machine interfaces, different from standard WIMP interfaces. They tend to emphasize the use of richer and more natural ways of communication, such as speech or gestures, and more generally all the five senses. Hence, the objective of multimodal interfaces is twofold: (1) to support and accommodate users' perceptual and communicative capabilities; and (2) to integrate computational skills of computers in the real world, by offering more natural ways of interaction to humans.

Multimodal interfaces were first seen as more efficient than unimodal interfaces; however, evaluations showed that multimodal interfaces only speed up task completion by

10%. Hence, efficiency should not be considered the main advantage of multimodal interfaces. On the other hand, multimodal interfaces have been shown to improve error handling & reliability: users made 36% fewer errors with a multimodal interface than with a unimodal interface. Multimodal interfaces also add greater expressive power, and greater potential precision in visualspatial tasks. Finally, they provide improved support for users' preferred interaction style, since 95%-100% of users prefer multimodal interaction over unimodal interaction.

Features

Compared to other types of human/computer interaction, multimodal interaction seeks to offer users a more natural and transparent interaction, using speech, gestures, gaze direction, etc. Multimodal interfaces are hence expected to offer easier, more expressively powerful and more intuitive ways to use computers. Multimodal systems have the potential to enhance human/computer interaction in a number of ways:

- Enhanced robustness due to combining different partial information sources;

- Flexible personalization based on user and context;

- New functionality involving multi-user and mobile interaction.

When comparing multimodal user interfaces (MUI) with standard graphical user interfaces (GUI), it is possible to draw the following differences:

Table: Differences between GUIs and MUIs.

GUI	MUI
Single input stream	Multiple input streams
Atomic, deterministic	Continuous, probabilistic
Sequential processing	Parallel processing
Centralized architectures	Distributed & time-sensitive architectures

In standard WIMP interaction style (Window, Icon, Menu, Pointing device), a singular physical input device is used to control the position of a cursor and present information organized in windows and represented with icons. In contrast, in multimodal interfaces, various modalities can be used as input streams (voice, gestures, facial expressions, etc.). Further, input from graphical user interfaces is generally deterministic, with either mouse position or characters typed on a keyboard used to control the computer. In multimodal interfaces, input streams have to be first interpreted by probabilistic recognizers (HMM, GMM, SOM, etc.) and thus their results are weighted by a degree of uncertainty. Further, events are not always clearly temporally delimited and thus require a continuous interpretation. Due to the multiple recognizers necessary to interpret multimodal input and the continuous property of input streams, multimodal systems depend on time synchronized parallel processing. Further, the time sensitivity of multimodal systems is crucial to determining the order of processing multimodal commands in parallel or in sequence. Finally, multimodal systems often implement a distributed architecture, to deal out the computation and insure synchronization. Multimodal systems can be very resource demanding in some cases (e.g., speech/gesture recognition, machine-learning augmented integration).

Cognitive Foundations

The advantages of multimodal interface design are elucidated in the theory of cognitive psychology, as well as human-computer interaction studies, most specifically in cognitive load theory, gestalt theory, and Baddeley's model of working memory. Findings in cognitive psychology reveal:

- Humans are able to process modalities partially independently and, thus, presenting information with multiple modalities increases human working memory;

- Humans tend to reproduce interpersonal interaction patterns during multimodal interaction with a system;

- Human performance is improved when interacting multimodally due to the way human perception, communication, and memory function.

Researchers experimented with presenting students content using partly auditory and partly visual modes. The split-attention effect that resulted "*suggested that working memory has partially independent processors for handling visual and auditory material.*" The authors argued that if working memory is a primary limitation in learning, then increasing effective working memory by presenting information in a dual-mode form rather than a purely visual one, could expand processing capabilities. The results of researchers were confirmed by Tindall-Ford, who used more general types of tasks than pure mathematical ones, and by Mayer & Moreno who studied the same effect with multimedia learning material. All this work is in line with the cognitive load theory, which assumes a limited working memory in which all conscious learning and thinking occurs, and an effectively unlimited long-term memory that holds a large number of automated schemas that can be brought into working memory for processing. Oviatt applied these findings to educational interface design in testing a number of different user centered design principles and strategies, showing that user-interface design that minimizes cognitive load can free up mental resources and improve student performance. One strategy for accomplishing this is designing a multimodal interface for students.

In the design of map-based pen/voice interfaces, Oviatt demonstrated that Gestalt theoretic principles successfully predicted a number of human behaviors, such as: users consistently followed a specific multimodal integration pattern (i.e. sequential versus simultaneous), and entrenched further in their pattern during error handling when you might expect them to switch their behavior. Gestalt theory also correctly predicted in this study a dominant number of subjects applying simultaneous integration over sequential integration.

The original short-term memory model of Baddeley & Hitch , refined later by Baddeley, described short-term or working memory as being composed of three main components: the central executive (which acts as supervisory system and controls the flow of information), the phonological loop, and the visuo-spatial sketchpad, with the latter two dedicated to auditory-verbal and visuo-spatial information processing, respectively. Although these two slave processors are coordinated by a central executive, they function largely independently in terms of lower-level modality processing. This model was derived from experimental findings with dual-task paradigms. Performance of two simultaneous tasks requiring the use of two perceptual domains (i.e. a visual and a verbal task) were observed to be nearly as efficient as performance of individual tasks. In contrast, when a person tries to carry out two tasks simultaneously that use the same perceptual domain, performance is less efficient than when performing the tasks individually. As such, human performance is improved when interacting with two modalities that can be co-processed in separate stores.

Seminal Works, Findings and Guidelines

Multimodal interfaces emerged approximately 30 years ago within the field of human/computer interaction with Richard Bolt's "Put-That-There" application , which was created in 1980. First multimodal systems sought ways to go beyond the standard interaction mode at this time, which was graphical interfaces with keyboards and mice. Bolt's "Put-that-there" processed spoken commands linked to a pointing gesture using an armrest-mounted touchpad to move and change shapes displayed on a screen in front of the user. multimodal interaction practitioners have strived to integrate more modalities, to refine hardware and software components, and to explore limits and capabilities of multimodal interfaces. Historically, the main trend has focused on pointing and speech combined using speech/mouse, speech/pen, speech/gesture, or speech/gaze tracking. Later multimodal interfaces evolved beyond pointing into richer interaction, allowing users to produce symbolic gestures such as arrows and encircling.

Another direction in multimodal research has been speech/lip movement integration, driven by cognitive science research in intersensory audio-visual perception. This kind of work has included classification of human lip movement (visemes) and the viseme-phoneme mappings that occur during articulated speech. Such work has contributed improving robustness of speech recognition in noisy environments.

In more recent years, research has also focused on mainstreaming multimodal interfaces. In this trend, Reeves defined the following "guidelines for multimodal user interface design":

- Multimodal systems should be designed for the broadest range of users and contexts of use, since the availability of multiple modalities supports flexibility.

For example, the same user may benefit from speech input in a car, but pen input in a noisy environment.

- Designers should take care to address privacy and security issues when creating multimodal systems: speech, for example, should not be used as a modality to convey private or personal information in public contexts.

- Modalities should be integrated in a manner compatible with user preferences and capabilities, for example, combining complementary audio and visual modes that users can co-process more easily.

- Multimodal systems should be designed to adapt easily to different contexts, user profiles and application needs.

- Error prevention and handling is a major advantage of multimodal interface design, for both user- and system-centered reasons. Specific guidelines include integrating complementary modalities to improve system robustness, and giving users better control over modality selection so they can avoid errors.

Principles of User-Computer Multimodal Interaction

The driving principles of multimodal interaction are well described in numerous surveys. The following concepts are popularly accepted: fusion (also called multimodal signal integration), fission (also called response planning), dialog management, context management and time-sensitive architectures. We introduce these concepts, at a high level first to illustrate how they are organized around a common conceptual architecture, and later at a lower level to probe key principles.

Theoretical Principles

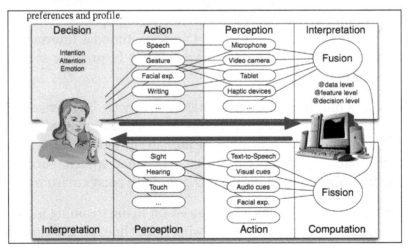

Figure: A representation of multimodal man machine interaction loop. The following model of multimodal man-machine communication can be drawn, together with the major concepts that should be considered when building a multimodal system: the fusion of multimodal inputs, and the multimodal fission to generate an adequate message to the user, according to the context of use, preferences and profile.

When a human interacts with a machine, his communication can be divided in four different states. The first state is a decision state, in which the communication message content is prepared consciously for an intention, or unconsciously for attentional content or emotions. The second state is the action state, where the communication means to transmit the message are selected, such as speech, gestures or facial expressions. The machine, in turn, will make use of a number of different modules to grasp the most information possible from a user, and will have similarly four main states. At first, the messages are interpreted in the perception state, where the multimodal system receives information from one or multiple sensors, at one or multiple levels of expression. In the interpretation state, the multimodal system will try to give some meaning to the different information it collected in the perception state. This is typically the place where fusion of multimodal messages takes place. Further, in the computational state, action is taken following the business logic and dialogue manager rules defined by the developer. Depending on the meaning extracted in the interpretation state, an answer is generated and transmitted in the action state, in which a fission engine will determine the most relevant modalities to return the message, depending on the context of use (e.g. in the car, office, etc.) and the profile of the user (blind user, elderly, etc.).

Computational Architecture and Key Components

We describe multimodal interaction from the machine side, and the major software components that a multimodal system should contain. The generic components for handling of multimodal integration are: a fusion engine, a fission module, a dialog manager and a context manager, which all together form what is called the "integration committee". Figure illustrates the processing flow between these components, the input and output modalities, as well as the potential client applications. As illustrated in the figure, input modalities are first perceived though various recognizers, which output their results to the fusion engine, in charge of giving a common interpretation of the inputs. The various levels at which recognizers' results can be fused are described together with the various fusion mechanisms. When the fusion engine comes to an interpretation, it communicates it to the dialog manager, in charge of identifying the dialog state, the transition to perform, the action to communicate to a given application, and the message to return through the fission component. The fission engine is finally in charge of returning a message to the user through the most adequate modality or combination of modalities, depending on the user profile and context of use. For this reason, the context manager, in charge of tracking the location, context and user profile, closely communicates any changes in the environment to the three other components, so that they can adapt their interpretations.

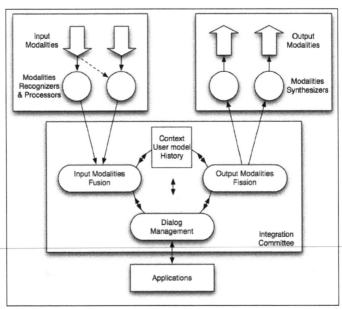

The architecture of a multimodal system, with the central integration committee and its major software components.

Fusion of Input Modalities

Fusion of input modalities is one of the features that distinguish multimodal interfaces from unimodal interfaces. The goal of fusion is to extract meaning from a set of input modalities and pass it to a human-machine dialog manager. Fusion of different modalities is a delicate task, which can be executed at three levels: at data level, at feature level and at decision level. Three different types of architectures can in turn manage decision-level fusion: frames-based architectures, unification-based architectures or hybrid symbolic/statistical fusion architectures.

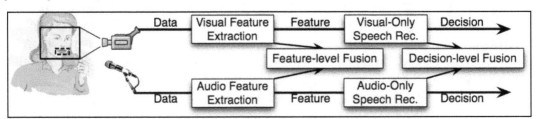

The various levels of multimodal fusion.

Consider these three levels for fusion of incoming data. Each fusion scheme functions at a different level of analysis of the same modality channel. As a classic illustration, consider the speech channel: data from this channel can be processed at the audio signal level, at the phoneme (feature) level, or at the semantic (decision) level.

- Data-level fusion is used when dealing with multiple signals coming from a very similar modality source (e.g., two webcams recording the same scene from different viewpoints). With this fusion scheme, no loss of information occurs, as the signal is directly processed. This benefit is also the main shortcoming of data- level fusion. Due to the absence of pre-processing, it is highly susceptible to noise and failure.

- Feature-level fusion is a common type of fusion when tightly-coupled or time synchronized modalities are to be fused. The standard example is the fusion of speech and lip movements. Feature-level fusion is susceptible to low-level information loss, although it handles noise better. The most classic architectures used for this type of fusion are adaptive systems like artificial neural networks, Gaussian mixture models, or hidden Markov models. The use of these types of adaptive architecture also means that feature-level fusion systems need numerous data training sets before they can achieve satisfactory performance.

- Decision-level fusion is the most common type of fusion in multimodal applications. The main reason is its ability to manage loosely-coupled modalities like, for example, pen and speech interaction. Failure and noise sensitivity is low with decision-level feature, since the data has been preprocessed. On one hand, this means that decision-level fusion has to rely on the quality of previous processing. On the other hand, unification-based decision-level fusion has the major benefit of improving reliability and accuracy of semantic interpretation, by combining partial semantic information coming from each input mode which can yield "mutual disambiguation".

Table below summarizes the three fusion levels, their characteristics, sensitivity to noise, and usage contexts.

Table: Characteristics of fusion levels.

	Data-level fusion	Features-level fusion	Decision-level fusion
Input type	Raw data of same type	Closely coupled modalities	Loosely coupled modalities
Level of information	Highest level of information detail	Moderate level of information detail	Mutual disambiguation by combining data from modes
Noise/failures sensitivity	Highly susceptible to noise or failures	Less sensitive to noise or failures	Highly resistant to noise or failures
Usage	Not really used for combining modalities	Used for fusion of particular modes	Most widely used type of fusion
Application examples	Fusion of two video streams	speech recognition from voice and lips	Pen/speech interaction

Typical architectures for decision-level fusion are frame-based fusion, unification-based fusion and hybrid symbolic/statistical fusion.

- Frame-based fusion uses data structures called frames or features for meaning representation of data coming from various sources or modalities. These structures represent objects as attribute-value pairs.

- Unification-based fusion is based on recursively merging attribute-value structures to obtain a logical whole meaning representation.

- Symbolic/statistical fusion is an evolution of standard symbolic unification-based approaches, which adds statistical processing techniques to the fusion techniques. These kinds of "hybrid" fusion techniques have been demonstrated to achieve robust and reliable results. An example of a symbolic-statistical hybrid fusion technique is the Member-Team-Committee (MTC) architecture used in Quickset.

Fission of Output Modalities

When multiple output modalities such as text-to-speech synthesis, audio cues, visual cues, haptic feedback or animated agents are available, output selection becomes a delicate task to adapt to a context of use (e.g. car, home, work), type of task (e.g., information search, entertainment) or type of user (e.g. visually impaired, elderly). Fission techniques allow a multimodal application to generate a given message in an adequate form according to the context and user profiles. Technically speaking, fission consists of three tasks:

- Message construction, where the information to be transmitted to the user is created; approaches for content selection and structuring revolve mainly around either schema-based approaches or plan-based approaches.

- Output channel selection, where interfaces are selected according to context and user profile in order to convey all data effectively in a given situation. Characteristics such as available output modalities, information to be presented, communicative goals of the presenter, user characteristics and task to be performed are forms of knowledge that can be used for output channel selection.

- Construction of a coherent and synchronized result: when multiple output channels are used, layout and temporal coordination are to be taken into account. Moreover, some systems will produce multimodal and cross-modal referring expressions, which will also have to be coordinated.

Dialogue Management and Time-sensitive Architectures

The time constraint is highly important in multimodal systems and all the modalities should be properly time-stamped and synchronized. Time-sensitive architectures need to establish temporal thresholds for time-stamping start and end of each input signal piece, so that two commands sequences can be identified. Indeed, when two commands are performed in parallel, in a synergistic way, it is important to know in which order the commands have been entered because the interpretation will vary accordingly. For instance, in the following application, in which voice and gestures are used simultaneously to control a music player, depending on the order in which modalities are presented the interpretation varies:

- <pointing> "Play next track": will result in playing the track following the one selected with a gesture;

- "Play" <pointing> "next track": will result in first playing the manually selected track and then passing to the following at the time "next is pronounced";

- "Play next track" <pointing>: In this case, the system should interpret the commands as being redundant.

The dialog management system and synchronization mechanism should consider multiple potential causes of lag:

- Delay due to technology (e.g. speech recognition);

- Delay due to multimodal system architecture;

- User differences in habitual multimodal integration pattern.

For this reason, multi-agent architectures (or similar architectures such as components-based systems) are advantageous for distributing processing and for coordinating many system components (e.g., speech recognition, pen recognition, natural language processing, graphic display, TTS output, application database).

Bui considers four different approaches to dialog management:

- Finite-state and frame-based approaches: In this kind of dialog management approach, the dialog structure is represented in the form of a state machine. Frame-based models are an extension of finite-state models, using a slot-filling strategy in which a number of predefined information sources are to be gathered.

- Information state-based and probabilistic approaches: These approaches try to describe human-machine dialog following information states, consisting of five main components: informational components, formal representations of those components, a set of dialog moves, a set of update rules and an update strategy.

- Plan-based approaches: The plan-based approaches are based on the plan-based theories of communicative action and dialog. These theories claim that the speaker's speech act is part of a plan and that it is the listener's job to identify and respond appropriately to this plan.

- Collaborative agents-based approaches: These approaches view dialog as a collaborative process between intelligent agents. The agents work together to obtain a mutual understanding of the dialog. This induces discourse phenomena such as clarifications and confirmation.

Multimodal Interaction Modeling

Modeling multimodal interaction is no simple task, due to the multiple input and output channels and modes, and the combination of possibilities between data coming from different sources, not to mention output modality selection based on context and user profile.

The shape taken by formal modeling of multimodal interaction depends on the level of abstraction considered. At lower levels of abstraction, formal modeling would focus on tools used for modality recognition and synthesis. At higher levels of abstraction, multimodal interaction modeling would focus more on modality combination and synchronization.

Formal modeling can also focus on the "pure" technical part as well as on the user- machine interaction. Two formal models exist for modality combination description:

- The CASE model, focusing on modality combination possibilities at the fusion engine level;

- The CARE model, giving attention to modality combination possibilities at the user level.

The CASE model introduces four properties: Concurrent – Alternate – Synergistic– Exclusive.

Each of those four properties describes a different way to combine modalities at the integration engine level, depending on two factors: combined or independent fusion of modalities, and sequential or synergistic use of modalities on the other hand. "Fusion of modalities" considers if different modalities are combined or managed independently, whereas "Use of modalities" observes the way modalities are activated: either one at a time, or in a synergistic manner.

		USE OF MODALITIES	
		Sequential	Parallel
FUSION OF MODALITIES	Combined	ALTERNATE	SYNERGISTIC
	Independant	EXCLUSIVE	CONCURRENT

The CASE model.

The CARE model is more focused on the user-machine interaction level. This model also introduces four properties, which are Complementarity – Assignment – Redundancy – Equivalence. Complementarity is to be used when multiple complementary modalities are necessary to grasp the desired meaning (e.g. "put that there" would need both pointing gestures and voice in order to be resolved). Assignment indicates that only one modality can lead to the desired meaning (e.g. the steering wheel of a car is the only way to direct the car). Redundancy implies multiple modalities which, even if used simultaneously, can be used individually to lead to the desired meaning (e.g. user utters a "play" speech command and pushes a button labeled "play", but only one "play" command would be taken into account). Finally, Equivalence entails multiple modalities that can all lead to the desired meaning, but only one would be used at a time (e.g. speech or keyboard can be used to write a text).

Multimodal Interfaces in the MMI program

The IM-HOST project, is representative of one class of multimodal applications, although it focuses on a single modality: speech, which has been historically the leading modality in multimodal interaction. The IM-HOST project targets voice-enabled man-machine interaction in noisy environments. However, still, current performances of voice applications are reasonably good in quiet environments but the surrounding noise in many practical situations drastically deteriorates the quality of the speech signal and, as a consequence, significantly decreases the recognition rate. The major scenario considered in this project is a person using voice command in an outdoor environment: a racing boat. For this reason, the project explores new interaction paradigms enabling voice recognition in a hostile environment.

The MeModules project, has the objective of developing, experimenting and evaluating the concept of tangible shortcuts to multimedia digital information. Moreover, it investigates the opportunity of a more complex, multi-sensorial combination of physical objects with multimedia information by associating tangible interaction with multiple other interaction modalities such as voice, gesture, etc. One of the expected research outcomes of the project is to assess which modalities are best combined with tangible interaction depending on the context and application.

Future Directions and Conclusions

Although many issues have been addressed well in the multimodal interaction research and systems literature, such as fusion of heterogeneous data types, architectures for real-time processing, dialog management, map-based multimodal interaction, and so forth, nonetheless the field is still young and needs further research to build reliable multimodal systems and usable applications. Machine learning methods have begun to be applied to a number of different aspects of multimodal interfaces, including individual modality recognition, early or late modality fusion, user-machine dialog management, and identification of users' multimodal integration patterns. But future work clearly is needed to work toward the design of usable adaptive multimodal interfaces. Multimodal dialog processing also will gain in the future from the recent and promising subfield of social signal processing, which can assist dialog modeling by providing a dialog manager with real-time information about a given user's state and her current social and collaborative context.

Other important future directions for multimodal research include human/machine interaction using new tangible interfaces such as digital paper and pen, and multi-touch tables, surfaces and screens. Further modeling of multimodal interaction still is needed too, in areas such as multimodal educational exchanges, collaborative multimodal interaction, multimodal interaction involving diverse and underserved user groups, and mobile multimodal interaction with emerging cell phone applications. Finally, further work is needed to improve tools for the creation of multimodal applications and interfaces so they can become more main stream, especially since multimodal interfaces are viewed as the most promising avenue for achieving universal access in the near future.

Gestures and Image Recognitions

Human-Computer interaction (HCI) relies on multiple modalities such as speech, faces or gestures. Faces and gestures are one of the main nonverbal communication mechanisms between humans and computers. Therefore, a real-time processing of faces and gestures is important for HCI. Moreover, in recent years the field of computer vision has been progressed rapidly and the efforts have been made to apply research results in the real-world scenarios. When applying research findings, hardware cost becomes an important issue. The HCI system can be used.

The HCI system can be used towards robot tour guidance, recreational, home and health-care applications. In museums, the traditional keyboard and mouse setup can be replaced with a robot tour guidance system. The robot can detect which exhibitions the visitors are interested in and introduce them directly. This not only makes exhibitions more interesting, but also reduces the tour guidance personnel training cost for the museums. For recreational usage, users can substitute wired controllers with hand gestures and enjoy the hands-free control of electronic devices. In household uses, we can combine head movement with simple hand gestures to control air conditioners, lighting, and other home appliances. It may also be used to aid patients in all kinds of situations when their body mobility is limited.

The proposed HCI system not only can detect face features in head-tilted situations, but also can recognize hand gestures correctly anywhere in the whole image. It is also robust to busy backgrounds and different clothing situations, extracting hand regions, and recognizing hand gestures efficiently using a trained neural network. In applications, we apply the proposed HCI system to a real-life scenario. We give commands wirelessly to trigger the head movement of the robot. Figure shows the diagram of the proposed HCI system.

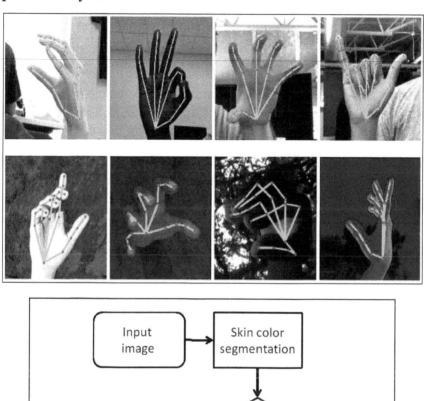

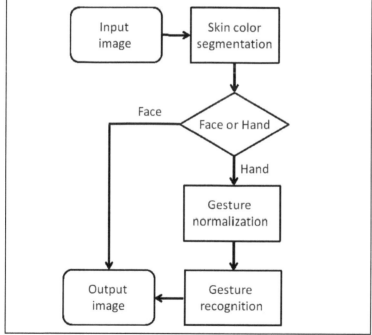

Diagram of the Proposed HCI System.

The Human-Computer Interaction System

We combine the results of both face detection and hand gesture recognition, and show them on the screen to verify the correctness of the detection and recognition results.

Skin Color Segmentation

The first step is skin color segmentation, which is an important preprocessing stage. We analyze a few skin color detection methods. Color spaces such as NCC r-g, RGB ,YC-bCr, hue-saturation-value (HSV) color spaces have their pros and cons. We group them into categories based on which color space is used to accomplish skin color detection and select the most suitable one to apply to our HCI system.

The experiments show that the NCC r-g color space gives the best result. This combined skin locus and color space keeps the calculation cost low, and also copes well with the skin color change due to varying lighting conditions. After this analysis we decide to use the NCC r-g color space skin locus model in our HCI system.

For skin color segmentation, first we label the areas of an image using skin colors, which act as candidates for the face or hand. Second, connected components are discovered from these image areas. Third, we set a threshold for the connected components to remove noise and eliminate the areas which are too small to be candidates for the face or hand.

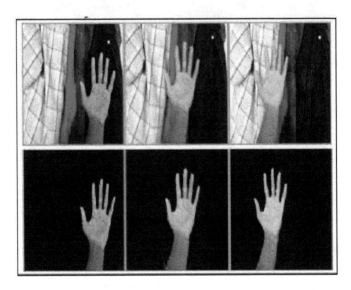

Face Detection

For face detection, we declare search areas for the eyes and mouth from the remaining succeeded candidates. We search for the eyes using the black and white color feature characteristics. We find the mouth using the distinct redder color tone of the lips compared to face skin. After retrieving the eyes and mouth, we use a simple isosceles triangle geometric shape to find a best match and output the resulting triangle model for the detection of the face.

When developing a real-time face detection system, reducing computational cost is a critical issue. In normal situations, a person's face features locate in fixed relative positions. Thus, we can use this characteristic to define the search windows and search range when searching for them. Figure shows the diagram of the search windows for the eyes and mouth.

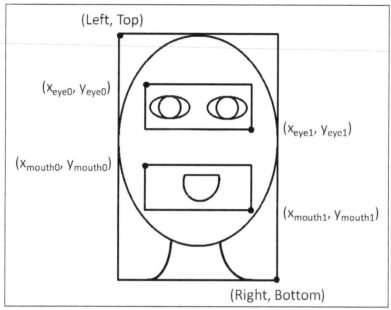

Search Window for the Eyes and Mouth.

The search window for the eyes is defined by:

$$x_{eye0} = Left + \frac{Right - Left}{10} \text{ and } y_{eye0} = Top + \frac{Bottom - Top}{5},$$

$$x_{eye1} = Right - \frac{Right - Left}{10} \text{ and } y_{eye1} = Top + \frac{Bottom - Top}{2}.$$

The search window for the mouth defined by:

$$x_{mouth0} = Left + \frac{Right - Left}{5} \text{ and } y_{mouth0} = Top + \frac{Bottom - Top}{2},$$

$$x_{mouth1} = Left - \frac{Right - Left}{5} \text{ and } y_{mouth1} = Top + \frac{3(Bottom - Top)}{4}.$$

The eyes tend to have a darker tone and have a more distinct characteristic than other face features. If we express this characteristic in color space, the three channels in the RGB color space tend to have similar intensity values. We can distinct the eyes with other face features using this observation. We can extract eyes from other areas of the face by:

$$|R - G| + |G - B| + |B - R| < T_{eye,}$$

where T_{eye} is the parameter for extracting the eyes.

The RGB channel intensities have values ranging from 0~255. After performing multiple evaluations, setting T_{eye} to 100 is a suitable threshold for extracting the eyes. We can locate the eyes in an image. Moreover, we propose a new method to locate the mouth. Using the previous analyzed skin color information, we dynamically adjust the mouth extraction threshold values. The specific steps are as follows:

1. From the previous skin color pixels of the image, we calculate the average of R and G color channel intensities by:

$$R_{avg} = \frac{1}{n}\sum_{i=1}^{n} R_i \text{ and } G_{avg} = \frac{1}{n}\sum_{i=1}^{n} G_i,$$

where n indicates the total number of skin color pixels in a frame.

2. People's mouth color tends to have a redder tone compared to the rest of the skin. The R/G channel intensity ratio is higher than all other skin color pixels. This can be expressed by:

$$1.2 \times \frac{R_{avg}}{G_{avg}} < \frac{R_{mouth}}{G_{mouth}} < 1.5 \times \frac{R_{avg}}{G_{avg}}.$$

Although some unwanted small areas are extracted using the above method, we can locate the exact position of the mouth by retrieving the largest extracted redder tone skin area and calculating the center of gravity of that specific area.

When we extract the eyes from other face features, sometimes eyebrows are extracted accidently at the same time. We define three rules to avoid this problem. Using accurate mouth position data acquired from the previous step, we use the rules below to find the best match for the eyes while eliminating the eyebrows.

1. The width between eyes D_{eye} is limited by:

$$\frac{width}{4} < D_{eye} < \frac{3width}{4} \text{ and } D_{eye} = \sqrt{\left(x_{eyeR} - x_{eyeL}\right)^2 + \left(y_{eyeR} - y_{eyeL}\right)^2},$$

where width is the width of the face.

2. The distances between the eyes and mouth D_{mouth} are also limited by:

$$\frac{width}{4} < D_{mouth} < \frac{3width}{4} \text{ and}$$

$$D_{mouth} = \sqrt{\left(x_{mouth} - \frac{x_{eyeR} + x_{eyeL}}{2}\right)^2 + \left(y_{mouth} - \frac{y_{eyeR} + y_{eyeL}}{2}\right)^2}.$$

3. The mouth must lie between the eyes by:

$$x_{eyeR} < x_{mouth} < x_{eyeL}.$$

Using the above rules, we eliminate eyebrows and other unwanted areas. Hence, we can retrieve the correct eye positions.

In our system, the goal is to control the hardware by mixing the eye movement and hand gestures. We now discuss how to recover orientation (pose) of a moving head. Ohayon et al. proposed a method that requires the construction of a head model using 3D points. Although the accuracy is high, it can only process 4 frames per second due high computational cost. Instead, we propose a low complexity method suitable for real time systems. First we calculate the centroid of the triangle connecting eyes and the mouth. We then compare it with the detected head's centroid. By doing this, we can estimate the tilt position of the head. In figure (x_{head}, y_{head}) is the centroid of the detected head, and (x_{face}, y_{face}) is the centroid of the triangle formed by connecting the eyes and mouth with:

$$x_{face} < \frac{x_{eyeR} + x_{eyeL} + x_{mouth}}{3} \text{ and } y_{face} < \frac{y_{eyeR} + y_{eyeL} + y_{mouth}}{3}.$$

We calculate the projection distances D_x and D_y to the x and y-axis of points (x_{head}, y_{head}) and (x_{face}, y_{face}), respectively, by:

$$D_x = x_{head} - x_{face} \text{ and } D_y = y_{head} - y_{face}.$$

Using the projection distances, we can estimate the tilt position of a person's head. For example, if D_x is a positive value, the head tilts to the right. The head tilts to the left if the value is negative. D_y indicates if the person tilts his/her head upward or downward.

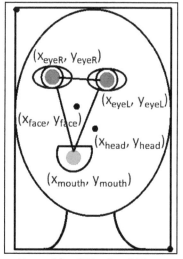

Centroids of Head and Face.

Hand Gesture Recognition

For hand gestures, we eliminate the arm and elbow first, then search for the long-axis of the hand, and normalize the hand to a certain fixed angle. We input the normalized hand to a trained and weighted neural network for hand gesture recognition.

We apply a particular type of neural network model, known as a feed-forward back propagation neural network. This neural model is easy to understand, and can be easily implemented in image processing tasks. With traditional techniques, one must understand the inputs of the algorithms and the outputs for correct implementation. For a neural network, you do not have to know these details at all. You simply show the relation of the output associated with the given input. With an adequate amount of training, the network mimics the function that you are demonstrating. With a neural network, it is possible to apply some inputs irrelevant to the solution. During the training process, the network learns to ignore any inputs that do not contribute to the output. If some critical inputs are left in the training process, the network fails to result in a correct solution.

Back-propagation Neural Network: A back-propagation neural network is a kind of feed-forward network. In a 3-layer feed-forward network, the information moves in only one direction, forward, from the input layer $(X_1, X_2, X_3, X_4, ...)$, through the hidden layer $(H_1, H_2, H_3, H_4, ...)$, and to the output layer $(Y_1, Y_2, Y_3, Y_4, ...)$.

Below are specific settings used in our neural network:

1. Network layer: We use the basic 3-layer neural network model for our real-time system. Although increasing layers in a neural network system has a higher accuracy rate, it also increases the complexity of the network. Adding layers will increase the learning and recalling time in the training process, which is not suitable for real-time systems. To increase accuracy, we add more neurons in the hidden layer instead.

2. Hidden layer neurons: A common approach to decide how many neurons are located in this layer is to double the number of neurons in the input layer. We give 16 neurons in the input layer and 30 neurons in the hidden layer.

3. Learning rate: Since learning is usually done in post-process, it will not affect the real-time performance when used. We choose a learning rate of 0.01 to maintain the system's stability.

Hand Gesture Segmentation and Recognition: We use the skin color to locate the hand's position. If a person wears a long sleeve shirt, the captured image area is the hand gesture candidate. But if one wears short sleeve clothing, we need to exclude the whole arm and preserve the hand section only.

From observations, we find the almost fixed width from the elbow to the wrist. Using this characteristic, we can eliminate the arm and capture only parts of the hand needed for hand gesture recognition. We first convert the hand image into a binary image, and then project the binary image onto the y-axis (x-axis indicates black pixel count of the same yaxis value). There is a large difference in terms of the change of the black pixel count from the wrist to the hand. We segment the whole hand based on the difference.

After obtaining the segmented hand, we first compute the hand's long axis that passes the centroid of the hand. Then we rotate the hand to the upright position based on the long-axis. Finally, we normalize the size of the hand image to 40×40. Figure shows (a) the long-axis of a hand, (b) the hand in the upright position, and (c) the normalized hand.

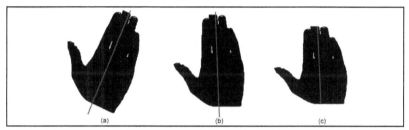

(a) The Long-axis of a Hand, (b) the Hand in the Upright Position, and (c) the Normalized Hand.

In the hand gesture normalization process, some gestures will show different results. For example, a "Roll Right" gesture could be normalized to a thumb down or a thumb up position. Figure shows two gestures with different results. This can be solved in the neural network training process. We can allow the output of both these images to have the same output results.

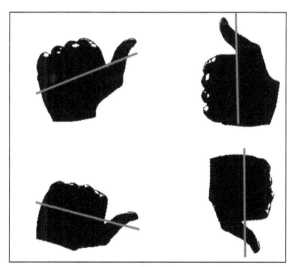

Two Gestures with Different Results.

After the above steps, we are ready for hand gesture recognition. Based on the gesture recognition approach of Wagne, we segment the hand image into 16 pieces and each piece has 100 (10×10) pixels. We record how many black pixels are in each piece, and normalize the pixel count from 0~100 to 0~1 for the inputs of the neural network. We define 11 hand gestures, and give the input of each hand gesture with 10 images for the training process of the neural network. For consistency, all images used for training are first segmented, and normalized into the upright position beforehand.

References

- Why-mvc-architecture: medium.com, Retrieved 05 June, 2019

- Post-WIMP: wikiwand.com, Retrieved 21 May, 2019

- S. Siddharth and A. Rautaray, "Vision based hand gesture recognition for human computer interaction: a survey," Springer Journal Artificial Intelligence Review, (2012), pp. 1-54

- Multimodal-Interfaces-A-Survey-of-Principles-Models-and-Frameworks- 225159733: researchgate.net, Retrieved 24 April, 2019

- Y. Tu, C. Kao and H. Lin, "Human computer interaction using face and gesture recognition," Proceedings of IEEE conference on Signal and Information Processing Association Annual Summit (APSIPA), (2013), pp. 1-5

5

Applications of Human-Computer Interaction

Human-computer interaction can be applied to various areas such as virtual reality, locomotives, game design, vehicle information system, hospitality, business management, finance, etc. The topics elaborated in this chapter will help in gaining a better perspective about these applications of human-computer interaction.

Human-Computer Interaction in Virtual Reality

The goal of *virtual reality* (VR) systems is to immerse the participant within a computer-generated, *virtual environment* (VE). Interacting with the VE poses issues unique to VR. The ideal VE system would have the participant fully believe he was actually performing a task. Every component of the task would be fully replicated. The environment would be visually identical to the real task. Further, the participant would hear accurate sounds, smell identical odors, and when they reached out to touch an object, they would be able to feel it. For example, in a VR system to examine designs for product assembly, the ideal system would present an experience identical to actually performing the assembly task. Parts and tools would have mass, feel real, and handle appropriately. The participant would interact with every object as if he would if he were doing the task. The virtual objects would in turn respond to the user's action appropriately. Training and simulation would be optimal.

Obviously, current VEs are still a ways from that ideal system. Participants use specialized equipment, such as tracked displays and gloves, to track movement, interpret actions, and provide input to the VR system. Interactive *three-dimensional* (3D) computer graphics and audio software generate the appropriate scenes and auditory cues. Finally, the participant receives the VE output (e.g. images, sounds, haptic feedback) through visual and audio hardware.

Here, we focus on immersive virtual reality systems. Immersive VR is characterized – though not universally – by participant head tracking (monitoring the participant's position and orientation) and stereo imagery (providing different views of the VE for each eye).

Interestingly, VR *human-computer interaction* (HCI) issues can be strikingly different than traditional 2D or 3D HCI.

- The participant views the virtual environment from a first person perspective projection point of view.

- VR interaction strives for a high level of fidelity between the virtual action and the corresponding real action being simulated. For example, a VR system for training soldiers in close quarters combat must have the participant perform physical actions, and receive visual, audio, and haptic input, as similar to the actual scenario as possible.

- Some virtual actions have no real action correlate. How do system designers provide interactions, such as deletion and selection, as naturally as possible?

- Typically most – if not all – objects in the virtual environment are virtual. That is, when a participant reaches out grab a virtual object, there will no physical object to give an appropriate feel. For hands-on tasks, such as assembly design verification, having nothing to feel or handle might be so detrimental to the experience as to make the VR ineffective.

Immersive VR systems that satisfy the high fidelity interactions requirements can become an important tool for training, simulation, and education for tasks that are dangerous, expensive, or infeasible to recreate. Examples of a near perfect combination of real and virtual objects are flight simulators. In most state-of-the-art flight simulators, the entire cockpit is real, but a motion platform provides motion sensations, and the visuals of the environment outside the cockpit are virtual. The resulting synergy is so compelling and effective it is almost universally used to train pilots.

VR Interaction: Technology

Tracking and signaling actions are the primary means of input into VEs.

Inputs

Tracking is the determination of a object's position and orientation. Common objects to track include the participant's head, participant's limbs, and interaction devices (such as gloves, mice or joysticks). Most tracking systems have sensors or markers attached to the objects. Then, other devices track and report the position and orientation of the sensors.

Commercial tracking systems employ one or a combination of mechanical, magnetic (Polhemus Fastrak and Ascension Flock of Birds), optical (WorldViz PPT, 3rdTech Hiball), acoustic (Logitech 6D Mouse), inertial (Intersense IS-900), and *global position satellites* (GPS) approaches. Each method has different advantages with respect to cost, speed, accuracy, robustness, working volume, scalability, wirelessness, and size. No one tracking technology handles all tracking situations.

Different tasks have varying requirements on the accuracy, speed, and latency of the tracking system's reports. VEs that aim for a high level of participant sense of presence – a measure of how much the participant believes they are 'in the VE' – have stringent head tracking requirements. Researchers estimate that the VR and tracking systems need to accurately determine the participant's pose and to display the appropriate images in under 90 milliseconds, and preferably under 50 milliseconds. If the lag is too high, the VR system induces a "swimming" feeling, and might make the participant disoriented and hamper the quality of interactivity.

Tracking the participant's limbs allows the VR system to 1: present an avatar, a virtual representation of the user within the virtual environment, and 2: rough shape information of the participant's body pose. Researchers believe that the presence of an avatar increases a participant's sense of presence. The accuracy and speed requirements for limb tracking are typically lower than that of head tracking.

Finally object tracking, usually accomplished by attaching a sensor, allows a virtual model of an object to be registered with a physical real object. For example, attaching a tracker to a dinner plate allows an associated virtual plate to be naturally manipulated. Since each sensor reports the pose information of a single point, most systems use one sensor per object and assume the real object is rigid in shape and appearance.

Since humans use their hands for many interaction tasks, tracking and obtaining inputs from a hand-based controller was a natural evolution for VR controllers. A tracked glove reports position and pose information of the participant's hand to the VR system. They can also report pinching gestures (Fakespace Pinchglove), button presses (buttons built into the glove) and finger bends (Immersion CyberTouch). These glove actions are associated with virtual actions such as grasping, selecting, translation, and rotation. Tracked gloves provide many different kinds of inputs and most importantly, are very natural to use. Glove disadvantages include sizing problems (most are a one size fits all), limited feedback (issues with haptic feedback and detecting gestures), and hygiene complications with multiple users.

The most common interaction devices are tracked mice (sometimes called bats) and joysticks. They are identical to a regular mouse and joystick, but with an integrated 3 or 6 *degrees-of-freedom* (DOF) tracking sensor that reports the device's position and orientation. Tracked mice and joysticks have numerous buttons for the participant to provide input, and they are cheap, easily adaptable for different tasks, and familiar to many users. However, they might not provide the required naturalness, feel and functionality for a given task.

A compromise to get ease of use, numerous inputs into a system, and proper feedback is to engineer a specific device to interface with the VR system. For example, the University of North Carolina (UNC) Ultrasound augmented reality surgery system attached a tracking sensor to a sonogram wand. The inputs from the sonogram wand buttons were passed to the VR system. This enabled the AR system to provide a natural interface for training and simulation. However, this required developing software and manufacturing specific cables to communicate between the sonogram machine and a PC. Creating these specific devices is time consuming and the resulting tools are usable for a limited set of tasks.

Outputs

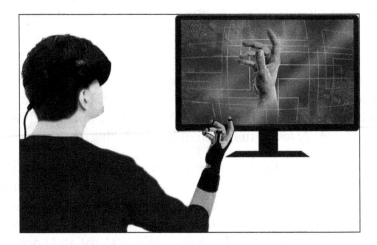

Given the system inputs, the resulting VE (visuals, audio, tactile information) is outputted to the participant. For example, as the participant changes their head position and orientation, the tracking system passes that information to the VR system's rendering engine. 3D views of the VE are generated from the updated pose information.

The visual output is typically presented either in a *head-mounted display* (HMD) or a multiple-wall back projected CAVE environment. HMDs are head-worn helmets with integrated display devices. The helmet has two screens located a short distance from the user's eyes. HMDs can be thought of as the participant "carrying" around the display. There are many commercial HMD solutions including the Virtual Research V8, VFX ForteVR, and Sony Glasstron.

CAVE environments have multiple back projected display walls and data projectors. The virtual environment is rendered from multiple views (such as forward, right, left, down) and projected onto the display walls. Fakespace, Inc. provides commercial CAVE solutions.

VR systems use either stereo headphones or multiple speakers to output audio. Given the participant's position, sounds sources, and VE geometry, stereo or specialized audio is presented to the user. Common audio packages include Creative Lab's EAX and AuSIM's AuTrak.

VR haptic (tactile) information is presented to the participant through active feedback devices. Examples of force feedback devices include a vibrating joystick (e.g. vibrating when the user collides with a virtual object) and the Sensible Phantom, which resembles a six DOF pen. Active feedback devices can provide a high level of HCI fidelity. Two examples of effective systems are the dAb system, which simulates painting on a virtual canvas, and Immersion CyberGrasp glove, which allows design evaluation and assembly verification of virtual models.

VR Interaction: Locomotion

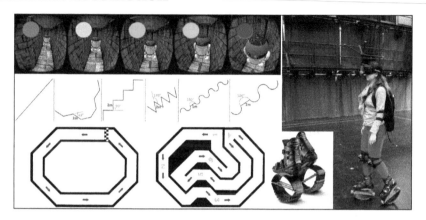

VR locomotion, the movement and navigation of the participant within the VE, is one of the primary methods of VR interaction. VE locomotion is different than real world locomotion because:

- The virtual space can be of an extremely different size and scale compared to the real space tracked volume. For example, navigation in a VE on the molecular or planetary scale requires special considerations.

- The method of VE locomotion might have a physical equivalent that is difficult or undesirable to emulate. For example, consider the navigation issues in a VE that simulates emergency evacuations on an oil platform to train rescue personnel.

The most common method for locomotion is *flying*. When some input, such as a button press, is received, the participant is translated in the VE along some vector. Two common choices for this translation vector are the view direction of the user and along a vector defined by the position and orientation of an interaction device, such as a tracked joystick or mouse. While easy to use and effective, flying is not very natural or realistic.

In *walking in place*, when the participant makes a walking motion (lifting their feet up and down, but not physically translating), the participant is translates in the VE along a vector. By monitoring the tracker sensor's reports, the VR system can detect walking motions.

Specific devices have been engineered to provide long distance locomotion. Treadmills such as the Sarcos Treadport and ATR ATLAS allow the user to physically walk long distances in the VE. Sometimes a steering device is coupled to change direction of VE.

Unfortunately, treadmills do not easily handle rotations or uneven terrain, and they are growing more uncommon. Further, there were safety issues in simulating high speeds and collisions with virtual objects.

Other locomotion devices include specialized devices such as motion platforms and exercise cycles. A motion platform is a mechanical stage whose movement is controlled by the VR system. For example, flight simulators use motion platforms to physically move and rotate the participant to simulate the sensations of flight. Of course, there are limitations to the range of motions, but for many applications, motion platforms provide an extremely valuable level of realism.

VR locomotion approaches have to deal with a finite – and typically quite limited – tracked space within which the participant can physically move around. Further, the participant typically has numerous wires connecting the tracking sensors and display devices to the VR system. Motorized methods for VR locomotion also have safety issues in the speed and methods they move the user.

New commercial and research approaches to VR locomotion look to provide a more natural and effective locomotion over larger spaces. New tracking systems, such as the WorldViz PPT, Intersense IS-900, and the 3rdTech HiBall, are scalable wide area trackers with working volumes approaching 40' × 40'. This allows the participant to physically navigate large VE distances. Studies have shown that real walking is better than walking in place which is better than flying for participant sense of presence.

NRL's GAITER system is a combination of harnesses and treadmills that allows soldiers to emulate running across large distances in combat simulations. The Redirected Walking project at UNC looks to expand the physical tracking volume by subtly rotating the virtual world as the participant walks. This causes the participant to physically walk in a circle, though in the virtual world, it appears as if they have walked along a straight line. This could allow a finite real world space to provide an infinite virtual walking space.

VR Interaction: Interacting with Virtual Objects

Training and simulation VR systems, which make up a substantial number of deployed systems, aim to recreate real world experiences. The accuracy in which the virtual experience recreates the actual experience can be extremely important, such as in medical and military simulations.

The fundamental problem is that most things are not real in a VE. Of course, the other end of the spectrum – having all real objects – removes any advantages of using a VE such as quick prototyping, or training and simulation for expensive or dangerous tasks. Having everything virtual removes many of the important cues that we use to perform tasks, such as motion constraints, tactile response, and force feedback. Typically these cues are either approximated or not provided at all. Depending on the task, this could reduce the effectiveness of a VE.

The participant interacts with objects in the VE, simulations, and system objects. The methods to interact will vary on the task, participants, and equipment (hardware and software) configuration. For example, the interactions to locate 3D objects in orientation and mobility training for the vision impaired are different than those in a surgery planning simulation. Variables to consider include accuracy, lag, intuitiveness, fidelity to the actual task, and feedback.

Virtual Object Interaction

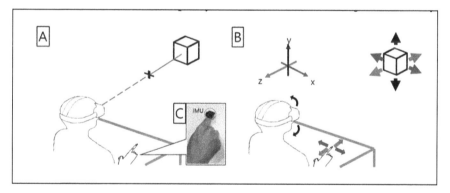

Applying 3D transformations and signaling system commands are the most common virtual object interactions. VR issues include the lack of a registered physical object with the virtual object and the limited ways for getting inputs to the system. This poses difficulties because we rely on a combination of cues including visual, haptic, and audio, to perform many cognitive tasks. The lack of haptic cues from a VE with purely virtual objects could hinder performance.

Given that most objects are virtual, can a system without motion constraints, correct affordance, or haptic feedback still remain effective? Is it even possible? These are some of the basic research questions that are being explored, and it is the system designers' job to provide interaction methodologies that do not impede system effectiveness.

VR Simulation Interaction

VR systems use simulations for a variety of tasks, from calculating physics (i.e. collision detection and response) to lighting to approximate real world phenomena. Most VR systems require participant interaction to control simulation objects and the simulation itself. For example, in a military solider simulation, the participant affects a soldier's view and battlefield location and provides input such as pressing buttons for firing his weapon.

Many simulations focus on recreating realistic experiences for the participant. Having a natural means of interaction improves realism. However, this adds to the difficulty in high-quality VR interaction. We can engineer specific objects, for example a prop machine gun with the trigger sensor connected to the computer, but that increases cost and reduced generality (the prop has limited uses in other applications). On the other end of the spectrum, using a generic interaction device, such as a tracked joystick, might prove too different than the actual task to provide any benefit.

VR System Interaction

The third object of VR interaction is system objects, such as menus and dialog boxes. As in traditional users of 2D or desktop 3D systems, VR participants need to execute commands such as opening files, changing system settings, and accepting incoming messages. VR systems have unique issues dealing with the following:

- First person perspective of the environment

- Natural methods to present the system interface

- Desire to avoid lowering the participant's sense of presence

- Accept participant input.

Most VR systems provide the system interface as virtual objects attached either to the virtual environment (world coordinate system), tracked device (local coordinate system), or the participant (user coordinate system). Attaching the system interface to the world coordinate system (the interface would appear as an VE object, such as a computer panel), provides a way to keep the interaction with the virtual environment (both virtual objects and the system interface) consistent. But for some VEs – such as a solider simulation – the scale (large distances) or the subject matter (realistic combat) do not naturally lend themselves to such a system interface.

Attaching the system interface to a tracked device, such as a participant-carried tablet or mouse, allows the system to provide a consistent virtual world. Previous studies have shown the presence of a physical surface enhanced task performance over the purely virtual surface implementations.

Attaching the user interface to the user has the menus and dialog boxes appear relatively stationary to the user, even as they navigate around the world. This is similar to implementing a standard 2D desktop interface in a 3D environment. In this case, the interface is always within reach of the participant, but its appearance and integration with the rest of the VE is typically not as seamless.

Future Directions in VR Interaction

VR interaction is constantly evolving new hardware, software, interaction techniques, and VR systems; the topics covered here are by no means a comprehensive list.

New products, such as the Immersion Haptic Workstation, provide high quality tracking of the participant's hands coupled with force feedback that will allow the participant to "feel" the virtual objects. The improved interaction could enable VR to be applied to hands-on tasks that were previously hampered by poor haptic feedback.

VEs populated with multiple participants (often physically distributed over great distances) have unique interaction issues. In a University College London study, two participants, one at UCL (England), and the other at UNC at Chapel Hill, (United States of America), are tasked with navigating a virtual maze while carrying a stretcher. How do the participants interact with a shared virtual space, simulation, and each other? Researchers are interested in how important audio, gestures, and facial expressions are for cooperative interaction.

Combining several interaction methods might develop into solutions which are greater than a sum of its parts. For example, the BioSimMER system seeks to train emergency response medical personnel. The system interprets hand gestures and voice commands in conjunction with traditional interaction methods to interact with the simulation. Researchers are also investigating passive techniques that use image processing and computer vision to aide in tracking and interpreting the participant's actions and gestures.

There is also research into new types of VR systems. Hybrid environments – VEs that combine real and virtual objects – focus on providing natural physical interfaces to virtual systems as well as intuitive virtual interfaces. There exists a spectrum of environments, from augmented reality – supplementing display of the real world with virtual objects – to mixed and augmented virtual reality – supplementing display of the virtual world with real objects.

Hybrid systems look to improve performance and participant sense of presence by having real objects registered with virtual objects. Studies into passive haptics had major virtual objects, such as the walls and unmovable furniture, registered with stationary physical objects. It was found that passive haptics did improve sense of presence.

New methods to navigate and interact with virtual objects are constantly being developed, and there are movements to formalize the description and evaluation of *interaction technologies* (IT). This allows VR system engineers to make interface design decisions confidently and reduce the ad hoc nature of IT creation. Formal evaluation also promotes a critical review of how and why people interact with VEs.

As the types of interactions grow more complex, higher order interactions with simulation objects are becoming a major research focus. Interpreting the participant's facial expressions, voice, gestures, and pose as inputs could provide a new level of natural interaction. Also, participants will interact with more complex objects, such as deformable objects and virtual characters.

As the hardware, interactions technologies, and software progress, VR system designers develop a more natural and effective means for participants to interact with the VE.

Human-Computer Interaction in the Car

Automobile has become a complex interactive system. Mechanical devices are transformed to the digital realm. It is common that drivers operate a vehicle and at the same time, interact with a variety of devices and applications. Looking up an address in the map and taking a phone call are such examples that help the driver in driving but also increase the risk on the road. The need to have a car with decent and safer usability from driver drives the researchers and auto companies discover the possibilities of driving with a friendlier and more powerful human-computer interaction interface in the car. As a result, various inventions on usability have been made and they together make the interaction with automobile an easy and safe thing.

The design of usability in automotive domain generally focuses on multiple goals including safety, comfort, enhancement, networking, etc. Actually in some cases the convenience is the same meaning with safety, i.e. the easier the driver finishes one task when driving, the safer he would be. Generally manufacturers improve the feeling of convenience by adding automatic features to devices in the car, a proper example here is power window which greatly reduce the complexity of controlling window in driving. For the need of entertainment, manufacturers usually upgrade the interaction with audio system – more functional buttons, and better effect – since people need to take an eye on the traffic but their ears are available.

Beyond the basic enhancements in HCI in automobile, recent years manufacturers are trying to integrate some more amazing features into the car by providing a powerful microcomputer and a central console with touch screen named vehicle telematics. These novel features include navigation system, auto drive and remote control etc.

Imagine this scenario: you start a new day with a cup of coffee in the car, watching the morning news from holographic projection that projected on the windshield. Following the presetting route, the car drives you to office after sending your children to school. You have a quick review on the whole day agenda while the car looks for a best place to park. After the car is parked, you leave it without locking with a key – the car will unlock itself when sensing your biometric identification around. Some parts of this fantastic scenario have been realization by the cutting edge technologies in automotive usability aspect.

Safety

Automobile safety is the study and practice of design, construction, equipment and regulation to minimize the occurrence and consequences of automobile accidents. Road traffic safety more broadly includes roadway design. One of the first formal academic studies into improving vehicle safety was by Cornell Aeronautical Labs of Buffalo, New York. The main conclusion of their extensive report is the crucial importance of seat belts and padded dashboards. However, the primary vector of traffic-related deaths and injuries is the disproportionate mass and velocity of an automobile compared to that of the predominant victim, the pedestrian. In the United States a pedestrian is injured by an automobile every 8 minutes, and are 1.5 times more likely than a vehicle's occupants to be killed in an automobile crash per outing.

Improvements in roadway and automobile designs have steadily reduced injury and death rates in all first world countries. Nevertheless, auto collisions are the leading cause of injury-related deaths, an estimated total of 1.2 million in 2004, or 25% of the total from all causes. Of those killed by autos, nearly two-thirds are pedestrians. Risk compensation theory has been used in arguments against safety devices, regulations and modifications of vehicles despite the efficacy of saving lives.

Two Systems

Technology is increasingly being seen to have a critical role to play in alleviating the negative aspects of road transport, such as congestion, pollution and road traffic accidents. Many technological initiatives are considered under the umbrella term, Intelligent Transport Systems (ITS), where "ITS provides the intelligent link between travelers, vehicles, and infrastructure". In this respect, in-vehicle computing systems are an important facet of ITS. Specifically, there are two core types of computing and communications systems which are either being implemented or developed for use in vehicles.

1. Information-based systems: which provide information relevant to components of the driving environment, the vehicle or the driver. Examples of systems include navigation (facilitating route planning and following), travel and traffic information (traffic conditions, car parking availability, etc.), vision enhancement (providing an enhanced view of the road ahead, when driving at night, in fog or in heavy rain), driver alertness monitoring (informing the incapacitated driver if they are unfit to drive) and collision warnings (presenting warnings/advice regarding hazards). Typically all lamps in panel should be classified into this kind of system. These lamps can warn you whether your car is in a good condition, is there something wrong with your engine. Also, when you leave your car with door opened, you will be warned by hearing continues sound. Information-based systems can improve safety for you and your car.

2. Control-based systems: which affect the routine, operational elements of the driving task. Examples of systems include adaptive cruise control (where the car is kept at a set time gap from a lead vehicle), speed limiting (the car speed cannot exceed the current limit), lane keeping (the driver's vehicle is kept within a given lane), self parking (vehicle automatically steers in low speed operation to position itself within a selected

parking space) and collision avoidance (the vehicle automatically responds to an emergency situation). Clearly, such systems fundamentally change the nature of what we consider to be 'driving'.

Safety Equipments

These two systems are major implications for safety. Then we will introduce specific facilities of automobile to keep safety.

Driver assistance

A subset of crash avoidance is driver assistance systems, which help the driver to detect obstacles and to control the vehicle. Driver assistance systems include:

- Automatic Braking systems to prevent or reduce the severity of collision.

- Infrared night vision systems to increase seeing distance beyond headlamp range.

- Adaptive headlamps control the direction and range of the headlight beams to light the driver's way through curves and maximize seeing distance without glaring other drivers.

- Reverse backup sensors, which alert drivers to difficult-to-see objects in their path when reversing.

- Backup camera.

- Adaptive cruise control which maintains a safe distance from the vehicle in front.

- Lane departure warning systems to alert the driver of an unintended departure from the intended lane of travel.

- Tire pressure monitoring systems or Deflation Detection Systems.

- Traction control systems which restore traction if driven wheels begin to spin.

- Electronic Stability Control, which intervenes to avert an impending loss of control.

- Anti-lock braking systems.

- Electronic brakeforce distribution systems.

- Emergency brake assist systems.

- Cornering Brake Control systems.

- Precrash system.

- Automated parking system.

Crashworthiness

Crashworthy systems and devices prevent or reduce the severity of injuries when a crash is imminent or actually happening. It includes:

Seatbelts limit the forward motion of an occupant, stretch to absorb energy, to lengthen the time of the occupant's deceleration in a crash, reducing the loading on the occupants body. They prevent occupants being ejected from the vehicle and ensure that they are in the correct position for the operation of the airbags.

Airbags inflate to cushion the impact of a vehicle occupant with various parts of the vehicle's interior. The most important being the prevention of direct impact of the driver's head with the steering wheel and door pillar.

Laminated windshields remain in one piece when impacted, preventing penetration of unbelted occupants' heads and maintaining a minimal but adequate transparency for control of the car immediately following a collision. It is also a bonded structural part of the safety cell. Tempered glass side and rear windows break into granules with minimally sharp edges, rather than splintering into jagged fragments as ordinary glass does.

Crumple zones absorb and dissipate the force of a collision, displacing and diverting it away from the passenger compartment and reducing the deceleration impact force on the vehicle occupants. Vehicles will include a front, rear and maybe side crumple zones (like Volvo SIPS) too.

Safety Cell - the passenger compartment is reinforced with high strength materials, at places subject high loads in a crash, in order to maintain a survival space for the vehicle occupants.

Side impact protection beams, also called anti-intrusion bars.

Collapsible universally jointed steering columns, along with steering wheel airbag. The steering system is mounted behind the front axle - behind and protected by, the front crumple zone. This reduces the risk and severity of driver impact or even impalement on the column in a frontal crash.

Pedestrian Protection Systems

Padding of the instrument panel and other interior parts, on the vehicle in areas likely to be struck by the occupants during a crash, and the careful placement of mounting brackets away from those areas.

Cargo barriers are sometimes fitted to provide a physical barrier between passenger and cargo compartments in vehicles such as SUVs, station wagons and vans. These help prevent injuries caused by occupants being struck by unsecured cargo. They can also help prevent collapse of the roof in the event of a vehicle rollover.

However, can we say that with all these safe systems, we can assure safety on the road and never got car accident? The answer is no.

All of our proud, graphically oriented screen devices, especially those with touch-sensitive screens and a paucity of physical controls, may be delightful to use while in a comfortable environment, but they become safety hazards when also attempting to drive a car. If the eyes of the driver are off road for two seconds, studies show a dramatic rise in accident rate. Can you try programming a street address into a navigation system in less than two seconds? Impossible, you need more time. Moreover, because the driver is attention switching, not only must the eyes shift from road to device, and back again, but all the context must be restored: memory structures, intentions, planned activities. Task switching lengthens the time to do each task considerably, thereby magnifying the danger.

The way to alleviate dangerous while you are driving is using acoustic warning system instead of visual warning system. New car should have sound to report current speed coordinates with speed panel. Thus when driver drives on a speed limit road, driver only need focus on front views and see if other cars runs in left or right lane, acoustic warning system will report whether the car is surpassing speed limit.

Comfort

Original Entertainment Equipments

More and more people not only care about the driving experience of a car, but also care about the comfort of a car, this is the reason why more and more advertisement focusing on interior trim. With CD/FM becomes the common equipment in a car, more and more people treat car as a "small home", not only a driving tool.

Of course if you want to pay more money, you can have more entertainment equipment in your car. In-Car Entertainment is a collection of hardware devices installed into automobiles, or other forms of transportation, to provide audio and audio/visual entertainment, as well as automotive navigation systems (SatNav). This includes playing media such as CDs, DVDs, Free view/TV, USB and other optional surround sound, or

DSP systems. Also increasingly common in ICE installs are the incorporation of video game consoles into the vehicle.

In-Car Entertainment systems have been featured TV shows such as MTV's Pimp My Ride. In Car Entertainment has been become more widely available due to reduced costs of devices such as LCD screen/monitors, and the reducing cost to the consumer of the converging media playable technologies. Single hardware units are capable of playing CD, MP3, WMA, DVD.

New Facilities

As the time change, In-Car Entertainment systems also involved new features, such as AUX, heat seat and Internet. When you get tired of listening FM music and tired of changing CD one by one. You can just link iPod or MP3 into your car by AUX. Then you can listen all music in that iPod or MP3. For heat seat, imagine this, in a cold winter, you got up really early and you saw snow covered everything near you. Is there something better than seating into a warm seat while driving to company? Internet is an increasingly popular option in cars. According to a study by market researcher Invensity that by the year 2013 every new car built in Europe will be equipped with Internet connection.

Comfort of car may make us love to drive, however, it also bring negative effect to our safety while driving. It is important to note that there is actually a third category of in-car computing system, include those systems which do not provide any functionality to support the driving task. These systems are an important consideration though, as they can negatively influence safety, particularly through the potential for distraction. Such systems may aim to enhance work oriented productivity whilst driving (e.g. mobile phones, email/internet access) or be primarily conceived for entertainment/comfort purposes (e.g. music/DVD players, games).

Enhancement

Modern world has completely changed our lives by providing us with new technology and advancements. Automobiles possesses an important place in everybody life. Even though there are lots of types of cars that serve different purposes of various customer groups, the very basic functionality of automobiles is always driving. As automobile industry is such a large and profitable industry, manufacturers make every effort to research and apply new technologies to enhance people's driving experience. Automatic transmission has made driving an easy task to almost every person. Other techniques like cruise control and auto-piloting aims at continuing save people further from driving control. Indeed, an age of driverless car is approaching to totally free users from driving.

Automatic Transmission

Automatic transmission is one type of motor vehicle transmission that can automatically change gear ratios as the vehicle moves, freeing drivers from having to shift gears manually.

Besides automatics, there are also other types of automated transmissions such as a continuously variable transmission and semi-automatic transmissions, which free the driver from having to shift gears manually, by using the transmission's computer to change gear, if for example the driver were redlining the engine. Despite superficial similarity to other transmissions, automatic transmissions differ significantly in internal operation and driver's feel from semi-automatics and continuously variable transmissions.

A conventional, 5-speed manual transmission is often the standard equipment in a base-model car. Manual transmissions generally offer better fuel economy than automatic or continuously variable transmissions. However the disparity has been somewhat offset with the introduction of locking torque converters on automatic transmissions. For most people, there is a slight learning curve with a manual transmission, which is likely to be intimidating and unappealing for an experienced driver. And because manual transmission require the operation of an extra pedal, and keeping the car in the correct gear at all times, they require a bit more concentration, especially in heavy traffic situations. The automatic transmissions, on the other hand, simply require the driver to speed up or slow down as needed, with the car doing the work of choosing the correct gear.

Automotive Navigation System

An automotive navigation system is a satellite navigation system designed for use in automobiles. Many modern vehicles are equipped with in-vehicle navigation systems that utilize global positioning systems (GPS), digital maps, and automatic route calculation. An navigation system typically uses a GPS navigation device to acquire position data to locate the user on a road in the unit's map database. Using the road database, the unit can give directions to other locations along roads also in its database. Just entering a destination will typically generate an accurate route that is displayed to the driver. Although the activity of entering a destination is not easy, especially while driving, voice activated systems are bringing to the market to solve this problem. These systems can greatly improve the driving experience by helping drivers navigate in unfamiliar setting and reduce the mental load of remembering where to go.

Navigation systems rely on good human-computer interaction. A quality design here helps drivers find their location and directions easily. As the driver approaches a change in direction, the application warns him in advance of an upcoming change. These systems typically include calculations and displays of time and range to destination. It would be easy to ignore safety issues by pointing out the troubles with driving and looking at a paper map.

The introduction of information systems into vehicles is a growing trend that can provide drivers with useful tools for navigation, communication, and exploration. However, in-vehicle information system (IVIS) cannot be allowed to distract users from the demanding task of driving. Among these IVIS, car navigation systems have been among the most widely adopted technologies. The decision to open up the map is the driver's own. However, car navigation system manufacturers have a responsibility to society to produce safe systems in addition to possible liability caused by their systems facilitating accidents. There are lot of research focusing on exploring the safest ways to present navigational vehicles.

Cruise Control

Cruise control, sometimes known as speed control or auto cruise, is a system that automatically controls the speed of a motor vehicle. The system takes over the throttle of the car to maintain a steady speed as set by the driver.

Modern cruise control was invented in 1945 by the inventor and mechanical engineer Ralph Teetor. His idea was born out of the frustration of riding in a car driven by his lawyer, who kept speeding up and slowing down as he talked. Daniel Aaron Wisher invented Automotive Electronic Cruise Control is 1968. His invention was the first electronic gadgetry to play a role in controlling a car and ushered in the computer-controlled era in the automobile industry. Two decades lapsed before an integrated circuit for his design was developed and as a result, cruise control was eventually adopted by automobile manufacturers as standard equipment.

Cruise control is really useful for long drives, in which it helps reduce driver fatigue, improve comfort by allowing positioning changes more safely, across highways and sparsely populated roads. This also results in better fuel efficiency. Besides, a driver who tends to unconsciously increase speed over the course of a highway journey may avoid a speeding ticket by using cruise control.

The advantage of electronic speed control over its mechanical predecessor, which was featured on luxury models but never gained wide acceptance, was that it could be easily integrated with electronic accident avoidance and engine management systems.

Some modern vehicles have adaptive cruise control systems, which is a general term meaning improved cruise control. These improvements can be automatic braking, which allows the vehicle to keep pace with the car it is following, or dynamic set-speed hype controls which uses the GPS position of speed limit signs to dynamically control speed.

Autopilot

When it comes to driving, human beings have an appalling safety record. With motor-vehicle accidents claiming more than a million lives worldwide annually, car companies are pushing the development of technology that increasingly borrows control from erratic human beings allowing the car to drive itself.

An autopilot is a mechanical, electronically, or hydraulic system used to guide a vehicle without assistance from a human being. An autopilot usually refers specifically to aircraft, self-steering gear for boats, or auto-guidance of space craft and missiles. But because of its technical constraints and great expenses, autopilot has been evolved to common motor vehicles until the recent years. However, low-level autonomous safety features have been around in various forms for decades.

Antilock brake systems, which automatically sense when a wheel is skidding and reduce brake pressure, were introduced back in 1971. In 1997, General Motors introduced an Electronic Stability Control system that can sense the difference between the direction a car is going and the angle of the steering wheel, and then pump the brakes to keep the car on course. These safety features are so commonplace today that federal legislation requires they be installed on all new cars, along with airbags and seatbelts.

And the next generation of autonomy is already here. The 2010 Ford Flex boasts Active Park Assist — just target a spot and the car uses ultrasonic range finders to park itself. The 2010 Toyota Prius has a Lane Keep Assist system that uses a camera to detect lane markers and automatically steers the car toward the center of the lane. And the Honda Accord comes standard with Adaptive Cruise Control, which uses a radar pulse to scan ahead for other vehicles and then increases or decreases speed to maintain a safe following distance. The current set of semi-autonomous safety features can quickly combine into something more. For example, a car could use Lane Keep Assist and Adaptive Cruise Control together to drive itself under highway conditions, sticking to one lane and not hitting the car in front. The next step is to expand these capabilities. Adaptive Cruise Control currently works only over 25 mph, but the next version (called Full Speed Range ACC) lowers that number to zero so that cars can begin to handle traffic jams in the city.

Driverless Car

Fully autonomous vehicles, also known as robotic cars, or driverless cars, already exist in prototype, and are expected to be commercially available around 2020. According to urban designer and futurist Michael E. Arth, driverless electric vehicles—in conjunction with the increased use of virtual reality for work, travel, and pleasure—could reduce the world's 800 million vehicles to a fraction of that number within a few decades. This would be possible if almost all private cars requiring drivers, which are not in use and parked 90% of the time, would be traded for public self-driving taxis that would be in near constant use. This would also allow for getting the appropriate vehicle for the particular need—a bus could come for a group of people, a limousine could come for a special night out, and a Segway could come for a short trip down the street for one person. Children could be chauffeured in supervised safety, DUIs would no longer exist, and 41,000 lives could be saved each year in the US alone.

Networking

Before the computer technology evolved to be good enough, manufacturers brought the usability of automobile to customers with a focus mostly on driving itself. The traditional solution were consist of a bunch of on-board embedded electronics systems that performing various operational functions focusing on different purposes, such as seat heating for comfort, cruise control for enhancement, parking sensor for safety, etc. While these helpers are already utilized in most of today's modern vehicle, new need on networking is raising recent years due to the development of Internet digit devices such as tablet and smart phone. Seeing this potential usability area, manufacturers begin to research and install more and more in-vehicle embedded system that focus on providing better functionalities, robust operation and higher degree of convenience to the in-vehicle users in the networking level. Within this trend, advance of wireless communication and information technology in the digital era has promoted new killer applications to the in-vehicle drivers and occupants. Among these advanced killer applications, services provided in the area of the telematics and information/entertainment have attracted most attention in the automotive industry.

Telematics Service

Telematics were considered as the system that provides location-based services for mobile vehicles over wireless communication networks. Typical example of automotive telematics services includes emergency call system, which instantly connects vehicle users to a service center for emergency assistance or roadside services while automatically reporting the vehicle's position. Normally the emergency call system requires a wireless transceiver for voice and data communication and an on-board GPS receiver for positioning. Telematics system was considered as the core technology in an Intelligent Transportation System (ITS) and applications of telematics services to ITS have been proposed and developed in some countries. An integrated positioning system were developed to realize an efficient and cost-effective GPS based electronic road pricing system by He, Law, and Ling. In, the importance of "situational awareness" in conveying the state of the automobile to other parties across a communication link was addressed and a novel interactivity environment for integrated intelligent transportation and telematics systems was proposed.

Information and Entertainment Services

As more and more people are traveling with Internet-enabled information appliances (IA) such as laptops, tablets, smart phones, digital cameras, MP3 players, etc., there is a desire to connect to the Internet permanently from anywhere, at any time, without any disruption of service, particularly for those people who spend a significant amount of time in mass transportation systems in weekdays or in their own vehicle during weekend. In order to access the Internet, an in-vehicle local area network or personal area network environment must be established, and the in-vehicle embedded system shall become the mobile gateway for these Internet-enabled IA. Ernst, Uehara, and Mitsuya, detailed the networking requirements for connecting vehicles to the Internet by displacing an entire IPv6 network and network mobility support in the InternetCAR project. The software and hardware requirements in designing human-computer interface for an in-vehicle information system were proposed such that the safety of the in-vehicle drivers is discussed. A distributed service-based architecture were proposed to provide fault tolerant application services to remote in-vehicle computers and mobile devices, such as Wi-Fi-enabled tablet and smart phone. It seems that research trend has shifted to providing an infotainment server system for the in-vehicle users such that the network-enabled IA can access the information from the in-vehicle network and also obtain the entertainment services from the entertainment server.

Products in Practice

A well-known example of telematics system is GM's OnStar service which provides multiple emergency services. Typically the OnStar in installed in the bottom of rearview mirror. The OnStar service relies on CDMA mobile phone voice and data communications well as location information using GPS technology. Drivers and passengers can use its audio interface to contact OnStar representatives for emergency services, vehicle diagnostics and directions. The OnStar service allows users to contact OnStar call centers during an emergency. In the event of a collision, detected by airbag deployment or other sensors, Advanced Automatic Collision Notification features can automatically send information about the vehicle's condition and GPS location to OnStar call centers. This Advanced Automatic Collision Notification service is designed to assist emergency response efforts. All OnStar equipped vehicles have Stolen Vehicle Tracking, which can provide the police with the vehicle's exact location, speed and direction of movement.

Human-Computer Interaction in Game Design

Game Design is the process of designing the content and rules of a game in the pre-production stage and design of gameplay, environment, storyline, and characters during production stage. In this topic, only some of the aspects of the Game Design are presented such as the culture of Game, Game Design by definition, an introduction to some popular genres in Video Game and Computer Game, and the Game Designers and their skills.

Game design is the process of creating content and rules of a game. And according to Jesse Schell said that Game Design is the act of deciding what a game should be. That's it. On the surface, it sounds too simple. The notion of Game Design is quite easily explained; it is what determines the form of the gameplay. So, the Game Design determines what choices players will be able to make in the game-world and what ramifications those choices will have on the rest of the game. Moreover, the Game Design determines what win or loss criteria the game may include, how the user will be able to control the game, and what information the game will communicate to him, and it establishes how hard the game will be. In short, the Game Design determines every detail of how the gameplay will function.

A good Game Design is the process of creating goals that a player feels motivated to reach and rules that a player must follow as he makes meaningful decisions in pursuit of those goals. Therefore, Game Design has to be player-centric. That means that the player and his or her decision are truly considered. Rather than demanding that the player do something by following the rules, the gameplay itself should motivate the player in the direction the Game Designer wants him or her to go. This technique is widely used in persuasive design, which is about making the user follow the Designer intent, and also helping the user to follow his or her intent.

In addition, a good Game Design happens when the game is viewed from as many perspectives as possible. Those perspectives are usually referred as lenses. Each lens is a way of viewing the design; they are small sets of questions that the Game Designers should ask themselves about their design (E.g. The lens of Fun, The lens of Challenge, The lens of Character, etc.). They are not blueprints or recipes, but rather are tools for examining the design. And it should be important to mention that none of the lenses are perfect, and none are completed, but each is useful in one context or another, for each gives a unique perspective on the design of game. The idea is that even though the design cannot be assembled in one complete picture, but by taking all of those small imperfect lenses and using them to view the problem from many different perspectives, the Game Designer will be able to use his or her discretion to figure out the best design.

Anthropology of Games

By definition a game is an activity involving one or more players. This can be defined by either a goal that the players try to reach, or some sets of rules that determine what the players can or cannot do. Games are played primarily for entertainment or enjoyment, but may also serve as exercise or in an educational, simulative or psychological role.

While games are well known for their enjoyable ability, they can also be used for educational purpose. This was mentioned in the previous paragraph. In fact, play is human nature; people play in order to learn and practice; for example, sensorimotor, intellectual and social skills. Throughout the history of human, games have been implied as an important part of the human's life. The Chinese strategy game Wei-Hai from 3000 BCE is the oldest known game, which has been used for military simulations. In physical education, Polo is known as one of the oldest known ball games, which were born in around 500 BCE. Furthermore, as role-playing games became popular in the social sciences and management decision-making, the first widely known business game. The Top Management Decision Simulation, was developed in 1956 by the American Management Association.

Furthermore, the year 1947 was noted as the turning point in the history of game, it is believed to be the first year when a game was designed for playing on a Cathode Ray Tube (CRT). This very simple game was designed by Thomas T. Goldsmith Jr. and Estle

Ray Mann. Although the history of computer and video games spans five decades, computer and video games themselves did not become part of the popular culture until the late 1970s. The first significant computer game, Space War, was release by MIT student Steve Russell and his team in 1962. In a way, it was recognized as the starting point of the video game industry. Over the decades, video games have become extremely popular, either in the form of hand held consoles, or with games that run on computers or attached to TVs. The term _digital game' is used to cover all the game played on digital devices.

Since it was created, digital games have evolved into many genres. The first commercial video game, Pong, was a simple simulation of table tennis. As processing power increased, new genres such as adventure and action games were developed that involved a player guiding a character from a third person perspective through a series of obstacles. This "real-time" element cannot be easily reproduced by a board game, which is generally limited to "turn-based" strategy; this advantage allows video games to simulate situations such as combat more realistically. Additionally, the playing of a video game does not require the same physical skill, strength and danger as a real-world representation of the game, and can provide either very realistic, exaggerated or impossible physics, allowing for elements of a fantastical nature, games involving physical violence, or simulations of sports. Lastly, a computer can, with varying degrees of success, simulate one or more human opponents in traditional table games such as chess, leading to simulations of such games that can be played by a single player.

Genres in Video Game

Video game genres are used to categorize video games based on their gameplay interaction rather than visual or narrative differences. Video game genres are defined by a set of gameplay challenges. They are classified independent of their setting or game-world content, unlike other works of fiction such as films or books. The following is a listing of commonly known video and computer game genres with brief descriptions and an example of each:

Action: The action genres consist of two major sub-genres: first person shooters and third person games. Although the first-person games are played as if the screen was the player's own vision, third person, on the other hand, is played with avatars that are fully visible to the player. These sub-genres are demarcated through a remediation of terminology from cinematic perspective, which is based on the literary definitions of narration. In reality, there is an invisible link between these two sub-genres. Whether the perspective is first or third person, in order to experience the virtual world of the game, the player and game must be linked by a static physical locator that acts as an indexical axis that connects the player's gaze and kinesthetic actions to the virtual game world.

Moreover, action games in particular are often intensive performativity, in a manner distinctly different from other genres of performativity games, since action games will often require the player to engage in extreme non-trivial action in order to make them enjoyable. In many action games, the player must actually perform a desired action by selecting the correct inputs, while in other genres of video games, the player will merely select the desired action and the computer will determine the performance of that action. For example, in the action game The Lord of The Rings, in order to attack a foe, the players must maneuver their avatar in range of the selected foe and then select an attack based on a combination of buttons.

Adventure: The adventure games were some of the earliest game created, beginning with the text adventure Colossal Cave Adventure in the 1970s. Unlike adventure films, adventure games are not defined by story or content. Somewhat, adventure describes a manner of gameplay without reflex challenges or action. They normally require the player to solve various puzzles by interacting with people or the surrounding environment, most often in a non-confrontational way. Because they put little pressure on the player in the form of action-based challenges or time constraints, adventure games have had the unique ability to appeal to people who do not normally play video games. The first form of adventure games were text adventures, also known as interactive fiction. Games such as the popular Zork series of the late 1970s and early 1980s allowed the player to use a keyboard to enter commands such as "get rope" or "go west" while the computer describes what is happening. A great deal of programming went into parsing the player's text input.

Educational games: These games emphasize learning. They are designed to teach or reinforce a learned concept. Educational games look like games of other genres, but they are their own genre because they emphasize education. The most basic educationally designed game would be text exercises like fill-in-the-blank, multiple choices, or essay. With a little imagination, the player could turn the multiple-choices game into a fun game show where the host asks the student an educational-oriented question and correct answers earn points or virtual cash. History games could be also turned into adventure games or RPGs, where the student plays the key character and must answer relevant historical questions or resolve a historical situation properly.

Role-playing: Role-playing games (RPGs) are vast worlds to explore where parties of players roam the terrain seeking treasures, objects of desire, and ways to increase their experience and health status, to destroy monsters and obstacles that get in their way. RPGs started as dungeon crawls through paper labyrinths created by—masters (dungeon designers). A master would create an elaborate labyrinth filled with traps, monsters, and evil magic. The party would enter the maze armed with individual skills, magical abilities, and weapons. On each turn the party would try to outwit, out-spell with magic, and outfight the master's creation. The world of the Internet has enabled millions of RPG fans to explore larger terrain and more exotic quests.

Additionally, one of the form belongs to the RPG is MMRPG. This acronym stands for massively multiplayer RPG (Role-playing game), a game in which parties of friends or groups from around the world form to explore, collect, and fight other parties and monsters. MMRPGs have numerous parties, each on various quests and with their own goals. An RPG has a specific goal, and after many hours of play, there is an ending. Conversely, MMRPGs may have no specific ending and can be played until players have completed all the quests or until another MMRPG or Internet game requires their time and attention.

Simulation: The simulation genres include video games that simulate sport, flying and driving, and games that simulate the dynamics of towns, cities, and small communities. Simulation games (or Sims) let gamers experience real-world situations from a safe, practice area. Since the 1950s, the Departments of Defense in developed countries such as USA has trained the military with computerized simulators like flight Sims, tank Sims, and war-gaming Sims (missiles launching and combat). Simulations are exciting and have a real world feeling to them. Since most of the real-world applications that the gamers are trying to simulate would be extremely dangerous and very expensive outside of the computer, navigating and reproducing practice scenarios are more practical and easier to set up inside a simulator.

What is more, simulations can be classified as either a vehicle simulation or a managing simulation. Vehicle Sims are trucks, cars (stock, Formula-1, high-performance), airplanes, helicopters, boats, submarines, spaceships, space stations and motorcycles.

Managing Sims include managing a nuclear power plant, a brokerage company trying to predict the stock market, being mayor of a city or president of the United States, being owner of a golf club, being manager of the city zoo, being Emperor of the Roman Empire, being owner of an amusement park (rollercoasters and rides), and even managing the lives of families.

Strategy: Strategy video games focus on gameplay that requiring careful and skillful thinking and planning in order to achieve victory. Strategy games differ from other genres not only because the Designer creates rules and goals, but also it is the gamer who decides what strategy to use to achieve those goals and outwit one or more opponent(s). War games are strategy games although they are usually simulations of actual or fictitious events.

Strategy games can be played as real-time or turn-based games. Both of these sub-genres give a similar aesthetic, a general god's eye-view of the actions taking place. However, in real-time strategy, this sub-genre is usually applied only to certain strategy games. The actions in these games are continuous, and players will have to make their decisions and actions within the backdrop of a constantly changing game state. Real-time strategy gameplay is characterized by obtaining resources, building bases, researching technologies and producing units. One of the most popular real-time strategy games is Blizzard's Starcraft (1.5 million copies were sold in two-day sales). Turn-based strategy games, on the other hand, are characterized by the expectation of players to complete their tasks using the combat forces provided to them, and usually by the provision of a realistic (or at least believable) representation of military tactics and operations. A player of a turn-based game is allowed a period of analysis before committing to a game action, and some games allow a certain number of moves or actions to take place in a turn. The first game of the genre was Combat Mission in 1999.

Furthermore, in the recent years, there have been some changes in the statistical data of the best-selling video game and computer game super genres. More new types of game have made their way into the league of popular game genre, including children and family entertainment. The rapid improvement of new technologies has opened new ways of entertainment. An example for this statement would be the Xbox 360 Kinect, a controller-free gaming and entertainment experience. Since it was first announced on June 1 st 2009, the Kinect has introduced to the players a whole new level of experience for the party games (e.g. Kinect Sports, Dance Central and Kinect Adventures). Moreover, it is also interesting to point out that, from 2005 to 2010, the action genre had dominated in video game (30.1% and 22.3% respectively), while the most popular game genre in computer game is strategy (30.8% and 33.6% respectively). For the reason, the main input devices of strategy games are keyboard and mouse.

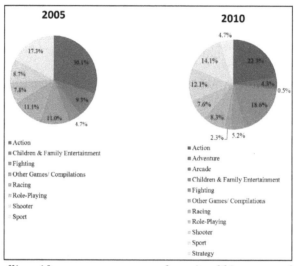

Best-selling video game super genres by unit sold in 2005 and 2010.

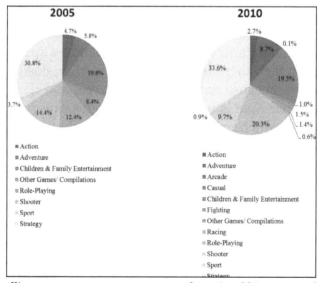

Best-selling computer game super genres by unit sold in 2005 and 2010.

Principles of Game Design

Many people assume that to best study the principles of Game Design, one would naturally study the most modern, complex, high-tech games that are available. However, this approach is completely wrong. Video games are just a natural growth of traditional games into a new medium. Therefore, the rules that govern them are still the same. A Game Designer must, at first, understand the simplest forms of game. According to Marc Prensky, here are what a game should be:

1. Games are a form of fun. That gives us enjoyment and pleasure.

2. Games are form of play. That gives us intense and passionate involvement.

3. Games have rules. That gives us structure.

4. Games are interactive. That gives us doing

5. Games have outcomes and feedback. That gives us learning.

6. Games are adaptive. That gives us flow.

7. Games have win states. That gives us ego gratification.

8. Games have conflict/competition/challenge/opposition. That gives us adrenaline.

9. Games have problem solving. That sparks our creativity.

10. Games have interaction. That gives us social groups.

11. Games have representation and story. That gives us emotion.

During the past decade, many Game Designers have argued about what are the best principles for Game Design, and which of them should be applied for all game designing's processes. In fact, there is no such thing as that; design principles should come from everywhere because design is everywhere, and design is the same everywhere. With each principle is based on the design's experiences and intuitions, the process of deciding which principle to choose should be an open book between Game Designers.

There are ten principles in total, and according to Roger E. Pedersen and Bob Bates, these principles can efficiently and effectively enhance the playing experience for the user:

Understand the role of the Designer: The Game Designer is the visionary, somewhat like a book's author. This person has outlined the scope and description of the product with sufficient detail so that others can understand and develop the product. Just as a book author sees his creation develop differently when made into a film, the Game Designer needs to accept and solicit modifications from the team members, the publisher, and the public during the development process. Often one of the Game Designer's tasks is to create the project bible - the game's lengthy design specification. This document details the gameplay, describes characters and settings (possibly including diagrams or drawings), includes level descriptions and possibly maps of areas to explore, positions and actions for each character or class of character.

Moreover, Game Designers should research their subject matter and evaluate outside suggestions and opinions. The audience demands and expects films and books to seem realistic and accurate. The computer and video game's audiences should accept nothing less. For instance when undertaking the development of a sports game (e.g. baseball), a Game Designer may feel that he knows the sport from playing it and viewing it on TV. However, much more research must be undertaken to create an immersive experience for consumers. Whether the game genre is sports, RPG, adventure, or simulation, the first step is to research similar titles in that game genre. There are many to accomplish this step such as surfing the Internet, visiting the local store and purchasing competitive games, reading reviews of similar genre titles, collecting marketing materials and advertisements from other publishers'web sites. This information is invaluable when put in use to design a new product.

Player Empathy: A good Game Designer always has an idea of what's going on in the player's head. This empathy for the player is crucial, since the Designer must develop the ability to put himself/herself in the player's shoes and anticipate his reaction to each element of the game. He or she must be able to imagine what the game will look like, all before a single line of code has been written. Naturally, no Designer has completely accurate foresight. That's one reason you have testers. Testers not only hunt for bugs, but also provide feedback on things they want to try in the game but can't.

Feedback: The basic interaction between a player and a game is simple: if the player does something, the game will do something in response. This feedback is what distinguishes a game from every other form of entertainment. It is the interactivity that makes games unique. Without it, the player would just be watching a movie on the screen. Every input the player makes in the game should give him a discernible response. No input should go unanswered. This answer can take many forms. It can be visual feedback, aural feedback, or even tactile feedback (if the controller is so equipped). It can be positive feedback or negative feedback, but there must be some feedback. Generally, this is easy when the player understands the game and is progressing nicely through it. It becomes more difficult when he is doing something wrong. Because nothing is more frustrating for a player than pressing a key, clicking the mouse, or pushing on the controller and having nothing happen. For every conceivable input, be sure to give the player some feedback about it.

Grounding the Player: The player should always know where he is in the game and why he is doing what he is doing. At any given point, he should have a long-term goal, a medium-range goal, and an immediate goal (This is true even of software toys, games that ostensibly have no goals, but in reality have a series of goals the player creates for himself.) Computer and video games are usually huge, and it is easy for a player to feel lost. Also, games are not always played start-to-finish in one sitting. If a player has an overall map in his head; it encourages him to come back to the game again and again until he is done.

Interface Design: Creating a good-looking yet functional interface is one of the most underrated tasks of Game Design - but it is vital to get it right. The Designer must decide what the game looks like on the screen, how information is passed along to the player, and how the player uses the controller, keyboard or mouse to input commands. So, he or she cannot rely on the instincts to get this right. The interface needs to be tested, first with team members and later with testers. What is intuitive to you can be awkward to someone else.

Moreover, elegance and ease of use are more important than increased functionality. Achieving this compromise is never easy. Frequently, the team will have to argue about it for months. If including a non-vital feature comes at the cost of messing up the interface, it is much better off without it. Usually, there are several interfaces within a game. Look at all of them. Get people to test them early, and listen to their feedback. Most importantly, the Designer must play his/her own game before everyone else.

Customizable Controls: Giving the player as much control over the interface as possible, and making everything as adjustable as the Designer can are important tasks. This includes game controls, monitor settings, volume. It is important to provide the users with everything, and let them change whatever and whenever they want. Since, different things are important to different players, one player might want to optimize for speed instead of graphics because he is an action addict. Another might prefer a higher resolution, even though it slows down the game, because he likes to look at the pictures. A third might want to remap the commands to different buttons or keys, because that is what he is used to. Whenever possible, the player must be able to customize the game to his/her liking.

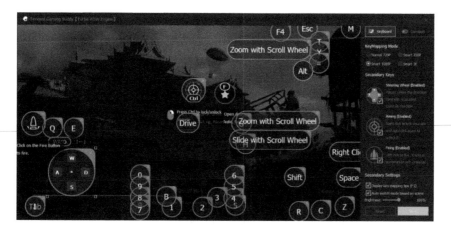

Design within Limits: Designers often forget that building a game is actually a software development project. Thus, it has a cost and a schedule, and its ultimate success or failure hinges not just on good gameplay, but on whether the team can deliver that gameplay on time, on budget, with technical features that work, and without crashing the player's machine. The person who makes this happen is the tech lead, and the Designers must work with him to make his job easier to accomplish. Even if Game Designers are not a programmer, they should read books about the software development process and adapt their design to the technical specifications and the budget. Consequently, as a Designer, he/she must limit him/herself to features that can possibly be implemented on the target machine.

Schedules are like Laws: Laws are created by legislative bodies and meant to be obeyed, but they are also designed to allow exceptions if evidence warrants special circumstances. Likewise, milestones created at the beginning of the project may need to be changed based on problems that occur during development. For instance, the decision to change the original game specification (e.g. to support a new computer, a new 3D card, alter preplanned artwork or audio clips) in order to make a better product is a situation that may warrant breaking the law of the schedule. If another month of development time would greatly improve the gameplay, remove non-show stopping bugs, or allow for better visuals or audio effects, then circumstances justify deviating from the schedule. To ship a game on a target day, month, or year, regardless of the state of the product at that time, can spell disaster for that product (not to mention the harm it does to the publisher's reputation). The team and publisher must agree that the additional time will substantially benefit the product.

Be truthful to your license: Games are based on licensed products often cause players to make certain assumptions about those titles. There are preconceptions about the gameplay, content, and target audience. In stores, it is the licensed titles that get noticed first, regardless of their marketing and advertising. Game Designers must understand this customer mentality. And the Designer must understand everything about that license in order to provide the kind of entertainment that the target consumers have anticipated. For instance, a baseball game that uses a particular baseball team's manager in its title suggests a strategy sports game. Players would probably assume that they would be responsible for making decisions about the players and batting order. On the other hand, a licensed product linked to a professional baseball player would suggest an emphasis on sports action, such as pitching and batting. There is one reason why licenses are expensive. Therefore, Designers and producers must use the license and the game's characters to leverage consumer preconceptions to the title's benefit.

There is no magic formula for success: It is essential to keep in mind that no one individual or company of any size has discovered the formula for what makes a successful product. Like film, art, and music, games appeal to a variety of consumer tastes, and of course taste is subjective. Some developers of past hits have credited their success to the underlying technology that their game used. Other developers claim that their game transports the player into a surreal and immersive universe. Nevertheless, others feel their game is success is due to the way it engrosses the player in a realistic simulation and challenges them with its compelling design. Behind each successful title is a unique list of traits that made it popular with consumers. The bottom line is quite simple. A well-designed product based on a team effort with a simple, user-friendly interface developed within a reasonable time frame will be successful.

The Game Designer

By this point it should be obvious what a Game Designer does; he determines what the nature of the gameplay is by creating the game's design. The terms Game Designer and Game Design have been used in such a wide variety of contexts for so long that their meanings have become diluted and hard to pin down. Some seem to refer to Game Design as being synonymous with Game Development. These people refer to anyone working on a computer game, whether artist, programmer, or producer, as a Game Designer.

Although, it is important to make the distinction between Game Developer and Game Designer, noted that Game Designers are just one of species of Game Developer, Designer is rather referred as a role than a person. So, anyone who makes decisions about how the game should be is a Game Designer. Almost every developer on a team makes some decision about how the game will be, just though the act of creating content for the game. These decisions are Game Designer decisions; therefore, when a person makes them, he or she is a Game Designer. For this reason, no matter what role on a Game Development team, an understanding of principles of Game Design will enhance the quality of a game.

Furthermore, there are some tasks in which the Game Designer may be involved. Firstly, the Game Designer may do some concept sketches or create some of the art assets that are used in the game. Secondly, the Game Designer may write the script containing the entire dialog spoken by the characters in the game. Thirdly, the Game Designer may contribute to the programming of the game or even be the lead programmer. Fourthly, the Game Designer may design some or all of the game-world itself, building the levels of the game (if the project in question has levels to be built). Fifthly, the Game Designer might be taking care of the project from a management and production standpoint, keeping a careful watch on the members of the team to see that they are all performing their tasks effectively and efficiently. These are some tasks that may be the job of the Game Designer; however, he may not need to do all of them. All someone needs to do in order to justifiably be called the Game Designer is to establish the form of the game's gameplay. Without a doubt, many Game Designers perform a wide variety of tasks on a project, but their central concern should always be the Game Design and the gameplay.

After having a better understanding about the role of a Game Designer, in the next part of this chapter, a list of skills is presented, which are required for any Game Designer to have. It should also be mention that Game Development is a collaborative process involving multi-disciplinary teams. Designers must be able to communicate their vision to artists, programmers, producers, marketing staff, and others involve in the development process, and accept feedback on their work. This involvement is presenting their ideas both verbally and on paper, for which they need writing and basic visual design and drawing skills. A good technical knowledge is also needed, with some programming skills at least at scripting level and awareness of the various games platforms and technologies.

Animation: Modern games are full of characters that need to seem alive. The very word animation means to give life.—Understanding the powers and limits of character animation will let you open the door for clever Game Design ideas the world has yet to see.

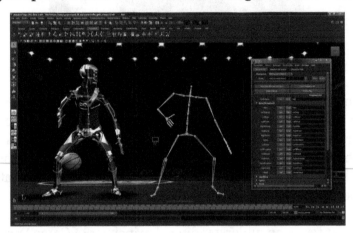

Anthropology: Game Designers will need to study their audiences in their natural habitat, trying to figure out their heart's desire, so that their games might satisfy that desire.

Architecture: Game Designers will be designing more than buildings — they will be designing whole cities and worlds. Familiarity with the world of architecture, in this case, understanding the relationship between people and spaces, will give them a tremendous leg up in creating game worlds.

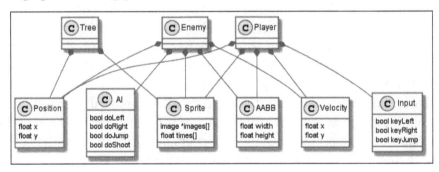

Brainstorming: Game Designers will need to create dozen or even a hundred ideas for a game.

Business: The game industry can be considered as an industry. Most games are made to make money. The better you understand the business end of things, the better chance you have of making the game of your dreams.

Cinematography: Many games will have movies in them. Almost all modern video games have a virtual camera. Game Designers need to understand the art of cinematography if they want to deliver an emotionally compelling experience.

Communication: Game Designers will need to talk with people in their team, and even more. They will need to resolve disputes, solve problems of miscommunication, and learn the truth about how their teammates, client and audience really feel about their game.

Creative Writing: Game Designers will be creating entire fictional worlds, populations to live in them, and deciding the events that will happen there.

Economics: Many modern games feature complex economies of game resources. An understanding of the rules of economics can be surprisingly helpful.

Engineering: Modern video games involve some of the most complex engineering in the world today, with some titles counting their lines of code in the millions. New technical innovations make new kinds of gameplay possible. Innovative Game Designers must understand both the limits and the powers that each technology brings.

History: Many games are placed in historical settings. Even ones placed in fantasy settings can draw incredible inspiration from history.

Management: Any time a team works together toward a goal, there must be some management. Good Designers can succeed even when management is bad, secretly managing from below to achieve a successful result.

Mathematics: Games are full of mathematics, probability, risk analyses, and complex scoring systems, not to mention the mathematics that stands behind computer graphics and computer science in general. A skilled Designer must not be afraid to delve into math from time to time.

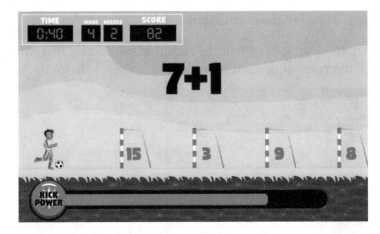

Music: It is the language of the soul. If a game is going to truly touch people, to immerse, and embrace them, it cannot do it without music.

Psychology: The goal is to make a human being happy. Game Designers must understand the workings of the human mind; otherwise, they are designing in the dark.

Public Speaking: Game Designers will frequently need to present their ideas to a group. Sometimes they will speak to solicit their feedback; sometimes they will speak to persuade other people of the genius of their new idea. Whatever the reason, the Game Designers must be confident, clear, natural, and interesting, or people will be suspicious that they do not know what they are doing.

Sound Design: Sound is what truly convinces the mind that it is in a place; in other words, hearing is believing.

Technical Writing: Game Designers need to create documents that clearly describe their complex designs without leaving any holes or gaps.

Visual Arts: Every game will need to be full of graphic elements. Game Designers must be fluent in the language of graphic design and know how to use it to create the feeling they want their game to have.

Of all the skills mention in the previous sections, one is far and away the most important. In fact, the most important skill for a Game Designer to have is listening. So, Game Designers must always listen to many things. These can be grouped into 5 major categories: Team, Audience, Game, Client, and Self.

Firstly, the Game Designers will need to listen to the team, since they will be building their game and making crucial Game Design decisions together with them. A team can bring together a big list of skills. If the Designers can listen deeply to their team, and truly communicate with them, all will function as one unit, as if sharing the same skills. As the result, tasks are easier to be done, and problems are simpler to be resolved.

Secondly, the Game Designers will need to listen to the audience because these are the people who will be playing the game. Ultimately, if they are not happy with the game, it means failure. And the only way to know what will make them happy is to listen to them deeply, getting to know them better than they know themselves. You will need to listen to your game. What does this even mean? It means you will get to know your game inside and out. Like a mechanic who can tell what is wrong with a car by listening to the engine, you will get to know what is wrong with your game by listening to it run.

Thirdly, the Game Designers will need to listen to the client. The client is the one who is paying the Designers to design the game, and if they do not give them what they want, they will go to someone else who does. Only by listening to them, deeply, the Game Designers will be able to tell what they really want, deep in their hearts.

And lastly, the Game Designers will need to listen to themselves. This may sounds easy; however, it is considered the most difficult kind of listening. A clear understanding of how to use it will be one of the powerful tools that can support their creativity.

Applying Human-Computer Interaction in Game Design

Computer games and video games are one of the most successful application domains in the history on interactive system. This success has appeared despite the fact that games were considered to be different from most of the accepted paradigms for designing usable interactive software. What has made games different is they focus on system performance over consistency; games have always ignored the windowing systems, the standard widget libraries, and the toolkits that define the look and feel of conventional systems which leads to a very different design environment. This environment does not place restrictions on how thing must look or how interaction must be carried out with the user. Instead, it does strongly reward innovation and performance – the driving forces in Game Design are user performance, satisfaction and novelty. As a result, games have both become early adopters of new HCI technologies as well as innovators in the area of HCI interaction design.

Understanding the important roles of Human-Computer Interaction which is not only in the Computer Science field, but also in Game Design, is essential. Therefore, it is necessary to discuss how the HCI has been implementing in the Game Design process.

Key Issues of HCI in Gaming

It is important to understand what Human-Computer Interaction is, and why it is so important in gaming. A relatively new field, HCI was founded in 1983 with the following definition which is still applicable today: The key notion, perhaps, is that the user and the computer engage in a communicative dialog whose purpose is the accomplishment of some task. All the mechanisms used in this dialog constitute the interface: the physical devices, such as keyboards and displays, as well as the computer's programs for controlling the interaction.

Consider every operating system found in the PC – whether Windows, Mac or Linux - and desktop or notebook which found in millions of homes and offices around the globe. The present PC is more powerful than it used to be; however, the methodology and technology for interacting with the PC remains little changed – a keyboard and mouse for input, and an LCD (or in the past CRT) display combined with speakers for output. These components are still considered as the basic interaction tools for computer games nowadays, especially in the strategy genres. The Total War series, Warcraft and Starcraft are the examples in this case.

Moreover, considering the modern gaming platforms in all their diversity – from the PC, through consoles (the Microsoft Xbox 360, Sony PlayStation 3, and Nintendo Wii), handhelds (Nintendo DS and Sony PSP) and the rapidly growing area of gameplay on mobile phones (best represented by the iPhone and other touch phones). On these platforms, gamers use devices ranging from microphones through touch-screens, accelerometers, cameras, gamepads and remotes to sing, strum, dance, swing, and otherwise conduct a range of physical activities – far richer than those afforded by a keyboard and mouse – in order to play their games. Without a doubt, in the past decade, the game industry has seen a genuine new start in HCI (Human-Computer Interaction) technology with new styles of interaction and play being supported, and these technologies achieving mass market penetration. Furthermore, new technologies such as several Brain Computer Interface (BCI) products have emerged in the past years (the NCI OCZ, the Emotiv EPOC headset) aimed squarely at, and priced for the game market.

What is more, despite the escalating economic importance of the computer and video games, indicated by the rapidly growing revenue within the game industry over the past few decades, it cannot be the sole value in measuring video game cultural value. As the matter of fact, although with some forms of play such as education and communication, computer and video games continue to receive negative recognition from the society. They are still held in rather low value by policy makers. Most schools and organizations have currently banned such form of activities in the class room or at the workplace.

This is intensified by an excess of research writing that over-emphasis the negative effect computer and video games have from various perspectives. At first, it is claimed that the prolonged use of computer games contributes obsessive, addictive behavior, dehumanization of the player, desensitizing of feeling, health problems, and other disorder. Others argue that computer and video games encourage the development of anti-social behavior among game players. In addition, perhaps, the most debated issue concerning games and players, especially teenagers, is their connection to violence. A growing body research is correlating violent computer games play to aggressive cognitions, attitudes, and behaviors. A number of studies have shown a positive association between the amount of video game play and aggressiveness among children, adolescents and even adults.

Consequently, there is an increasing interest in approaching game studies from the perspectives of HCI. Some researchers investigated novel forms of interaction such as tangible interfaces to encourage collaboration and techniques of gathering user requirement for design educational game. While other studies focused on the human behavior and physiological responses such as frustration in order to better understand the interface design toward building affective computer through the study of computer gameplay. In term of research in Game Usability, attempted to generate Heuristics and usability guidelines for the creation and evaluation of fun in video games by working closely with game developers. In addition, to the study of HCI in computer game, is the work of Malone on educational games. Malone in his early work on the motivation of computer game based learning proposes, the Heuristics for Game Designers and researchers. The Heuristics for the fun factor of computer games consists of three main elements that draw largely from Csikszentmihalyi's flow theory: challenge, fantasy and curiosity. Apart from these, there has also been research on the evaluation of the usability of games.

Game User Interface Design

An interface has many pieces; for instance, menus, text, buttons and icons. What is more, the interface is the part of the game that allows the user to interact with the game. Interaction is what makes a video game different from a movie. When playing a video game, the user can make choices and respond to events. An interface is the connection between the user and the game, and a well-designed interface makes the video game experience more fun.

Interface design is a creative, exciting, and challenging subject. However, it is necessary to point out that, too often, video game interfaces are an afterthought. The reason is too many project managers assume the most important part of a software development project is the programming, and then the interface can come later. As the result, insufficient time is assigned for interface design which may leads to a poor quality interface.

All this considered, the visual quality of a game is very important. A poor interface can ruin the entire video game experience. One of the negative example is the user is confused and cannot comprehend how to navigate the menu or if he/she cannot find the information while playing the game. The more the user tries to search for information in order to play, the less enjoyable the game becomes. On the contrary, if the game has a great interface, it can enhance the playing experience. A good-looking interface with a lot of well-designed features can actually be fun to use and even seem like a game itself. But more importantly, great game interface design can boost game sales.

The Game Interface Design Goals

A good way to for a Game Designer to make decisions about features of a game is to have goals. If he understands these goals, it will be much easier for him to make decisions about the interface. It is not always easy to define the overall game goals, but if the Game Designer takes the time to create concise goals for the entire game and clearly understands these, many decisions will be easier to make. In fact, goal oriented design produces great results.

In many cases, the Designer may be wondering, What kind of goals do you need to set when designing an interface? Thus, making the coolest interface ever may be the first thing that comes to mind. This goal sounds great, but it probably should not be the first priority. As much as everyone wants a cool interface, there may be other things that are more important. If making a kids' game; for example, it might be more important that the menu is easy for a six-year old to use than that it looks cool. More importantly, prioritization is the key to using these goals to guide the design.

In addition, below is a list of possible goals that a Designer may have. These goals may not match perfectly with every case, but it is important to understand the goals of the company, and to align these with the user's requirements. This list is by no means a complete list of goals that could ever be used for every Game Design case. In fact, it is a very brief list which meant to simulate thought about the real goals of the Game Designer:

- Promote an existing license or famous personality.
- Capitalize on an existing license or famous personality.
- Meet a particular schedule.
- Reach a particular audience.
- Create something completely unique.
- Outdo a competing game.
- Capitalize on the success of a competing game.
- Continue a successful series.
- Sell another product (other than the game itself).
- Promote a moral issue.
- Create an educational experience.
- Pass the approval process of the console manufacture.

- Please the marketing department.

- Tell a story.

Promoting and capitalizing an existing license or famous personality are the first goal for the Game Designer. It is important to have a good first impression from the users. The second goal is meeting a particular schedule. A game interface design should be treated equally as the other phases in the game development process. Therefore, a sufficient time should be scheduled for the design in order to create a well-made interface that can guarantee meeting the player's expectation. A further goal is reaching a particular audience. A targeted group of customer should be decided first, before starting to create an interface. For instance, different styles of interface will be made based on the information whether the game is for young audiences, or for more mature audiences. Consequently, if the target audiences are students or teachers, creating an education experience should be considered as one of the priority goals. The fourth possible goal is pass the approval process of the console manufacture – a game can be developed for playing in many platforms.

Furthermore, for a game manufacture to success in the market, it is essential for the Game Designer to create something completely unique. There is a variety of possible ways to achieve this goal. The Designer can outdo a competing game in features and effects; capitalize on the success of a competing game, continue a successful series or even promote a moral issue. But more importantly, the game should tell a story. For example, the strategy game Total War Shogun 2 promotes the Japan's warfare in the 16th century.

The final goals in this list are the Game Designer needs to please the marketing department and sell another product (e.g. a game is based on a movie or a novel). More innovative ideas can possibly be acquired by the collaboration between different departments. In this case, since the marketing people work closely to the customers, they understand clearly the customer's desires. Additionally, a game may be used in a promotion campaign to boost sale of another product, that is different than game.

What is more, it is essential to mentioned that every Designer should avoid the temptation to set one large goal that is actually several goals in one. This is often the easy way out, since it is more difficult to articulate specific goals than it is to generalize. But in comparison, a goal like Make a cool game is not nearly as clear as Add three new and creative features that are not found in competing racing games. The point is to define useful goals that will provide direction during development. As the result, understanding the motive behind the goal is very important.

Basic Design Principles

Every best Interface Designer knows and understands clearly the design principles. In fact, nothing will improve the design skills better than an understanding of basic design principles. Many Interface Designers learn these principles in college or a specialized art school but they forget them later, since it is easy to go out and find a job in the industry, start working on real games, and just gets sort of rusty on design basics. Ignoring or forgetting basic design principles will adversely affect the design ability. Once the Designer has learned basic design principles, it is important to keep using them to evaluate and improve the interfaces.

Understand the users and support their goals. Mitchell Kapor wrote a Software Design Manifesto back in 1991: If a user interface is designed after the fact it is like designing an automobile dashboard after the engine, chassis, and all other components and functions are specified. If these interfaces are designed after the fact, it is almost impossible for them to be able to meet all the user's goals. In other words, the Designer need to first understand the users (their needs and objectives) in order to create an interface that allows them to effectively access the system's functionality.

Get back to basics – using color. Color can be a very powerful design tool. One of the abilities of color is to set a mood; color can express emotion and set an atmosphere. For instance, a design that uses a lot of neutral gray and desaturated colors can bring the sad feeling. Moreover, one of the major challenges when working with color is finding a set of colors that work well together creating color harmony. Harmonious colors or complementary colors can include colors that are similar to one another like a range of blue colors can look good together.

Make the interface easy to learn and enjoyable to use. This is an important rule that helps the user maintain a sense of spatial orientation and sanity. It is essential to consider how the user will interface with the product before creating it. Additionally, a bonus point for a good interface is creating an interface that is enjoyable to use. The Designer can add a variety of effect like 3D transformation and adding light/shadow, instead of using only plain text and picture, into the design.

Organize the visual. A good rule when creating an interface is to space elements evenly and align them well. It is necessary to paying attention to spacing and alignment results in visual organization. If the elements in the design are scattered and the spacing between them is not consistent, the design will appear unorganized. This is displeasing to the user because most people are attracted to organization. Moreover, if the design calls for objects that are not aligned, then make sure that these elements are not positioned only slightly off-alignment with other objects, in other word, move them far enough out of alignment that there is no doubt that it was intentional. It can be very disconcerting to the user if objects look like they should be aligned but they are not. Many designs can be improved by simply fixing the spacing between objects.

Use Unity and Variation. When creating an interface design, one of the biggest challenges is striking a balance between unity and variation. If the design is composed of a group of unrelated elements, then there is no unity. If all of the elements in the design are a different shape or color, then the composition will appear to be thrown together and it will lack the cohesiveness found in a good design. On the other hand, if all of the colors and shapes in the design are exactly the same, then this design will not be very visually interesting. A little variation is required to make a design pleasing to the eye. The best approach is to start with unity. Everything should feel like it fits together.

Be a problem free. The quickest way to inhibit enjoyment is to create frustration over simple interface and navigation issues. Although testing is never the most fun part of the process, it is vitally important. In a competitive marketplace, if the game's interface has noticeable bugs it risks losing the users no matter how good the content is. Interface problems can be more than just software bugs, however, as a poorly designed interface is still a major issue. A good way to test an interface is by watching people use this interface a real-world scenario, then arise with some possible questions: Are they able to navigate around and achieve their objectives with relative ease? Is the interface intuitive to both experienced and less experienced game players?

Develop for Console or PC. There are some big differences exist between video game development for consoles and development for PC games. Each platform has its benefits and drawbacks. One of the biggest and most apparent differences between the PC and a console is that they use different input devices. A mouse is very different from a controller. The entire game can change if it is on a console instead of a PC. Understanding these differences can help an Interface Designer create a better interface for either platform.

Methods of Presenting a Game User Interface

All the Game User Interfaces are made of two main elements: text and icon. Therefore, these two elements, in another word, are the two ways of presenting a Game User Interface:

The first element is Text. It is a powerful tool that is often overlooked or at least underestimate by Designer working on game interfaces. The style of text can also set mood of the game as well as color. Each font has a personality. A font that is handwritten and scratched up-looking might be a great choice for an extreme sport game, while a smooth and flowing script font might be great for a horse riding game targeted at young female players. It is also possible to make a great interface design using only text. Font choice, size, placement, color, and type effects can greatly improve the design of an interface.

Nonetheless, in reality, no one likes to read a lot of text when playing a video game. For this reason, text should only be used when it is absolutely necessary. If the information is so important that text must be put in the interface, then it needs to be easy to read. If text is hard to read because it is too small or is not clear enough, the user is likely to ignore it and move on. Additionally, in many cases, it has been proved that text can be used in the background merely as a design element. And the purpose of this background text is to set a mood.

Furthermore, fonts or text styles are an essential element in design text. Fonts can easily be made by using software to manipulate the font design. Most game engines require that an artist create all the fonts. Some advanced engines have tools that can take a standard font and convert it to game format. Even in these cases, it is good to understand how a font works because it is often helpful to edit the font directly. The most common format for a game font is white text placed in a grid. Fonts can also be a great place to put all kinds of images; numbers, dashes, symbols, and icons can all be put into a font file. These icons and images can be used in the game just like a font. A common example of using icons in a font is when creating a console game and small images of the controller buttons are placed in the font (e.g. the Xbox 360 icon).

The second element is Icon. Beside text, it is another important method of communication in an interface. Nevertheless, displaying information graphically is always more interesting than displaying a lot of text. For instance, if an amount of money must be shown, consider using gold coins instead of a number amount. If the amount of energy character has left must be displayed, consider using a fill-bar. So, icons can be used for almost everything in the interface. Although they usually take a lot more time to create than would a paragraph of straight text, they make the game a whole lot more fun to play.

What is more, great icons can accommodate the game to the user without text. Text can used to reinforce an icon, but the better the icons are, the less text will be needed. The key to creating a great icon is choosing the right image to represent the functionality. For example, for a button that allows the player to attack an enemy, a crossed sword icon may be a great solution. Many standard icons, or icons that always mean the same thing, are used in video games. Players already know what these icons mean and can get up to speed more quickly if these standard icons appear in the game. For instance, many game have a save feature, and a common icon for the save feature is a floppy disk. Consequently, it is important to take advantage of player's past experiences by using images that they are familiar with. However, in order to have a better impression from the players, these icons should be customized to fit the look of the game. Moreover, for nongame standard icons; for instance, a symbol used in a bathroom door, a stop icon in music player software, or even a minus and plus sign, these icons can also be used in designing a game icon, since most people can recognize their meaning.

HCI Evaluation Techniques

Evaluation is concerned with gathering data about the usability of a design or product by a specified group of users for a particular activity within a specified environment or work context.

Evaluation can be divided into 2 types: an informal evaluation which only requires a quick feedback of the users, and an evaluation that are much more rigorously planned and controlled (e.g. use laboratory experimentation or large scale surveys). However, regardless of the type evaluation being done, it is important to consider the four aspects: the characteristics of the user who is chosen to participate in the evaluation (e.g. age, gender and experience), the types of activities that the user will do, the environment of the study and the stage of the game that is evaluated (whether it is a demo version or a completed version).

Furthermore, the evaluation methods that are used in game serve three main goals. First of all, it is used to access the functionalities, in the extent of accessibility, that is are provided by the game. Second of all, these methods are used to record the user's reaction and experience when playing the game. And lastly, they are used to identify any specific problem with the game. So, without evaluation the games reaching consumer would be premature; they would reflect the intentions of the design team but there would be no study of the actual relationship between design and use. As the result, it may lead to the failure of games in the market. For the reason, Heuristic Evaluation is one of the most powerful techniques that currently used in the computer game and video game industry; it focuses on evaluating the usability of game interface.

Heuristic Evaluation for Games

Most of video games require constant interaction, so Game Designers must pay attention to usability issues; for example, the degree to which a player is able to learn, control and understand a game. Having failure to design usable game interfaces can interfere with the larger goal of creating a compelling experience for the users, and can have a negative effect on the overall quality and success of a game. Additionally, Game Designers need a method for identifying usability problems both in early designs and in more mature prototypes. However, there are few formal methods for evaluating the usability of game interfaces.

But first, there is a necessity to understand to word Heuristic. It is a set of usability principles that is used by the evaluators to explore an interface. And unlike many common usability inspection techniques which are not appropriate for games since they either rely on formal specifications of task sequence or are oriented around user interface concepts used in desktop applications. Conversely, the Heuristic Evaluation does not make any assumptions about task structure, and it is flexible enough to be adapted to specialized domains.

What more is the Heuristic Evaluation has the potential to improve the Game Design process. Unlike play-testing (one of the most common ways to uncover design problems using playable prototype of a game), it does not require user participation. Instead, Heuristic Evaluation relies on skills of evaluator who inspects the user interface and identifies usability problems. In addition, it is in-expensive and can be carried out in a short amount of time. As the result, Heuristic Evaluation gives the evaluators significant freedom in how they conduct the evaluation, and it also helps the Game Designers find important classes of problems that are not always found with user testing.

One of the first set of Heuristics was developed by Nielsen which is primarily used for desktop applications. It refers to common user interface concepts such as dialogs, undo and redo, and error prevention. However, many of these ideas have limited application in the game context, for the reason, it does not address several important usability issues. An example is the necessity of providing intuitive control mappings when displaying the game world. Similar to the Nielsen case, also compiled a list of Game Heuristics that concentrates on four areas: game interface, game mechanics, story and playability. Some of the usability issues were mention in both the cases, but they were not described in detail. For instance, Federoff's Heuristics include: for PC, consider hiding the main interface and the interface should be as non-intrusive as possible, while Desurvire's Heuristics include: players do not need to use a manual to play game and provide immediate feedback for user action.

Among all, the most appropriated Heuristics, which can be used for the Game Usability inspection, are probably from Pinelle and his associates. What make these Heuristics be different from previous mentioned Heuristics are they consider on the detail of usability. Pinelle and his associate believed that a set of Heuristics that focuses on Game Usability can help improve the video game process. As the result, they created a set of Heuristics to serve as a set of design principle, and to implement the usability inspections at the same time.

Game Heuristics

- Provide consistent responses to the user's action:

Games should respond to users' actions in a predictable manner. Basic mechanics, such as hit detection, game physics, character movement, and enemy behavior, should all be appropriate for the situation that the user is facing. Games should also provide consistent input mappings so that users' actions always lead to the expected out-come.

- Allow users to customize video and audio settings, difficulty and game speed:

The video and audio settings, and the difficulty and game speed levels seen in games are not appropriate for all users. Therefore, the system should allow people to customize a range of settings so that the game accommodates their individual needs.

- Provide predictable and reasonable behavior for computer controlled units:

In many games, the computer helps the user control the movement of their character, of a small group of teammates, or of a large number of units. Computer controlled units should behave in a predictable fashion, and users should not be forced to issue extra commands to correct faulty artificial intelligence. The game should control units so that path-finding and other behaviors are reasonable for in-game situations.

- Provide unobstructed views that are appropriate for the user's current actions:

Most games provide users with a visual representation (i.e. a view) of the virtual location that the user is currently occupying. The game should provide views that allow the user to have a clear, unobstructed view of the area, and of all visual information that is tied to the location. Views should also be designed so that they are appropriate for the activity that the user is carrying out in the game. For example, in a 3D game different camera angles may be needed for jumping sequences, for fighting sequences, and for small and large rooms.

- Allow users to skip non-playable and frequently repeated content:

Many games include lengthy audio and video sequences, or other types of non-interactive content. Games should allow users to skip non-playable content so that it does not interfere with gameplay.

- Provide intuitive and customizable input mappings:

Most games require rapid responses from the user, so input mapping must be designed so that users can issue commands quickly and accurately. Mappings should be easy to learn and should be intuitive to use, leveraging spatial relationships (the up button is above the down button, etc.) and other natural pairings. They should also adopt input conventions that are common in other similar games (e.g. many first-person shooters and realtime strategy games use similar input schemes). Games should allow users to remap the input settings, should support standard input devices (e.g. mouse, keyboard, gamepad), and should provide shortcuts for expert players.

- Provide controls that are easy to manage, and that have an appropriate level of sensitivity and responsiveness:

Many games allow users to control avatars such as characters or vehicles. Controls for avatars should be designed so that they are easy for the user to manage, i.e. they are not too sensitive or unresponsive. When controls are based on real world interactions, such as steering a car or using a control stick in an airplane, the game should respond to input in a way that mirrors the real world. Further, games should respond to controls in a timeframe that is suitable for gameplay requirements.

- Provide users with information on game status:

Users make decisions based on their knowledge of the current status of the game. Examples of common types of information that users need to track include the current status of their character (such as their health, armor status, and location in the game world), objectives, teammates, and enemies. Users should be provided with enough information to allow them to make proper decisions while playing the game.

- Provide instructions, training, and help:

Many games are complex and have steep learning curves, making it challenging for users to gain mastery of game fundamentals. Users should have access to complete documentation on the game, including how to interpret visual representations and how to interact with game elements. When appropriate, users should be provided with interactive training to coach them through the basics. Further, default or recommended choices should be provided when users have to make decisions in complex games, and additional help should be accessible within the application.

- Provide visual representations that are easy to interpret and that minimize the need for micromanagement:

Visual representations, such as radar views, maps, icons, and avatars, are frequently used to convey information about the current status of the game. Visual representations should be designed so that they are easy to interpret, so that they minimize clutter and occlusion, and so that users can differentiate important elements from irrelevant elements. Further, representations should be designed to minimize the need for micromanagement, where users are forced to interactively search through the representation to find needed elements.

These Heuristics were developed by analyzing PC game review from a popular gaming website, and the review set covered 108 different games divided by 18 for each of 6 major game genres (e.g. action, strategy, simulation, etc.). In the conclusion, Pinelle and his associates believed that the Heuristics that they presented have provided a new way to adapt usability inspection for games, and allow Game Designers to evaluate both mockups and functional prototypes. Moreover, the Heuristics allow the Game Designers to evaluate Game Usability by applying design principles that are based on design trends seen in recent games, and that are generalized across major genres found in commercial games.

Evaluate Usability issues from a Case Study

Here, using the Heuristics from Pinelelle and his associates to evaluate the usability of the role-playing game (a third person view game) Final Fantasy XIII. The game belongs to the Final Fantasy series developed by Square Enix, and it was released on March 9th 2010. The evaluation process is presented in form of a table with the Heuristic's list as well as my comments related to each issue.

Usability Evaluation of Final Fantasy XIII

- Provide consistent responses to the user's action:

Character's movement responses consistently to the player's action.

- Allow users to customize video and audio settings, difficulty and game speed:

Final Fantasy allows the player to set the levels of difficulty (from easy to hard) for the game.

The player is also allowed to freely customize the video and sound settings before starting the game and during the gameplay.

- Provide predictable and reasonable behavior for computer controlled unit:

The game has a few problems with the computer controlled teammates. They are frequently fallen behind by the player's character which causing the troubles to engage the enemies and to explore maps.

- Provide unobstructed views that are appropriate for the user's current actions:

The game's views are built with two different modes: third-person and first-person view. The third-person camera is used for most of the gameplay, while traveling or during the battles. However, the player can also have the ability to switch to the first-person view in some actions that require an accurate aiming.

- Allow users to skip non-playable and frequently repeated content:

The game includes many cut-scenes during playing, and they can be skipped by the player's choice.

- Provide intuitive and customizable input mappings:

The attack and defense strategies, called paradigm, can easily be set by the player, and then be labeled automatically by the game (e.g. combat clinic, diversity and perpetual magic). In the battle, the player can switch between each paradigm quickly by choosing their names.

- Provide controls that are easy to manage, and that have an appropriate level of sensitivity and responsiveness:

The player only needs to control a single character at a time, when traveling. During the battle, the player can let the game choose a default set of actions on his/her behalf, some late-game battles benefit from a bit of skill micromanagement on top of the usual paradigm (or strategy) fiddling. There will be smart and more difficult challenges waiting for the player once he/she overcomes the ease of the early hours.

- Provide users with information on game status:

The information about the player's character (e.g. level, experience, attack and defense points, and status) can be easily access through the game menu.

- Provide instructions, training, and help:

The game provides a sufficient amount of instruction and help during the first few hours of gameplay. The player also has an option to skip these assistances. Some additional information; for example, the data of monsters that the player has fought or location that the player has travelled through, can be found during the gameplay by accessing the game's menu.

- Provide visual representations that are easy to interpret and that minimize the need for micromanagement:

During the gameplay, the player is provided with radar view and map which can be accessed by a short-cut button or accessing the game's menu. Objectives and treasure location icons are displayed in the game's map.

To sum up, Final Fantasy XIII had some glitches with the artificial intelligence which are one of the most common errors found in games. However, the game has successfully provided the players with an easy to use and learn interface, among its stunning beauty game world, dynamic battles and fantastic story. Nearly every battle and every leg of the journey moves fluidly made these errors seem minor. Thus, it almost goes without saying that Final Fantasy XIII is a fruitful product of the RPG genre in the past few years.

Human-Computer Interface Design for an In-vehicle Information System

Urban Traffic Flow Guidance System (UTFGS) is the core U research contents of Intelligent Transportation Systems (ITS). It synthetically applies detection technology, communication technology, computer technology, control technology, information technology, GPS and GIs etc to guide the car moving on the optimal mute which is calculated by In-Vehicle Information System (IVIS). UTFGS ultimately aims. to realize the reasonable distribution of traffic flow of the whole road network.

IVlS can connect with the world outside of the vehicle via wireless communication. The driver can receive current traveller information and road network conditions which are updated in real-time. The driver can use the input device to acquire the type of information required such as mute guidance or traveler information for a specified route or zone of road network. Increasingly it is becoming possible for drivers to use telephone. e-mail and the internet through the development of an in-vehicle office environment.

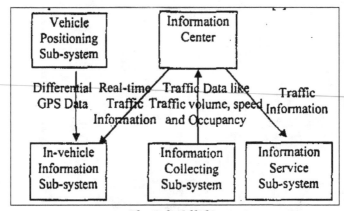

The Role Of IVlS.

Human-Computer Interface (HCI) also called user interface, is the cross-research domain of computer science, psychology, graphic an, recognition science and human-computer engineering. It is the media of delivering and exchanging information between human and computer. It is the user's comprehensive manipulation environment. Through look and listening provided by HCI, the user applies knowledge, experience, thinking etc. To acquire the interface information, then completes human-computer interaction, such as the input of command, parameter etc. After the computer deals with the information received, HCI provides the response information or the results.

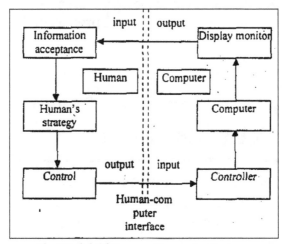

The Model Of Human-Computer System.

Restriction Factors of In-vehicle Information System

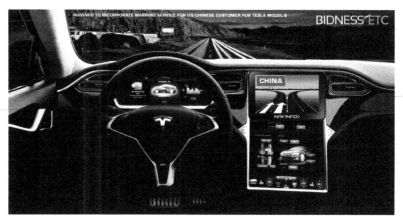

IVIS is the embedded computer system, which is dedicatedly designed for dynamic route guidance. It is restricted by some conditions as following:

Space Restriction

Because lVlS is usually installed in the dashboard, its space architecture and volume is restricted. This means that IVIS's configuration is compact.

Anti-shake Restriction

The function of dynamic route guidance of lVlS must be supported by electronic map. The calculation of the optimal route must be fulfilled in aver short time, so this means that IVIS read the electronic map data quickly. For satisfying this read speed: the electronic map should be stored in the DVD. Because the road condition varies, this requires that IVIS's anti-shake is good.

Speed of Calculation Restriction

Dynamic route guidance requires that the display of the optimal route is fulfilled in a very short time, so this requires that the route guidance software has the good data structure, human-computer interaction has the high efficiency.

Pressure Stability Restriction

The pressure provided by the car normally is twelve volt. So this restricts the working pressure of IVIS is twelve volt. When the car starts up, the volt is not stability. So the power circuit of IVIS has to be designed to support this.

Contrast Restriction

The contrast ratio describes the relation between the luminance of the foreground and background (contrast= ($L_{foreground} - L_{background} - L_{background}$). This should be a minimum of 3:1, whilst a ratio of 5:1 is recommended. Too high contrast can cause problems of glare, while two low contrast slows down the reading process. The ratio of area average luminance of the display and of the surrounding should not exceed.

Reflections and glare visible to the driver on both displays and windscreens reduce legibility, and should be avoided for example through:

- Provision of a display brightness control.
- Appropriate display surface texture and finish.
- Appropriate colour choice.
- Appropriate image polarity.

Colours Restriction

Colours should be used to make it easier to find the required information under both day and night-time viewing conditions. It should not, however, be used for actual messages, as this would increase the reading time. The use of too many colours should also be avoided. A maximum of five different easy to distinguish is recommended (excluding black and white).

Re-design of Hardwaers In-vehicle Information System

Hardware HCI of lVlS usually is control panel, on which there is control key and display monitor 141. The function layout of control key and display panel is one dimensional design. So during the hardware HCI design, we must take the proper proportion of control key and display monitor into account. lVlS may work on day or at night, in the sunshine sky or in the cloudy sky, so the display of IVlS should have day mode and night mode, strong light mode and faint light mode.

The Design of Software In-vehicle Information System

In the UTFGS, we adopt autonomous route guidance. HCI of lVlS provides two operating mode of route guidance: static mode (IVIS uses only in-vehicle route guidance map database) and dynamic mode (IVIS uses link travel time obtained from Information Center for route guidance). When dynamic mode is, selected, travel time for each link shall be provided from Information Center. If Information Center can't provide refreshed link travel time, lVlS shall use the latest set of data for route guidance. The driver also can convert into static mode that provides the shortest route.

With the advent of IVIS, there is an accompanying concern that it may interfere with the primary driving task, and impact negatively on both the safety of the driver and other road users. So the foremost issue for information services of lVlS is the assurance of safety. IVlS should have a safe and usable HCI.

Some Essential Elements Display

Software HCI of lVlS is the information interface between driver and IVIS [Z]. It is important to Human-Computer Interaction. Based on the characteristic of dynamic guidance, HCI design technologies of some essential elements should be considered.

The Electronic Map Display

Electronic map is the essential part of IVIS. Our purpose is dynamic route guidance, so we should intensify the road network information, weaken non-road network information. We label OUT interest point by text in the map. The electronic map should have the function of zooming in, zooming out, grabber, etc. During dynamic guidance, the electronic map should move as the car moves, so that the car icon is always in the middle of the display monitor.

The Car Icon Display

During the dynamic route guidance, the car icon denotes the car's location. An obvious car icon is very significant to the driver. Its color should be fresh, for example red, green, etc. Its shape may be the car or the arrow.

The Optimal Route Display

The role of the optimal mute is to tell how the driver goes. So the interface of the optimal route should be clear and friendly. We may adopt many arrows which points to the destination or the line which connects with the destination. When the car crosses the cloverleaf junction, the display monitor should be divided into two parts, one part displays in two dimensional mode, the other displays in three dimensional mode.

Requirements from HCI of IVIS

The driving task can be structured hierarchically into the levels:

Strategic Level

At this level the task concerns trip planning and mute selection. A high cognitive load for the driver is involved at this level: map reading, orientation of direction and distance. The information need during the trip is occasional at roundabouts, intersections or traffic interchanges.

The moment of presentation of the information is not crucial, this can be given a while before the roundabout etc. and can be repeated. The information should not be given (unless a repeated message) when the driver is preoccupied with tasks at lower levels.

Level

Manipulate the vehicle such as overtaking, car-following, crossing, turning. At this level a combination of cognitive load and skills based on experience are relevant.. The information need at this task level is frequent.

Operational Level

Steer. brake, manage the accelerator pedal. At this level the steering and braking etc. is almost done automatically based on skills. The information need is continuous, e.g. discontinuation of mad delineation can lead to cats driving off the road.

Basic Requirements

The principal requirements for conducting the driving task in a proper manner are:

- Both hands at the wheel.
- The senses directed on the road and surrounding traffic.
- Also the attention and thinking directed on the road and traffic.

HCI Design of Information Acquisition

For assurance of safety, inputs operations of IVlS for obtaining information and outputs form of IVIS for presenting information are two major problems.

Conventional Model and AutoDJ Model for Information Acquisition.

With the conventional model outlined in Figure, drivers must enter operational inputs several times via IVIS in order to obtain the information they want the screen menus of IVlS are generally structured in multiple hierarchical layers.

Drivers indicate their demands by making selections and narrowing down the choices at each menu level until they have determined what they want.

Drivers' demands are very diverse and one way of responding to their manifold demands is to increase the number of screen menus.

However, that results in a hierarchical menu structure and makes the operation of the system more complicated. In short, in determining the information they want, drivers themselves must perform the task of searching for a menu that satisfies their needs.

A major issue in connection with the operation of IVIS for obtaining information has been to eliminate complicated operating procedures while at the same time providing the information that meets the drivers' diverse needs.

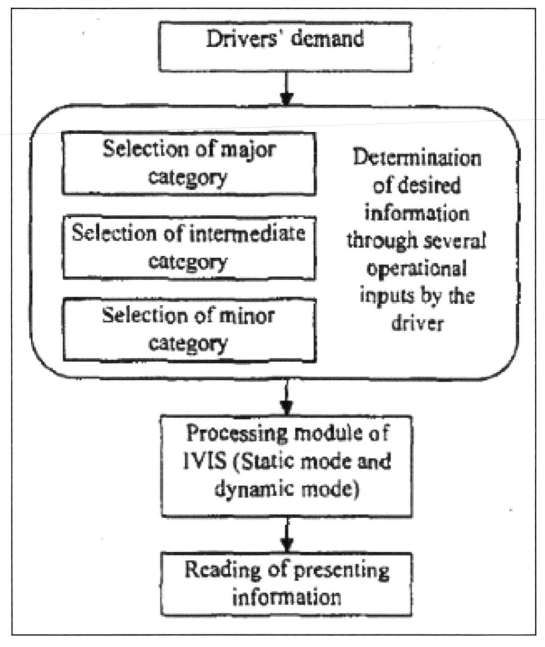

Conventional Model for acquiring information To simplify the task of obtaining information.

Optimal Artificial Speech Recognition Model

Though the viewpoints of AutoDJ model researched by Telematics System Engineering Group of Japan simplified the task of obtaining information, during en-route route guidance the driver has to shift the eyes from the road to the display monitor of IVIS. So it is not the optimal human-computer interface.

Compared to AutoDJ model, voice recognition input is a safe and usable solution. The model of voice recognition input is illumed in figure.

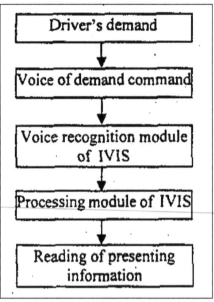

Voice recognition model for acquiring information.

TRL of Britain has putted forward four design guidelines of voice recognition system:

- The vocabulary used should be familiar to drivers and should avoid using similar sounding words or phases.

- The system should give immediate. feedback, (for example, within <250ms) to the driver in regards to the recognition results.

- The systems recognition accuracy should be high, particularly in safety. critical situations (for example, recognition 98% for hit rates and less than 5% false alarm rates).

- The system must be able to cope with expected amounts of background noise.

High voice recognition rate plays a predominant role of achieve this HCI. Under good recognition conditions, voice recognition HCI can solve the interference between primary and secondary task. In the noisy situations or problematic situations, the driver can shift to manual modality.

HCI Design of Information Presentation

Issues of Conventional Model for Information Presentation

The conventional method of presenting information has mainly been in a visual mode in which drivers read the information displayed on their navigation monitor. When presenting a large amount of information involving a sequence of screens, the trigger for changing screens has usually required an operational, input by the user. It has been difficult for drivers to operate the system to change screens while driving. Consequently, one problem has been that the amount of information which can be provided while a vehicle is moving has been limited. A major issue for the presentation of information via a navigation monitor is to provide necessary and sufficient information without requiring any operational inputs by the driver.

Optimal artificial speech model for information presentation. The artificial speech for information presentation can resolve this problem. During en-route dynamic route guidance, the artificial speech media has the merit as following:

- It can relieve the driver's time of seeing the display monitor. The research done in Japan indicates that artificial speech route guidance can reduce 5O percent to 70 percent of the driver's time of seeing the display monitor. While driving, the driver can't complete many operating tasks. If we only use the display monitor information for route guidance, the driver has to search route guidance information while driving. It is disadvantageous to traffic safety. But artificial speech route guidance can make the driver concentrating on the driving.

- It is not restricted by space.

- The guidance information provided by artificial speech media is intuitionistic to the driver. Thus this can reduce the driver's burden of-using IVIS. When the car moves at the intersection, the artificial speech can tell the driver to tum left or tum right via text-to-speech technology. It can also tell the driver the distance or time left.

This HCI is supported by the Text-to-Speech synthesizer. This enables the driver to listen passively [SI to information while driving. The volume and frequency of artificial speech have to be considered so that the driver's mental workload is approximately equal to the car radio 15). According to the guidelines provided by TRL of Britain, the volume of auditory output should be adjustable over a reasonable range; in most circumstances between 5OdB(A) and 90dB(A) is suitable, Higher than 90dB(A) should be avoided 131. Auditory information should always lie with the range of human hearing (for example, 200-8000Hz), but it is recommended in practice that it should lie between 500 and 4000Hz.

This makes it possible to present information to the driver not only visually as conventional systems do, but also by artificial speech. The driver first select the artificial speech for information presentation, when in the noisy situations or problematic situations, he can convent to visual modality.

System Fault and Input Error Warnings

If the IVlS is inoperative at the start of a drive or fails during driving, the driver needs to be made aware of the situation.

Drivers will make mistakes while using IVIS, so the systems must be tolerant of driver input errors. it must be possible to easily recover from errors and the consequence of potential errors must be minimized. Error messages should express in plain language. Precisely indicate the problem, and constructively suggest a solution. Some other guidelines for system faults and warnings are (European Commission, 1998 and ISo 15005- currently) being approved:

- The driver should have immediate and clear feedback for input errors.

- Provide driver-centered wording in messages.

- Avoid ambiguous messages, use plain language and indicate the precise problem.

- Avoid using threatening or alarming messages unless appropriate.

- Make the system 'take the blame' for errors (for example, systems should respond 'unrecognized command' rather than 'illegal command').

- Make driver actions easily reverse, allow 'undo' commands and other escape routes from operations.

HCI is the essential components of IVIS. 'the effect of HCI design directly has relation to the driver's safety. A bad HCI shall interfere with the driver's primary !ask and shift the driver's attention from the road to the display monitor of lVlS for searching information. So HCI of artificial speech recognition combined with auditory information feedback is a safe and usable solution.

Implementation of HCI in the Hospitality Workplace

A large amount of applications of human-computer interaction (HCI) were used by both employees and guests within the hospitality workplace. Some major hotel chains, including Marriott and Hyatt Corporation, introduced and expanded the management systems that control all hotel operations with a central computer since 1980s. This part will gather and group existing examples of HCI applications within the hospitality workplace to give readers a comprehensive understanding of HCI.

Hotel: Front Desk Operations

The major brands of hospitality industry are interested in clearing long check-in/checkout lines in hotel lobby by introducing the new ideas of paperless check-in, self-service kiosks, and even the online web check-in systems. Many people may remember the big board behind the front desk with all the room numbers on board and keys on chains before hotels have computer systems. The paper-based check-in is time consuming and inefficient. Nowadays, people have seen a lot of innovations happened to the hotel lobby where new technologies constantly implemented. One important change is the installation of computerized check-in system. Date back to early 1970s, the Westin Hotels and Resorts (then Western International Hotels) developed their own computerized reservation system named "Westron" which became the industry standard in subsequent years. With the computerized reservation systems, hotel front desk can easily check the resource of the hotel reservations, record guests' information, and check available rooms. Tourists can easily book hotel rooms through online travel companies and booking systems. This also allows hotels to spend less on expensive labor costs and to maximize room occupancy without wasting a lot of money on advertising. Moreover, it allows hotels to get efficient and rapid feedback form guests, so that hotels could predict the guests' preference and give them customized service.

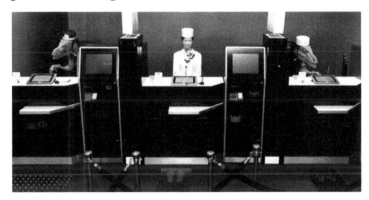

Starwood first implemented paperless check-in system globally that relies on credit card swipes rather than signed registration cards in 1999. It takes less than one minute to help a guest check into the hotel. The other reason that hotels use paperless is to reduce paper waste. For example, Kerry Hotel, Pudong, Shanghai introduced paperless check-in/checkout system recently. Guests will use stylus pen to sign on a tablet to complete check-in and check-out with the electronic receipts emailed upon check-out from the hotel.

However, the old computerized check-in/check-out systems used for hotel front desk in today's world are not efficient enough to satisfy hotel guests because people are still experiencing with crowed tourists who waiting in long lines in hotel lobbies. It still needs employees to interact with the machine when guests have to wait in lines. To solve this problem, self-service kiosk has been introduced to hotel lobbies in recent years. Hilton implemented about 100 self-service kiosks in its hotels in the year of 2004. The check in/check-out kiosks help hotel guests to view their reservation and to get the room key; by the end of their stay, guests could also view and confirm their bill and print the receipt. These hotel check-in/check-out kiosks increase guests' satisfaction by reducing waiting time. In addition, the kiosks are usually connected to hotels own technology platform, allowing guest service agents to provide their guests with value-added services according to their preference. Moreover, with the self-service kiosks, employees' effectiveness can be maximized because the staff would have more time to provide personalized customer service.

Hilton was also the first one to offer airline kiosks in hotel lobbies in 2004 to enable hotel guests to print boarding passes. The guests can view the airline websites to check in their flights, change seats, and request upgrades by using these kiosks.

Besides the self-service kiosks, a mobile phone check-in system and web-based check-in system are more and more popular among many hotels. Hilton provided mobile check-in system to their loyal guests in 2010; Starwood distributed the radio frequency identification (RFID) keycards to loyalty customers, so that the guests can directly go to the room using card sensor on the doorknob to unlock their room; InterContinental introduced a program that customers can scan an emailed barcode contained in their phone to the door's sensor for entry. Radisson allowed their guests to check into any of its branded hotels through internet seven days before arrival.

Hotel: Room Division

The innovation of HCI in hotels rooms or housekeeping department has been around for many years to please hotels guests. One change related to hotel check-in is the use of room keycards. The early hotel room keys were made of brass or bronze along with metal tags. But this kind of keys were heavy to carry and easy to duplicate, thus increased the possibility of illegal break-ins. Some guests even kept the keys as souvenir thus increased hotel costs to make those keys. In order to prevent burglaries, larger hotels such as Marriott start to use electronic key cards in late 1990s, which enhanced room safety for guests. The e-keycards have a magnetic strip which coded by hotel check-in computers and valid for one lock per stay. Although with the same key card, a new guest will have a different code that distributed by computer system. Thus, it is nearly impossible for burglar and illegal break-ins by duplicating a card. One of the electronic key cards systems help hotels significantly reduces energy waste by using room key cards switch that located at the main entry door. When guests take out the key cards and left hotel room, the light will power off automatically. Also, the guests will never worried about losing track of their key cards again since they needs their key cards to power the lights.

However, some drawbacks of electronic key cards system caused inconvenient to hotels and guests. First, the key cards are easily demagnetized when put near by cell phones or other magnetic strip cards. Second, sometimes the key cards do not work when they encoded incorrectly or swiped the wrong way. Third, the locks won't open when they are out of batteries. Moreover, guests worried about ID theft when their private information is encoded. In order to provide more convenience, some hotels start to try new room key programs, such as smart phone check-in program. This program integrates check-in procedure and room key system. Guests can just scan the barcode contained their phone on the door sensor to unlock the door instead of using a real key. However, this is still not an ideal room key especially when guests lost their phones.

With hotel guests expecting a luxury home experience, hotel operators complete premium accommodation with installation of high technology in rooms. For example, the Aria Resort & Casino Las Vegas installs the Control system, a remote control system displayed by room touch panel. Guests can control everything with just one-touch. Guests can play audio through connecting personal media devices to audio/visual connection panel; adjust room temperature and lights; request cleaning services; view room bills and check-out; check flight schedule; open or close the curtains in room; and set up a customized wake-up event such as wake up by opening the curtains or turning on the lights at a specific time.

Restaurant: Food Ordering

Similar as hotels, restaurants are also constantly introducing new technology. Although people experienced with face-to-face interaction when ordering food in most restaurants, some fast food restaurants such as McDonald's and Jack-in-the-Box installed self-service food ordering kiosks several years ago. The self-service food ordering kiosk is based on computer system that allows customers to order food directly and to pay checks themselves, using a touch screen with no employees involved. After an order is placed, customer would wait for the order number to be called to get the meal. The McDonald's has introduced such kiosks in the year of 2004, reducing the ordering waiting lines. Jack-in-the-Box also offered self-service kiosk in 2010 not only to reduce the waiting line but also to cut labor cost.

The online food ordering website allows customer to place an order with a local restaurant or a food cooperative. Some of these service websites make frequent ordering convenient by encouraging customers to keep accounts with them. Many restaurants use their own websites providing online food ordering as an alternative to help them provide more convenience to customers and expand business. For example, Pizza Hut in 2007 offered online ordering that allows customers to create "pizza playlists" with their favorite pizza orders for future visits; Papa John's International announced that its online sales were growing from $21.4 million in 2001 to $400 million in 2007, a big increase.

With growing trend of using iPad, some restaurants are also considering using iPads to order food. For instance, at Chicago Cut Steakhouse, Chicago, servers carry iPads with wine menus, containing detailed introductions and images of the products. Servers at Jose Garces' Jaleo at the Cosmopolitan Hotel, LasVegas, also use iPads for wine and cocktail menus.

A more recent innovation of food ordering solution introduced is restaurant e-tablets, such as MenuPad and eTab software. It allows customers to order and to pay at their tables through the touch screen computer. ETab uses a digital-menu interface wirelessly connect table to the restaurant's staff and point-of-sale system. It gives customers comprehensive understating of menu by providing abundant pictures of varies dishes; lets customers control ordering and paying time; and reduces restaurant order errors. In addition, the system accepts either cash or credit card payment and allows splitting bills, with receipts directly emailed or printed for customers. Moreover, restaurant could easily remove or add items to menus according to operation needs.

Restaurant: Shift Scheduling

Scheduling employees' work shifts perhaps annoy many restaurant managers, who may spend a lot of time on it but still get unsatisfied employees. However, there are some software such as Restaurant Scheduler which helps restaurant managers schedule employees' shifts efficiently at work or home at anytime. The software adopts drag-and-drop technology that allows managers quickly drag and drop employees on the specific shifts and easily change schedules. It can also automatically assign employees to available shifts. Moreover, it reduces communication errors between managers and employees by providing an online platform to record the employees' special request for managers.

Casino: Gaming Technology

The Cosmopolitan of Las Vegas opened in December of 2010 with sbX Experience Management System, a server-based slot gaming system developed by International Game Technology (IGT). Before sbX, casino slot technicians would spend hours going from one machine to another and individually change computer chips and slot machine theme programs. With sbX system, casino operators can easily download variety of game themes from the sbX sever network to individual electronic gaming machine. In addition, the system can distinguish the most popular games on the floor by tracking playing data from each machine and player. With the analyzed data reports, casino can effectively advertise to the target slot machine players.

References

- Disney-experiment-lets-you-catch-real-objects-in-virtual-reality: x-tech.am, Retrieved 22 June, 2019

- Disney-research-vr-object-tracking: immersed.io, Retrieved 28 July, 2019

- An-illustration-of-the-end-users-interaction-with-dataviz-in-VR-system- 328082088: research-gate.net, Retrieved 28 April, 2019

- Virtual-reality-simulation-transports-users-ocean-future: news.stanford.edu, Retrieved 14 May, 2019

- Stage-vorausschaender-fussgaengerschutz-stage-mobile, driver-assistance-systems-predictive-pedestrian, passenger-cars-and-light-commercial-vehicles: bosch-mobility-solutions.com, Retrieved 18 March, 2019

- Sherman, W. R. & Craig, A. B. Understanding virtual reality: Interface, application, and design. (Morgan Kaufmann, 2018)

Permissions

All chapters in this book are published with permission under the Creative Commons Attribution Share Alike License or equivalent. Every chapter published in this book has been scrutinized by our experts. Their significance has been extensively debated. The topics covered herein carry significant information for a comprehensive understanding. They may even be implemented as practical applications or may be referred to as a beginning point for further studies.

We would like to thank the editorial team for lending their expertise to make the book truly unique. They have played a crucial role in the development of this book. Without their invaluable contributions this book wouldn't have been possible. They have made vital efforts to compile up to date information on the varied aspects of this subject to make this book a valuable addition to the collection of many professionals and students.

This book was conceptualized with the vision of imparting up-to-date and integrated information in this field. To ensure the same, a matchless editorial board was set up. Every individual on the board went through rigorous rounds of assessment to prove their worth. After which they invested a large part of their time researching and compiling the most relevant data for our readers.

The editorial board has been involved in producing this book since its inception. They have spent rigorous hours researching and exploring the diverse topics which have resulted in the successful publishing of this book. They have passed on their knowledge of decades through this book. To expedite this challenging task, the publisher supported the team at every step. A small team of assistant editors was also appointed to further simplify the editing procedure and attain best results for the readers.

Apart from the editorial board, the designing team has also invested a significant amount of their time in understanding the subject and creating the most relevant covers. They scrutinized every image to scout for the most suitable representation of the subject and create an appropriate cover for the book.

The publishing team has been an ardent support to the editorial, designing and production team. Their endless efforts to recruit the best for this project, has resulted in the accomplishment of this book. They are a veteran in the field of academics and their pool of knowledge is as vast as their experience in printing. Their expertise and guidance has proved useful at every step. Their uncompromising quality standards have made this book an exceptional effort. Their encouragement from time to time has been an inspiration for everyone.

The publisher and the editorial board hope that this book will prove to be a valuable piece of knowledge for students, practitioners and scholars across the globe.

Index